$20 -

1999 PB

SHEER
WILL

SHEER WILL

THE INSPIRING LIFE AND CLIMBS OF

MICHAEL GROOM

RANDOM HOUSE AUSTRALIA

Random House Australia Pty Ltd
20 Alfred Street, Milsons Point, NSW 2061
http://www.randomhouse.com.au

Sydney New York Toronto
London Auckland Johannesburg

Hardcover published by William Heinemann Australia in 1997
This Random House Australia edition first published 1999

National Library of Australia
Cataloguing-in-Publication Entry

Groom, Michael.
   Sheer will.

   ISBN 0 091 84141 0.

   1. Mountaineers – Australia. 2. Mountaineering – Nepal. 3. Mountaineering
   accidents – Nepal. 4. Everest, Mount (China and Nepal) – Description and travel.
   I. Title.

796.522092

Cover photograph Michael Groom
Cover design by Yolande Grey
Typeset in 12/17 Galliard by Midland Typesetters, Maryborough, Victoria
Printed and bound by Griffin Press, Netley, South Australia

10 9 8 7 6 5 4 3

To my parents, Donn and Roma, and my wife, Judi

My grandmother, Marjorie Groom, died on the 5 June 1998. At her funeral I read this poem. It is also a fitting memorial for those who appreciate and respect the secrets of nature, particularly the people mentioned in this book who are no longer with us.

Do not stand at my grave and weep
I am not there
I do not sleep

I am a thousand winds that blow
I am the diamond glints on snow
I am the sunlight on ripened grain
I am the gentle autumn rain

When you awake in morning's hush
I am the swift uplifting rush
of quiet birds in circled flight
I am the soft stars that shine at night

Do not stand at my grave and cry
I am not there.
I did not die

Anon

FOREWORD

When Michael Groom asked me if I'd write a foreword to the first edition of this book, fourteen years had passed since we'd climbed together. Our last expedition had been to the huge unclimbed South Face of Annapurna II in 1983. Following the success of that climb I tackled a new route on Mount Everest, a project that was the culmination of six intense years devoted to high mountains. I turned back 500 metres short of Everest's summit because I ran out of energy and daylight. Afterwards, rather than vowing to return, I felt it was time to hang up my boots. I wanted to stay alive. I wanted to spend more time where it was warmer and the air was thicker. I wanted to pursue my ambition to become a writer, and I began by writing books about mountaineering.

These days I'm still invited to write about climbing, and I usually accept because some of my most vivid memories are of high times in the Himalayas, standing on summits, battling storms, and watching avalanches thunder down towards me. When I dashed off a couple of pages for Michael, I relived those past glories. His book was packed full of personal triumphs and tragedies, and when I compared these to my own experiences of Himalayan peaks, I felt a little inadequate. At the end of the foreword I pronounced that Michael's feat of becoming the first Australian to climb the four highest mountains in the world, all without supplementary oxygen, was the equivalent of four drug-free Olympic wins, an achievement that is especially notable because he made three of these climbs after he'd lost thirty per cent of each foot to frostbite.

Michael's achievements haven't stopped there, as he continues to climb at the highest level. I approached writing this foreword to *Sheer Will*'s second edition with very different eyes, because a month ago Michael and I returned from an expedition to Makalu, the world's fifth highest peak. He reached the summit, as you will discover when you read this book, but I was turned back by bad weather.

Makalu certainly refreshed my perspective on Himalayan climbing. Nepal was as entrancing as I remembered, the mountains as magnificent, the friendships amongst us as deep, and the dangers as apparent. However, the cold seemed more intense, the effort of high-altitude climbing greater and the sleepless nights at high camps more uncomfortable. It was not that I'd forgotten what mountaineering was about, because I'd spent the last three summers climbing in Antarctica. Rather, I saw that over the last fifteen years I'd let myself romanticise the hardships of climbing the world's highest peaks. Those illusions are now gone with the wind, literally.

Returning to the high Himalayas on Makalu made me appreciate more fully what Michael had put himself through. His feet were very much his limiting factor, not only because it was hard for him to climb but also because of the pain they gave him. Frostbite injuries remain susceptible to further cold damage, an after-effect I can vouch for twenty-one years after losing a couple of frozen toes. During our Makalu expedition, Michael's decisions about climbing were influenced by what he could and couldn't do with his feet, but he never asked us to compromise our plans for his sake. This turned out to be unnecessary because once we started reaching higher altitudes Michael was always up the front. He seemed to thrive in the thin air. His determination was extraordinary and yet he never wasted any effort. When he and I had climbed together in the early 1980s his strength was apparent but his determination hadn't been obvious. In those days he was coming to grips with the uncomfortable truths of high-altitude climbing, and he lacked the confidence to offer his opinions. Today he remains a quiet introverted man, but with a ready smile and a well thought out position on any problem at hand.

Now that I browse through the updated version of Michael's book, his achievements seem even more remarkable because I understand much more about what he has gone through since he learnt to walk again in 1988. He is delighted to have achieved his ambition of climbing the five highest mountains in the world. Invariably, he fails to mention that he has climbed the top six. His 1990 ascent of Cho Oyu, number six, is in one way the most significant of all his climbs. Life is pretty miserable at 7000 metres, but as you climb above 8000 metres there is an exponential worsening in the effects of the shortage of oxygen. Michael feels that there is such a quantum leap between the effort needed to reach Cho Oyu's summit at 8201 metres and Makalu's at 8461 metres that Makalu and the four higher peaks are in a league of their own. This distinction is recognised by the few other climbers qualified to comment. For Michael, Cho Oyu is special for a different reason. This peak is where he proved to himself that his high-altitude climbing days were not over, and that his childhood ambition of climbing Everest need not be an abandoned dream. His commitment to his goals is a dominant theme in what is a very inspiring book. And yet he is in no way a salesman for self-improvement; he preaches only by example.

On Makalu I found it frustrating that the weather prevented me from reaching my personal limits, which no doubt have been redefined by the passing of fifteen years. Yet I know very well that the mountains often call the shots. While I cursed the weather, Michael applied his experience from seventeen years of expeditioning to get himself in the right place at the right time. I was only a day behind him, but the weather turned bad as I climbed up with my partner, and Michael descended with his. He had been lucky, we had been unlucky, but as Michael had said a week or so earlier, 'On 8000-metre peaks you've got to make your own luck.' In reading this book you'll get an inkling of how such luck can be manufactured, and it's not by magic but by hard work and persistence, a formula that anyone can follow.

On many expeditions it has been Michael who has reached the top, alone or with a companion, while others have turned back. Perhaps I would have tagged Makalu's summit if I'd pushed myself to be at our high camp at the first glimmer of good weather, if I'd played the long chances as thoroughly, if I'd displayed as much sheer will.

Lincoln Hall

CONTENTS

ACKNOWLEDGEMENTS

The manuscript for this book was completed before I returned to Everest in 1996, but the very public disaster that unfolded towards the end of this expedition meant that another chapter had to be added whether I liked it or not. Needless to say, it was a difficult chapter to write and it could not have been done without the encouragement and valuable comments of Margaret Collins and my wife, Judi.

I am deeply indebted to Judi for her constant support. She has suffered long periods of loneliness while I have been away climbing, often not knowing our whereabouts and progress, whether I was alive or dead. She has tolerated my constant comings and goings on expeditions and, determined not to waste time worrying, has maintained her own interests in life. Most important of all is her love and understanding when things go terribly wrong—which they inevitably do in mountaineering.

I am also forever grateful to my parents, Donn and Roma, for introducing me to the outdoors and to Tim Macartney-Snape, Lincoln Hall, Greg Mortimer and Andy Henderson for taking me under their wing all those years ago.

Finally, to my climbing partners, past and present, thank you for the memories.

INTRODUCTION

From the half-open door of my tent I could see only one star but it signalled the beginning of another day on Mount Everest. It was 1.00 a.m., 20 September 1991.

Rummaging through my rucksack I found the small St Christopher's medal my mother had given me at the airport before leaving for my second attempt to climb Mount Everest. At the time I had thought it an unusual gift, until she told me that St Christopher was the protector of travellers. Alone in my tent at Camp 2 (C2), at 6450 metres above sea level, I tied the medal to my climbing-suit before wriggling out of my sleeping-bag.

An hour later, I crawled bleary-eyed from my tent, but the minus 15°C night air very quickly brought me to life as I trudged over to the French camp, ice axe in hand and ready for what I knew would be a long, hard day. We planned to fix the last section of rope between C3 and C4, while my team-mates would spend the day carrying supplies from C1 to C2.

We were forced to start early so we could stop climbing before the midday heat—around 30°C, despite being halfway up Everest—set off rockfalls and avalanches. For a moment, the brightness of the stars held my attention, the one I had seen from the door of my tent shining brighter than the others, but my subconscious interrupted with the thought that today an accident was going to happen. What type of accident and to whom it would happen I had no inkling.

In my day-to-day life I have always followed my instincts, and when climbing I do the same. But today, for no reason, I ignored them. The premonition passed as quickly as it came.

Three other expeditions, French, Korean and Basque, were on Everest this season. Our team had arrived at Base Camp (BC) a couple of weeks after them and this caused a small but embarrassing problem for us. The other teams had fixed a route of ropes and ladders through the Khumbu Icefall and we felt some obligation to help make the route up the mountain, instead of following in their footsteps. The three expeditions had worked well together and had prepared the route all the way to C3, with only the section between C3 and C4 to be done. Most commonly referred to as the Lhotse Face, this sweep of steep ice, at 45 degrees to 50 degrees with short, even steeper sections of ice and rock in between, has to be taken seriously. Six climbers have fallen from it. All of them died. Thousands of metres of rope are needed, as well as dozens of pitons to hammer into the rock to tie the rope to. Not all of the rope can be secured to pitons in the rock, so 600-millimetre to 800-millimetre lengths of angled aluminium, called snow-stakes, are driven into the snow in the same manner as pitons. We also use 200-millimetre-long ice screws with self-tapping threads to screw into the often concrete-hard ice. All this equipment creates a great deal of load-carrying to get it into a position to use. My climbing partners and I had been on the mountain a little over a week and had not yet acclimatised to the altitude of C2. Nor were we fit enough to climb and fix ropes all the way to C4 at 8000 metres. As I had been higher more often than my team-mates, I volunteered to help the French team between C3 and C4, knowing very well that I would be punished with nausea and crippling headaches from lack of acclimatisation.

When Deni, the leader of the French team, handed me 400 metres of rope to carry, it meant we were ready for departure from C2. Deni had already made a couple of climbs to C3 to carry equipment and the pace set by him and his three Sherpas was heart-breaking. He congratulated me on keeping up. I concentrated on keeping my breakfast down.

We arrived at C3 just on dawn and I was immediately impressed by the amount of work they had already done. Small ledges hacked out of blue ice supported three large tents. A web of ropes encased each to prevent them from falling into the valley; the web was in turn tied to several ice screws fixed into the ice on the uphill side of each tent. This finely balanced camp on the Lhotse Face was the only safe place that was sheltered from avalanches and rockfalls. Anything dropped outside the tent would not be seen again, including yourself.

Grateful for some shelter at last, I crawled into one of the tents to escape the cold. I massaged my painfully cold feet while the others sorted ropes and hardware for the pending ascent to C4. Thankfully Deni offered to lead while I belayed him from inside the tent, one hand on the rope, the other furiously rubbing my feet, as Deni climbed with short bursts of energy separated by long rests. Once this 200-metre section of rope was secured to a snowstake hammered deep into the snow with the rope tied to the top, the Sherpas and I headed up the rope ready for the next section.

We followed this routine until 10.30 a.m. The snow conditions indicated avalanche danger and I was nervously alert. Reaching the last tie-off point for the rope, we were unable to go any further until Deni had secured the other end of the next 50 metres. Deni yelled from above, his voice echoing around the Lhotse Face. He would finish for the day once he had overcome the short but steep Yellow Band, a significant landmark band of rock on the South Col route, in which he would pound the final piton. Once under the shelter of the Yellow Band, we could bury the equipment we had in our packs for another day.

Meanwhile the Sherpas made themselves comfortable beside me, laughing and joking as they stamped out a small ledge to stand on, and produced something to eat and drink. It was not a good place to stop in such an exposed position high on the Face, and, concerned with safety, I connected my harness to a small loop of rope, my suggestion for them to do the same falling on deaf ears. A tumble from here would mean death. It was becoming hot and I wanted to remove one of my three layers of clothing, but I remained tense and edgy.

Looking upward revealed what I had feared most: an avalanche had broken loose some 400 metres above us. I immediately shouted at the Sherpas who were facing in the opposite direction and their merriment quickly changed to panic. Swearing profusely, they scampered to the right as far and as fast as our precarious position would allow. One slip, one missed foot placement and they would fall down the Lhotse Face. I had only a few seconds to do the same but I quickly saw that the contours of the slope would take the avalanche into a gully on our left. Deni was the one in trouble. I yelled, 'Avalanche!' but he didn't hear me.

The contours were more defined than they looked and before I had a chance to repeat my warning, the avalanche was funnelled into a gully to the left of Deni and out of harm's way. With the danger past, I motioned for the Sherpas, who had reached a safer position 15 metres away, to come back, thinking the slopes were clear of further threat. Without warning another avalanche appeared from our right. A 1-metre-high wave of snow and ice plunged over the ice cliff that had hidden its approach from our view and I was in its direct path. There was no time to panic; in less urgent times I might have been frightened, but there was nowhere to run. In any case, I was still attached to the fixed rope. I had only a fraction of a second and it was no use contemplating untying; all I could do was duck in the hope that it would pass over the top of me. It was my last voluntary action.

There was only a short distance between me and the avalanche and I was spellbound by its terrifying speed. A shock wave travelled in front of the wall of snow. I felt its power the instant before it struck me—the force wrenched my climbing harness so powerfully that I thought I would be torn in half, and the rope snapped like a piece of cotton. I had placed all my confidence and indeed my life in that rope. The impact pushed me backwards into space like a rag doll, and I was forced through the air for another 30 metres before I fell back down into the belly of the avalanche. I tried to protect my mouth but I had no control over my actions and it was jammed so full of snow that from then on there was no chance of taking a breath. The noise in the avalanche was deafening: it sounded as if I had my ear stuck to a jet engine, and bowling ball-sized blocks of ice bashed into every inch of my body. I had plenty of time to think about dying. I didn't think I'd survive this, and my brain flashed: 'Michael Groom, dead at 32'. For many facing death is a frightening experience, but as I fell I did not feel fear. I resigned myself to meet my destiny, even though I found some small fascination in pondering whether there was life after death. Other parts of my mind, less concerned with my eulogy, were busy on survival. I told myself to stop fighting and go with the flow to avoid being torn limb from limb, and so I began to roll like a barrel.

I knew I could hold my breath for about a minute, maybe an extra thirty seconds in an emergency. After that the brain would send a message to start breathing no matter what. If you're under water the lungs are flooded and you drift into unconsciousness within seconds. If you are in an avalanche your mouth is jammed so full of snow the reflex action to breath is gagged by the wad of snow, and the more you gag the further down your throat it slips. The result, however, is still the same—unconsciousness within seconds. The reality was I was cartwheeling down the upper slopes of Everest at between 80 and 100 kilometres per hour and there was only one place I was going— all the way to the bottom. There was no-one waiting to pull my limp body out of the wreckage of this avalanche. I was dead for sure.

At no time did I get a glimpse of the outside world: it was either pitch black or there were flashes of brilliant diamonds before my eyes. At any moment it would be dark forever as I absorbed the last millilitre of air that was trapped in my lungs. I hoped the end would come soon.

Suddenly there was momentary respite from the bone-crushing pressure and thundering noise as the avalanche released me over a cliff. Flying through the air was a relief, even though I knew the landing would probably be fatal. Instead, it drove me relentlessly into the snow below like a pylon, and metres of snow began to bury me. Just when I thought my time had come and I felt as if I was going to burst with the weight on top of me, the snow started to move. I was off again.

I was hurtled over another cliff and across the yawning jaws of a 15-metre-wide bergschrund, with still no chance of catching a breath of air. Then as suddenly as it began, it stopped. A heavy weight again crushed my body and it was deathly silent. A pale blue light was my only focus.

Am I in heaven? Or have I checked into hell?

THE BEGINNING

chapter one

'Okay, Michael, you may sit down now.' My teacher tried to hide her laughter behind a cupped hand. I had just finished telling my class what I was going to be when I grew up.

It was an easy question to answer as I had been dwelling on this very subject for several days.

'I want to climb Mount Everest just like my dad,' I said proudly, expecting admiration and applause. They only giggled.

My father had climbed Everest just a few days before, so I thought. Before the laughter started I was imagining the gold star against my name for sharing with my fellow six year olds the name of the world's highest mountain, but now the joke was on me.

Red-faced, I walked back to my small wooden desk, my head bent. Miss Venner smiled. 'Michael, your father hasn't climbed Mount Everest.' I nearly replied, 'Yes he has, and so will I', but by now I was in tears. For the remainder of the school day I remained doggedly silent, humiliated by the amusement my confident prediction had caused.

My father, Donn Groom, had been an active rockclimber and mountaineer for as long as I could remember, and I was fascinated by his stories. Mount Barney—a mountain my father climbed frequently and talked of fondly—was the closest thing we had to a mountain in our area of south-east Queensland. It was during one of my earliest trips to Barney that I first heard of Mount Everest. My father was taking a photo of Barney and wanted me to stand to one side of the frame. Eager to join my younger and only brother, Terry, who was happily poking sticks into a large ants' nest, I fidgeted impatiently.

'Did you know there is a mountain seven to eight times higher than Mount Barney? It's called Mount Everest and it's the highest mountain in the world,' Dad said.

My attention was immediately captured.

'It's in another country a long way from here. Across the other side of the world.'

'Has anyone climbed it, Dad?'

'Not many, only a few. It's very difficult and costs lots of money to climb.'

I placed the height of Mount Barney between my thumb and index finger and started to measure seven times its height. Bent over backwards and convinced my measurement was accurate, I remained spellbound by its impossible height.

'Have you climbed Mount Everest, Dad?' There was no reply; he had gone.

So at school I considered myself an expert on mountains. But my father never got the chance to answer my final question and on this particular day at school I took it upon myself to steal some limelight. It seemed logical to me that if Dad had already climbed Mount Barney, during this week of school when I knew he was away climbing, the only other mountain he could possibly be climbing was Mount Everest. After all, a week was ample time to climb a mountain on the other side of the world.

How wrong I was, and the only lesson I learnt at school that day was that there are many people willing to laugh at what they see as the outrageous dreams of others. I hated school for the next two weeks and because I took the taunts of my schoolmates so seriously, it would be another twenty years before I mentioned climbing Everest again.

I later left the sleepy dairy farming district of Beechmont to attend the large Southport State High School. I found the dramatic change from twenty-three to 1500 students overwhelming and in little time my only ambition was to get out of school as soon as possible.

Even though I led an adventurous life bushwalking, camping and rockclimbing with my father and brother, the necessary skills and confidence of the mountaineer eluded me throughout my childhood. A chilling indication that I was not cut out to be a mountaineer came four years later.

It was my third abseil. My father was the instructor, and most important of all, I had just turned ten. As I waited anxiously for my go, I tried to convince myself that it would be easy, but the longer I waited, the more nervous I became.

Ballunjui Falls (Aboriginal for 'easterly') in Lamington National Park cascade in a dramatic series of three steep, 60- to 80-metre vertical drops to the valley below, the flow then continuing without interruption down to the Gold Coast. During the descent, in the mist and spray from the falls thundering down just metres away, there is a feeling of tremendous exposure. For anyone, let alone a ten year old, it is a daunting adventure.

The abseiling party of fifteen guests from Binna Burra Lodge, including my brother, was diminishing every ten minutes as each person, with one or two steps backwards, disappeared from sight. To make things seem worse, there was never any reply from the abseiler to my father's constant encouragement. Terry, who was two years younger than me, gave everyone a boost of confidence as he effortlessly dropped over the edge in a single bound, but this only put the pressure on me to do equally well.

I made the mistake of choosing to be the second last to abseil. In doing so I only prolonged the churning of my stomach to a point where I had to go to the toilet. I didn't dare tell my father this as he attached me to the abseil and safety ropes. As I backed up to the edge, I felt the warm updraft from the valley below, causing me to lunge forwards in panic. I fell flat on my face, unable to release my death grip on the rope.

I was too embarrassed to look my father in the eye, my legs were shaking, and I bit my bottom lip to stop it from trembling. My father's encouragement fell on deaf ears as I crept back towards the edge. Finally I dropped onto my elbows and knees and grovelled in a shower of dirt and rocks over the edge and down to the people waiting on the next ledge 70 metres below. I don't remember ever being so scared.

Abseiling and rockclimbing instilled an emotion I had never felt before: the fear of dying. Little did I know that it was just the beginning of a long relationship with fear and in years to come it would become no more controllable. Most people feel some sense of achievement in facing their fears, but this day went a long way towards proving to me that I would never be a climber like my father.

The legendary Italian mountaineer, Riccardo Cassin, says in his autobiography, 'Climbers, like sailors and poets are born not made.' And he says about the mountains, 'If you are born for them, sooner or later you will find yourself drawn towards them with an attraction that may be violent.'

In some ways this describes my attraction to the mountains. I am often asked how I became involved in climbing and I like to blame my heritage for at least the sense for adventure I have, in particular my grandfather, Arthur Groom, who died before I was born, and my parents, Donn and Roma. One day when Arthur was twelve or thirteen he argued so bitterly with his brothers and sisters that he left the family home in Ascot, Brisbane, with his younger brother, Jim, in tow. They said they were heading for America. It was not a hasty decision for they took with them a leg of lamb, a bottle of water, an atlas, a ruler and a pencil and set off into Moreton Bay in the family rowing-boat. They rowed for hours to get as far away from their siblings as possible. They stopped at nightfall when Jim started to cry and fortunately for them, Jim's sobbing was heard by a fisherman who towed them back to land.

As a young man Arthur Groom explored central Australia alone on foot, or with local Aboriginal people and camels trekked to the MacDonnell and Krichauff Ranges, Lake Amadeus, Ayers Rock and Mount Olga. He went on to co-found Binna Burra Lodge near Lamington National Park with Romeo Lahey. The lodge was built to allow people better access to the park. As small boys Terry and I had climbing competitions to see who could scale a rock memorial near our house at Binna Burra Lodge. We had no idea what the pile of rock was for. I have now grown as tall as the memorial, which is dedicated to my grandfather for the extensive work he did for the area.

But first my parents had to meet. Dad's idea of a date was to ask Mum to climb Mount Tibrogargan, one of the Glasshouse Mountains on the Sunshine Coast of Queensland. The climb was not by the walking track which Mum was expecting, but by an exposed rockclimb on the East Face. Their first date, it could easily have been their last as Mum had rarely climbed a ladder, let alone an exposed rock face. My mother followed Dad blindly that day, overcoming the hurdles one at a time until she reached the top. It was here that she fell prey to inexperience and believed it was over. But Dad had more surprises for her: an abseil over a part of the East Face, most of which is overhanging rock. This was also a first for Mum and she didn't know that once she stepped off the top, she would be hanging in thin air for most of the way down. There was none of the modern-day equipment to ease her descent and rope burn to her shoulders and hands were all part of it.

Terry and I were given the freedom to explore our backyard, Lamington National Park, with little restriction. At a young age we were given the responsibility of organising our own camping trips with school friends every school holiday. By the time I was twelve I had all my own camping gear, some of which I had made myself.

Just when I felt ready to progress to the greater challenges of rockclimbing, however, my brother and I were hit with the shocking news that our parents were separating. When Dad left, so did my chance to learn to rockclimb, and I succumbed to peer pressure to adopt the more acceptable and competitive sports of football, cricket, tennis and, later, motorcycle racing. However being quiet and lacking confidence meant that I didn't fit into the highly competitive sports. I became used to being ignored and grew comfortable with my own company and very much self-contained. I knew that one day I would return to the mountains and climbing.

EARLY DAYS

chapter two

I peered from the window of the plane. So this is Alaska, the Land of the Midnight Sun. There was not an igloo or Inuit in sight as I had imagined, only white-water rivers cutting between large sweeps of evergreens at the base of snow-capped mountains rising majestically from the ocean.

I grew nervous as we came in to land at Sitka. This was the first time I had seen my father in nine years. I was just shy of my twenty-first birthday and was not the twelve year old he remembered. Would he recognise me? Would I recognise him? What would I say?

My last memory of him was on the sad day he left home, riding a bicycle with his meagre possessions in a pack on his back. I'm sure he had no idea where he was going and never in his wildest dreams imagined he would end up in Alaska. He cycled around the USA for a while, odd-jobbing on the way and doing the occasional climb. After a few years he married Mary Jo from Wisconsin and they moved to Alaska, as work was easy to find in this frontier state. By then my father had more or less given up climbing because of the wear and tear on his knees.

So he turned to ocean sailing and bought a 38-foot sailing boat. It became home for them and their baby, Joshua.

It was a rare day for Sitka—about 27°C and not a cloud in the sky. Dad and Mary planned a barbeque followed by a climb up Harbor Mountain. It was after 6.00 p.m. and I thought the plan a little strange, until I was told the sun never sets in Alaska during the mid-summer months.

We loaded the Kombivan, including a 12-gauge shotgun to frighten the grizzly bears. The shotgun would become a regular piece of my climbing equipment in Alaska, especially when Dad was not able to accompany me.

The barbeque was not a big success as we had forgotten too many things, so we scrambled up the rocks and over the summer snowfields of Harbor Mountain. A sweeping panoramic view renewed my interest in the mountains—from the top Dad pointed out where he hunted deer with his Inuit friend, Ray, and where they dived for crab and abalone. We looked before us down on Sitka; a thin veil of smoke from the pulp mill hung over one end of the harbour, while puffs of blue barbeque smoke dotted the sky above the town. Behind us snow-capped peaks, glaciers and alpine lakes stretched to the horizon. I could not have been more excited by the prospect of spending the next twelve months there.

My first day in Alaska has lasting memories for me and the scramble up Harbor Mountain re-opened a chapter in my life that I had not finished. Weather-wise there would not be another day like it in the next twelve months. The cold and drizzle settled in the next day, and I found it increasingly difficult to remain inactive on board a cramped boat. I took every opportunity to venture upwards with an ice axe and, if alone, the 12-gauge shotgun. Some of the unroped climbs, juggling an ice axe and shotgun in one hand and hanging on with the other, were potentially deadly. It seemed only natural that for my twenty-first birthday Dad and Mary should give me a pair of mountaineering boots, crampons and an ice axe. Nobody could have guessed the path these tools would lead me along.

Dad had always wanted to climb Mount Adda, a spectacular shark-tooth-shaped mountain on the opposite side of Baranof Island from Sitka. To reach it, we sailed for two days around the island and anchored in a safe inlet beneath the mountain. We would attempt the summit and back in one day, sustained by the usual thermos of tea and peanut butter sandwiches.

As soon as we stepped ashore, I could smell rotting fish. Climbing through mossy forest, the smell grew stronger and we fell upon half-eaten salmon scattered around some boulders. Dad cocked the shotgun. We had walked into the middle of some bear dens. Not wanting to turn back, we continued cautiously upwards and climbed a small cliff out of harm's way.

For the next couple of hours we scrambled through bush interspersed with short rockclimbs. By the time we had reached the snowy col that led up the last 300 to 400 metres to the summit, it was late afternoon and the last 300 metres to the summit presented a technical challenge beyond our skill. It was time to head down.

I suggested to Dad that we descend by a different and

what seemed an easier way, a slab of rock angled down towards the boat for about 1000 metres.

He shook his head. 'There could be cliffs hundreds of metres high between us and the boat. It's always better on mountains like this to descend the way you came, than to take a chance on a descent route you don't know.'

'But you can see all the way down to the boat,' I argued.

I didn't expect to win so easily as we stepped off down the rock. It was the type of climbing I liked—clean rock. It was warm and, at the end of a long and tiring day, I was looking forward to reaching the boat and having a swim. We zig-zagged backwards and forwards across the slab to avoid some of the steeper sections. Occasionally I stopped and glanced across at the more rugged, forested ridge we had climbed up, grateful we were not descending it.

How wrong I was. With just 200 metres to go to the shoreline, our rocky slab ended abruptly in a vertical 200-metre drop. There was no way around it or down it with our short ropes.

Dad could have said, 'I told you so,' but there was no need. We had no alternative but to climb all the way back up to the snowline and descend the ridge we had climbed that morning.

The Mount Adda climb had taught me a hard-learnt but valuable lesson—descend the mountain the same way as you came up, unless you are familiar with the other descent route. It was one, however, I would ignore again in seven years' time when the same mistake on one of the world's highest mountains would very nearly cost me my life.

After the Mount Adda climb I was hooked on climbing

and it was all I wanted to do. Over-ambitious, I wanted to climb North America's highest mountain, Denali, also called Mount McKinley, at 6194 metres. Dad took me in hand again, insisting I do a climbing apprenticeship before tackling anything like Denali and expecting to live. From then on I closely followed his advice while climbing with him in Alaska, but there was only so much he could teach me, as the technical side of rockclimbing and mountaineering had changed dramatically in the few years since he had stopped regular climbing. He suggested a mountaineering course, followed by climbs under the guidance of the most experienced climbers I could find. In other words, to learn from the best.

My father had one lesson of caution, however: beware of the competitive side of climbing. He warned there were always those that fell prey to ego, taking ever greater risks in an attempt to be the first, the fastest and the most famous in the climbing world. I didn't understand at the time how climbing could be so competitive, but in the years that followed, I met some of the very types he described.

The best piece of climbing advice I ever received was from a short New Zealand film, *Fool on the Hill*. Two climbers battling on a particularly difficult pitch are cautioned by a narrative voice: 'No matter how good a climber you think you are, there always has been and always will be someone who can climb better than you.' It became an important motto and kept my head level in a world of soaring and aggressive egos.

I returned to Australia just in time to sign up for a ten-day
mountaineering course in New Zealand in the summer of
1981. Only shortly after the course, however, my climbing
career nearly came to a sudden end. I had decided to spend
the remainder of the summer climbing in the New Zealand
Alps and teamed up with Andrew, a fellow member of the
mountaineering course. We had been holed up with two
New Zealand climbers in the Colin Todd Hut in Mount
Aspiring National Park for three days because of bad
weather. If we did not climb Mount Aspiring the next day,
we wouldn't be climbing it at all, as our food was nearly
gone.

Thankfully the weather cleared and early next morning
the four of us set off to climb Aspiring by its North West
Ridge. During those pre-dawn hours we shadowed the
New Zealand pair closely as they knew the start to the
North West Ridge, having climbed it once before. Three
hours later the cold, grey light of dawn revealed that we
had passed the ramp leading to the ridge and were standing
at the base of the more difficult South West Ridge. Feeling
pressured by time and a strong ambition to reach the
summit, we passed the New Zealanders and continued
upwards.

Our confidence was severely undermined when the ridge
suddenly steepened and the New Zealanders, even without
our time restrictions, decided to retreat. Being aware of our
new position only heightened the fear we already had. I
suspect it came not from the climb ahead of us, but because
we were now on our own. Our climbing instructor was no
longer looking over our shoulders pre-empting careless

actions. Now we had to put into use the skills we had learnt on the course, make our own decisions and be responsible for our actions.

It would have been far easier to go down, but the ridge, although intimidating, would be a great learning experience and a feather in our caps. We decided to proceed with caution. My fear grew with every step upwards, but I enjoyed facing this fear and making progress. Momentarily it disappeared as I crested the summit ridge and saw the summit only 40 metres away. The pick of my ice axe stuck in the ice just before I crested the ridge. I yanked on it to proceed, but it released too suddenly and the adze bounced off the right lens of my sunglasses and dug deep into my cheek. The impact and fright threw me off balance and nearly sent me tumbling backwards down the South West Face. At the last second I managed to hook a chunk of ice with the pick of my axe. Regaining my balance and composure I looked down at Andrew, who was holding my ropes, for an encouraging comment, but he was staring intently at the view.

Another short spurt of climbing and we were on the summit. The area was so small we had to take it in turns to stand there. Although the South West Ridge of Mount Aspiring is a relatively straightforward climb, considering the level of our own experience we felt we had overcome great obstacles to get there. The compulsory summit photos were taken and, feeling less threatened by the descent of the North West Ridge, we unroped and climbed down independently via the route we had originally intended to climb. The rocky buttresses confused us and we were forever crossing from one side of the ridge to the other to find the easiest way down. We should have used a rope on some sections but in the euphoria the summit had given us we fell to a false sense of security. Stopping to wait for Andrew at the bottom of one buttress, I looked back up to see him heading towards the opposite side of the ridge to negotiate a buttress via a steeper and more difficult side. No amount of yelling or waving could attract his attention.

Frustrated by the wind which muffled any attempt to communicate, I gave up and waited impatiently. Seeing easier ground ahead I removed my crampons and placed them in my pack with my ice axe. At least an hour went by before I saw Andrew on safer ground. I started down again. The delay created some urgency but I quickly cautioned myself to stop hurrying. The message had not quite reached my feet when I slipped on a rock slab that angled down towards a snow slope. I fell the couple of metres off the end of the slab onto hard-packed snow and with my ice axe and crampons in my pack, there was no way I could stop myself. My speed increased and I hurtled towards a band of rocks that stretched across the width of the snow slope. My gloves were torn from my hands as I tried to dig my fingers into the snow and I knew the only thing that was going to stop me was the band of rocks. They were alarmingly big and capable of shattering an arm or a leg but I must have an armour-plated behind. The rocks separated like tenpins and I continued to fall.

Several large rocks that I had dislodged bounced along beside me. I continued my slide down a second snow slope. Another rock band loomed some distance below. It marked the edge of a 200-metre cliff. In no time I was upon this final barrier, travelling at a great speed. Too frightened to think about pain I braced myself for the collision but instead once more I effortlessly knocked the rocks out of the way. It was the last thing I wanted to happen. Skidding on my backside across the final 3 metres of bare rock, I came to rest on the very edge, my legs dangling over the ledge. There, some 200 metres below, framed between my feet, were the jaws of the biggest crevasse I had ever seen. My body lurched forward to follow my feet, but at the point of near-perfect balance, and just before the point of no return, I stopped. And so did my heart as I waited to see which way I would fall. No amount of reaction would save me now. It seemed the only things holding me onto the rock were the wrinkles in my pants and at that moment I fell backwards onto the rock slab. It was my lucky day. I wriggled back onto the ledge and collapsed.

My heart still thumping, I removed my ice axe and crampons from my pack and, with skinned and bloodied hands, used them to assist my lame legs back up to the ridge-line. I collected my gloves from the trail well marked with splashes of blood, and it was only when I reached the ridge that I regained some composure. Andrew appeared within a few minutes and remained unaware of my detour despite my limp. Feeling a little embarrassed, I hid the scars of my accident until the following morning when, unable to walk normally because of the sprains and bruising, I had to offload some of my gear onto Andrew as we walked from the park.

———

I returned to Australia to work in the building industry. The four-year plumbing apprenticeship I had completed before going to Alaska was the only full-time job I would ever have, much to the dismay of my mother. Despite this trade behind me she was unhappy that I spent so much of my time and money on climbing, although the possibility of a fatal accident caused her the most distress.

I led a frugal life, owning little and, more importantly, owing nothing. Every spare dollar went towards climbing gear or my next climbing trip. Some saw me as a no-hoper or non-achiever and my childhood ambition to climb Everest remained a secret—an ambition most climbers never realise. The sceptics couldn't have been further from the truth. Climbing Everest was a worthwhile goal, and to me it was an unparalleled achievement in life.

Brisbane became my home for a couple of years. I found odd jobs as a plumber and I rockclimbed on the local cliffs, each summer was spent in the New Zealand Alps. There were always plenty of climbers to rockclimb with, but few who shared the same keen mountaineering ambitions. Those mountaineers within Australia who were climbing at a level I aspired to seemed out of reach. I finally found the confidence, however, to approach Australia's leading Himalayan climbers, Tim Macartney-Snape and Lincoln Hall, for a chance to join one of their Himalayan expeditions. To my complete surprise they asked me to join an expedition to Changabang, a 6864-metre mountain in the Garhwal Range, northern India, in April 1982. No expedition book I had read or my experience so far could have prepared me for the real world of high-altitude moun-taineering.

———————

By the time my overhead locker on the Air India jumbo sprang open as we bounced onto the runway at Delhi air-port, the excitement of travelling to my first Himalayan climb was well and truly over. A restless flight in crowded smoking-class seats, delays, and excess baggage charges left me in no mood to face pompous Indian customs officials or struggle with my heavy packs through the onslaught of beggars outside the terminal. I looked for Lincoln Hall everywhere but gave up and jumped into a motorised rick-shaw to speed off to the youth hostel where the expedition members were meeting. I was promptly short-changed fifty dollars by the rickshaw driver before I knew it. Wandering around the hostel for hours, I searched for anyone who looked remotely like a climber but found no-one and began to wonder if I was in the right place. Walking the streets was not a wise thing to do, considering my experi-ence with the rickshaw driver, so I stayed in my room. There was no drinkable or hot water and the smell of sewage permeated from a small hole in the bathroom floor.

By the end of my second day in Delhi I had met all nine members of the expedition but I was so sick I couldn't recall any names. I suffered explosive diarrhoea, and painful stomach cramps gave only a thirty-second warning to find a toilet. On several occasions I failed. To save weight I had only brought three pairs of underpants for the six-week expedition, but by the time we were ready to leave Delhi, all three pairs were in the bin. In this condition, I was not looking forward to the slow and bumpy two-day bus trip up to the Garhwal Range.

Although our walk through the Rishi Gorge is still one of the most memorable I have ever done, we were plagued with the problem of porters who, demanding more money, either refused to walk the agreed distance for that day or went on strike at a moment's notice. The biggest concern for me, however, was not the porters—Tim and Lincoln handled them better than anyone could—it was my fear of losing too much weight because of my bout of diarrhoea. This was exacerbated by being a fussy eater. By the end of the second week, I was stripped of the fitness level I had trained so hard for in the pre-expedition months in Australia.

Porter problems persisted and it looked increasingly as if we would have to turn back the way we had come without setting foot on the mountain. On the sixth day of our ten-day walk into Changabang BC our porters went on strike again, this time refusing to carry any further with the threat of leaving everything where we were to return to their village. Fortunately Tim and Lincoln struck a reasonable but disappointing compromise. From this agreement the porters received more money for less work, carrying for two more days along an easier path to another mountain called Trisul. Without ever having experienced altitude before, I had already crossed Trisul off as a disappointing consolation prize. A rounded lump in appearance and 300 metres higher, it offered none of the challenge of the greyish-white, granite fang of Changabang. However, my

judgement was based on my inexperience with altitude—
even after a couple of days in BC I could barely drag one
foot after the other from lack of breath and motivation.

Being by nature quiet and by far the youngest in the
team I only made lasting relationships with Tim, Lincoln
and John Coulton. It was also John's first Himalayan climb
and we shared the highs and lows of this great adventure
and were captivated by Tim's and Lincoln's talk of going to
Everest in a couple of years' time. Already planning for this
expedition and with the lead-up climbs they had in the
making between now and then, they would reach Everest
at the peak of their climbing careers. Each of them had
crammed a wealth of climbing adventure into his life and it
shattered any illusion that there might be some shortcut to
Everest for me. I would have to earn my stripes the hard
way as they had done.

My home-made plan for dealing with the altitude wasn't
working. I had imagined I could stop for a short rest, catch
my breath and start again, just as I did when bushwalking.
It was a matter of fitness I thought: the fitter I was, the
faster I would climb and the shorter my rests would be.
Little did I know that at around 6000 metres I would
barely be able to string thirty steps together, that my head
would pound three times to every step, and I would be
overcome by nausea. I wanted to go home. Relief from a
long rest only lasted the first half-dozen steps before I felt
absolutely shattered. I had to find something extra within
me to make any progress up the mountain.

Over the next two weeks as we set up C1 and C2, there
was no relief from the headaches and nausea. Suppressed

appetite and the occasional spell of bad weather caused uncontrollable bouts of homesickness and depression. Fortunately Tim's advice that this would pass once my body adjusted to the altitude was right. Four weeks after leaving home, I emerged from my tent at C2 with a clear head and an eagerness to go up instead of home. The next morning we would climb to C3 at 6500 metres before the final 700-metre climb to the summit.

At C3 after an exhausting but encouraging day's climb, I meticulously prepared my gear for tomorrow's 4.00 a.m. start to the summit climb the next morning. At last I was excited to be here. High anxiety kept me awake for most of the night until the unthinkable happened, at least for a novice Himalayan climber like me. At midnight a storm blew away my summit dreams and destroyed one of our three tents. With nine climbers crammed into two two-man tents, we endured a second night in the same storm. Wind gusts lifted our tent, even with the combined weight of five climbers and nearly tipped the lot of us over the edge. The only way we could save ourselves was to dive to the wind-ward side. During the night our tent became a group body bag when the poles broke and the outer fly was ripped off, leaving only a thin layer of nylon between us and freezing to death. Being the smallest, I knelt in the middle of the tent to keep it off our heads. Two or three of the others lay motionless. They had foolishly taken sleeping-pills to help obliterate the misery of our situation, without first thinking about the life-and-death decisions that would have to be made if the tent ripped open.

My awkward stance kneeling in the tent made my arms

and legs ache and the noise of the incessant flapping around my ears was driving me insane. What would we do if this nylon sack we were sheltering in ripped open? Where would we go? How would we save ourselves from freezing to death? As many unlikely answers flashed through my mind, my worst nightmare was realised. Half a dozen rips appeared simultaneously in the stitched seams of our tent. As I was about to warn everyone that this was it, that our tent was about to explode like an expanding balloon, I realised with immense relief that the gaping holes were in fact sparks of static electricity chasing each other around the seams of our tent.

By early morning, the eye of the storm had passed over us. Battle worn and weary, we had just enough time to gather our belongings and descend the mountain. No-one cared about the summit any more.

This climb on Trisul, although unsuccessful, was a huge leap in my learning curve as a mountaineer, especially in the rigours of climbing and surviving at high altitude. It was a tough but necessary lesson. I was glad when it was all over and I vowed never to return to the Himalayas again.

In little time, however, my recollections of the worst faded and it left me with little choice but to return the following year.

ANNAPURNA II, 1983

chapter three

C3 7100m

C2 6600m

Easier and safer route taken after first climbing the ridge

C1 5800m

Route taken after avalanches take out fixed ropes over here

To ABC 4700m

I soon started to pester Tim and Lincoln for another chance to return to the Himalayas. While climbing Trisul, they had spoken at length about their next climb to Annapurna II in the Himalayan range west of Kathmandu in Nepal. The town of Pokhara has the magnificent Annapurna mountains as its immediate backdrop. As the months turned into a year, Tim and Lincoln did not respond to my persistent letters and phone calls. The expedition was well under way: Andy Henderson and Greg Mortimer, Australian climbers with similar experience, were joining them. It seemed they had no room for me and I had given up hope, when Lincoln arrived in Brisbane from Sydney to collect some custom-made clothing and sleeping-bags for the expedition. During his short and busy stay he found a day to do a multi-pitch rockclimb with me on our local Mount Maroon. As he threw his climbing gear into the boot of his car before leaving, he said almost non-chalantly, 'Better pack your bags for Annapurna, Mike.' I could hardly contain my excitement and my casual acceptance came more from shock than indifference. The final arrangements would have to be sorted out by phone with

Lincoln or Tim at some other stage, but for now all I knew was that I was going, and that was all that mattered. It was early June 1983 and I would have to be in Kathmandu on 3 August.

After two months of intensive training and preparation and an extra night job washing dishes at a restaurant, I finally made it: fit, with bags packed and enough money to pay my share of the expedition costs.

The South Ridge of Annapurna II had been attempted four times without success. Tim, Lincoln, Andy, Greg and I and a small team of Sherpas made the fifth attempt in August 1983. When I first saw the ridge, which dominates the Pokhara skyline, I could understand why they had chosen it as a training climb before their Everest attempt the next year.

After a six-day walk from Pokhara we reached BC. The final day reminded me of walking in Lamington National Park, only there was no track and we had to slash a path with machetes and construct the odd bridge to get across monsoon-swollen rivers. It was an unusual BC in that it was only temporary and sat in the middle of rainforest at only 2600 metres. It was far too low to operate from for a mountain as high and as difficult as Annapurna II but it was as high as we could go with our forty porters. Tim had an idea where our eventual Advanced Base Camp (ABC) would be, but in that stretch the terrain was too steep and dangerous for the porters. With enormous help from our two climbing Sherpas, Narayan and Tenzing, a couple of our strongest porters, and the occasional load-carry by our mail runner, Onche, we carried everything ourselves up to

ABC. Maila and Tomboy were our cook and kitchen boy and I'm not convinced they had the preferred job as they sometimes had to cook under the most trying conditions. Narayan I knew well from the Trisul climb and it didn't take long to befriend the others. Both Narayan and Onche were rogues, often plotting practical jokes on the climbing party and I regularly fell prey to their harmless fun. Thankfully on one occasion they targeted another. At BC we kept three or four able-bodied porters to help carry our loads up to the next depot camp. Because of our remote location, the porters were given food and an increase in their daily allowance. There was one porter, however, who was constantly seeking more food. Narayan was tired of such demands on our limited supplies, and when the porter approached the kitchen tent for another hot drink, Narayan seized the opportunity. 'Why don't you try some coffee? All the sahibs drink it.' The porter extended his hand greedily for the cup, which Narayan had filled with ten tea-spoons of coffee and eight of sugar. For someone who had never experienced caffeine before, it acted as a drug over-dose. In a few minutes the unfortunate fellow was curled up on the ground with dizzy spells and stomach cramps. Onche played along perfectly, 'You fool, Narayan! You've poisoned him. Now we'll have to carry his loads.'

The incident had its desired effect. The porter kept his distance from the kitchen and treated everything handed to him by Narayan or Onche with understandable suspicion.

The distance between BC and ABC was too far and dif-ficult to cover in a single day, so we established two inter-mediate camps. Every day over the next two weeks the five climbers and five Sherpas struggled with heavy, unwieldy loads through thick bamboo forests and up steep grass slopes that required the use of fixed ropes, as a slip would have been fatal. To make our task even more difficult, we had to tolerate the draining heat and humidity of the monsoon season.

It would often start raining around mid-morning and, if we were lucky, cease by late afternoon. Otherwise it would continue to rain into the night, and with it came the ankle-deep mud and leeches. I was used to leeches from bush-walking as a young boy, but nothing prepared me for the quantities of leeches that lie in wait below the southern slopes of Annapurna II. Repellent was washed off by the rain and the leeches quickly found their way into our tents and sleeping-bags. Bites, mainly around my ankles and lower legs, soon became infected because I could not stop scratching them. They turned into open sores and the daily removal of my socks only irritated the sores even more. It was impossible to prevent the bites; stopping to pull the leeches off only meant more latched on. I did, however, manage to wreak some revenge by standing around BC for an extra fifteen minutes to attract as many leeches as possible, then with boots full of them I would climb as quickly as the slippery trail would allow. It seems leeches die from a sudden change in altitude and some 800 metres higher I could stop to pick off countless rubbery and very dead blobs from my blood-soaked socks.

On most expeditions, you can only afford to bring a limited number of changes of clothes, maybe two or three sets. Normally I would have kept one set for the dirtiest work and changed at night, but here it was senseless to change at all because of the moisture in the air, which was saturated with either rain or humidity. At night, before crawling into our sleeping-bags, we tossed our daytime clothes into the corner of the tent, where they sat in a muddy, damp pile until morning. Wearing only one set of clothes in such conditions for so long meant that I eventually lost a sleeve and pocket due to rot.

We had many obstacles to overcome on our way to ABC and each night Tim would discuss the best way to overcome anticipated hurdles. One of these was a 70-metre-high rock face, down the centre of which tumbled a small waterfall. I was standing at its base next to Greg and Lincoln as one of them belayed Tim up the rock. We had hired a local Nepalese as a guide to ABC, as there were no trails to lead us there. Tim was halfway up, his long arms and legs searching for holds on the water-smoothed surface, when quite unexpectedly our guide started up the rock, scaling it barefoot and effortlessly without a rope. One look up his baggy trousers revealed he wore no underpants.

Tim had no idea he was being followed until he was overtaken. The guide politely stopped to tell Tim that he thought Tim was indeed a good rockclimber, then nimbly completed the remaining 30 metres, leaving Tim unsure which hand or foot to move next.

Our guide had no idea of the technical side of rockclimbing but was so confident in his footwork and his own ability—qualities that are essential to everyday survival in the rugged foothills of the Himalayas—that climbing this rock face was second nature to him, despite the fact that there was no room for error.

Returning from a carry to the higher of the two intermediate camps between BC and ABC, I slipped on a greasy rock and fell off the trail. My fall was cushioned a little by bushes that resembled wild raspberry. By the time I had thrashed around and found my feet, I was some 15 metres below the trail and a few metres above a high cliff. Standing in the middle of this prickly trap, I was not concerned so much about the exposure below me but more of what the others might think when they learnt I had fallen off the trail. Would they decide against me climbing above BC if I was having trouble staying on this easier trail? By the time I fought my way back up to our camp, I was covered from head to toe in bloody scratches, my rotting shirt torn even more. Lincoln and Tim caught me trying to sneak into one of the tents, and couldn't help laughing when I admitted what had happened. Over the next few days, I was beset by unbearable itching around the leech bites and newly acquired scratches.

Just getting to ABC at 4700 metres on Annapurna II was an expedition in itself, but the real climbing started just above it. After we had crossed a small glacier there was a 250-metre-high rock band to negotiate. From a distance it looked intimidating—the bottom half of smooth, rocky slabs was the most difficult; the top half relented to a slightly easier way via a steep chimney. We used pitons hammered into cracks to secure our ropes. But it was the upper part of the rock band that was the most dangerous, as the chimney acted as a funnel for loose rocks and the odd block of ice. One day during a load-carrying exercise, the word 'Rock!' echoed down the gully from above. Jumarring on a rope somewhere around mid-height, I could hear the rock coming. It sounded huge and my only escape was around the corner to the left of the gully. To get there required quick action and precise footwork on the minimal holds available. Before I had a chance to hesitate, I made the dicey moves across and was out of harm's way.

Finely balanced above a sizeable cliff face, the sound of the rock ricocheting off the walls of the gully above me was unnerving. I was thankful of my protected position, and began to gloat at the cockiness of my actions, when it suddenly dawned on me that my right hand was still holding onto a rock in the gully. I could not let go, as it was this hand that held me in place. For a couple of long seconds I listened, urging the rock to pass. Surely it wouldn't hit my hand. Sure enough it did. It hit so hard that I thought some of my fingers had been severed. I began to feel dizzy. Worst of all I knew I couldn't let go to relieve the pain and inspect the damage.

There was none of the cockiness in my actions as I reversed the moves back into the chimney and dared to peek at my hand. All the fingers and thumb were intact, but blood gushed from the back of my hand. Gritting my teeth with the pain, I used my left hand and feet to make the delicate moves into the middle of the chimney, where I slumped nursing my shattered hand. More rocks could have come tumbling down. If they had, I could not have cared less. I wrapped my hand in a dirty handkerchief and for the next two weeks managed with only my left hand.

Foolishly I did not tell the others for fear I would be seen as a walking disaster. All the accidents involving injuries were happening to me and I feared I could be banished to BC for the duration of the climb.

Once on top of the rock band, we turned right to follow a 6- to 8-metre-wide strip of rock that made up the distance between the edge of the rock band and a glacier off to our left. In some places it resembled a road, but this easy street lasted only 100 metres or so before ending in the jumbled wilderness of the glacier. Here we had two choices of route and, after much discussion among the group, there seemed to be no consensus on one particular way. While Tim stayed to organise ABC, the rest of us split into pairs and on alternate days one pair would explore an option to find a suitable site for C1. Lincoln and I chose the ridge route to C1, which we would explore the day after Greg and Andy had ventured onto their preferred glacier route.

I could tell it was going to be a long day. Lincoln was determined to investigate the full potential of the ridge and he telegraphed this intention right from the start via the tight rope that connected us. It would remain that way for the rest of the day as he practically dragged me up the ridge. Fortunately he was patient and understanding with the beginner floundering to keep up and stopped for regular rests, but it wasn't until 4.30 that afternoon that he finally stopped on a small rise on the ridge. I could go no further. My head, arms and legs ached, and my face, dry and sunburnt from the blistering sun, felt as if it had done several rounds in the microwave on high. It was hard to

imagine that at nearly 6000 metres in the Himalayas surrounded by snow, it was easily 30°C. When Lincoln told
me he could see a suitable site for C1 only 50 metres down
a gentle slope, I could not will myself to move. Never have
I felt so utterly exhausted from the effects of altitude.

The fact that we had found a site for C1 meant to me
that it would be the preferred option over the glacier route
favoured by Greg and Andy. I didn't know if I had the
energy to get down from C1, let alone do it all over again
tomorrow. I could only make that decision in the morning.
Meanwhile Lincoln strolled effortlessly down and levelled a
small area for the contents of his pack. He returned to collect mine and his energy made me feel guilty and even more
inadequate. I consoled myself with the knowledge that I
would eventually get used to high-altitude mountaineering. And somehow I did.

For the next week we operated out of ABC carrying
loads of food, fuel and climbing equipment such as stoves,
tents, ropes, pitons and snowstakes. No-one coped well
enough with the debilitating effects of the altitude to carry
two loads in a row. We needed more time at this altitude
for our bodies to adjust. This pleased me no end and the
difference a rest day made was all I needed to return and
do three more carries to C1.

Once we had settled into C1, we wasted no time making
an exploratory trip to find a safe route and site for C2. We
left C1 shortly after 7.30 a.m. and Greg, Andy, Tim and I
enjoyed an exhilarating day's climbing on the exposed
South Ridge leading up to C2. By the time Greg and I
arrived, Tim and Andy were already on their way down as

it was getting late. Although I was tired when I arrived at the site of C2, it was nothing compared to my first day's climb to C1, and I felt some satisfaction in feeling as though I was beginning to cope with the altitude. Because of the terrain on the South Ridge we had no choice in our placement of C2. At 6600 metres, on a small notch along the ridge, it became a wind tunnel and an unpopular camp in which to spend any length of time.

Long shadows heralded nightfall and reminded us that we had not brought our head-torches—we had mistakenly believed that the route to C2 was going to be straightforward. Greg led the way back down until we came to a section of the ridge that required careful climbing. Here we stood somewhat puzzled by the black void beneath us. Fortunately lightning strikes from a thunderstorm near Pokhara, 6000 metres below, lit up the mountain sufficiently to show a way down the next difficult section of the ridge. When a lightning strike gave us an image of the terrain below, we attempted to climb down, but sometimes my memory failed me and I would take a step into thin air, fortunately without mishap. The ridge eased considerably after an hour and it then became a casual stroll back to C1.

The ridge to C2 was never used again, as it would take more fixed rope than we had, so an alternative was found by abseiling off the eastern side of the ridge to start a long angling traverse up to C2. This route, although easier, had its dangers. Collapsing cornices and avalanche-prone slopes made it a run of the gauntlet. The closest call happened to Lincoln. One afternoon, as he hobbled slowly back to C1, I noticed new scratches on his helmet, and he was rubbing a limp right shoulder. He could not hide the pain as he told us how, when he had flicked one of the fixed ropes to start the jumar up to the crest of the ridge, he had dislodged a large block of rock onto himself. Lincoln was lucky as his shoulder was only badly bruised but he would need to rest a suspected broken foot for a week or two.

The onset of inclement weather meant we had to amuse ourselves for two long and dull days at C1. I found this more difficult to deal with than the altitude and, although a good book does help, I am not one to read all day. We had dug a snow cave for a kitchen and here I busied myself by melting snow on our kerosene stoves for hot drinks. The others all had Walkmans, so if one was left sitting idle for too long, I would sneak a half hour or so as battery power was always at a premium.

Lincoln continued to nurse his injured foot once the weather had cleared, so he volunteered to stay at C1 as chief cook, while the others continued carrying loads to C2. I was less fortunate. A badly infected split lip and the large, weeping leech bites on my feet forced me to return to ABC to clean and dry them out.

From the top of the rock band I was excited to see ABC on the grassy meadow just below the glacier. I had not been at this warm, sunny place for two weeks and I was looking forward to having a wash, a large plate of fried rice and some milk tea. But my descent was barricaded by large blocks of ice on what was once a wide strip of smooth rock. The glacier at the top of the rock band had started to move towards the edge under which our fixed ropes hung. Clambering over the jumbled mess of ice blocks, I located the top of our fixed ropes and began my abseil. Midway down there was a short traverse across the rock face to pick up a steep abseil to the glacier at the base of the rock band but here I found only fragments of crushed ice and the smell of powdered rock. The traverse rope dangled in space on the other side. Fortunately the traverse was not too difficult without a rope and I was able to retrieve it and knot together the two frayed ends.

We did not have radio communication, so I spent the next few days at ABC with Maila and Tomboy anxiously waiting for news from above. During this time large blocks of ice continued to crash down the rock band. At last after lunch one afternoon I saw a number of unidentifiable figures appear at the top of the rock band. They seemed to be taking much longer than normal to reach ABC and it wasn't difficult to guess why. When Andy, Tim, Greg and Lincoln arrived at ABC late that afternoon they told me they too had had to join damaged pieces of rope to get down. Over the next day or so we watched the glacier bombard our fixed ropes, and with binoculars we could see them hanging in tatters. I found this setback so discouraging that I felt it was futile for us to continue with the climb—I could have easily packed up and gone home. My companions, however, demonstrated the necessary motivation to get up one of these big Himalayan mountains. It was just one of many impressive examples I would store in the back of my mind as inspiration in years to come. We retrieved what ropes we could to prevent further damage to our limited supply before attending to a more urgent problem: we had run out of food at ABC.

We were now getting to the end of our sixth week. To continue the climb, a safer line up the rock band was essential, but more immediate was the restocking of food and fuel as we had only budgeted for six weeks. Once again it was an unexpected obstacle that would have defeated me, but motivated by the persistence of the others, I followed blindly. All of us with the exception of Maila, Tomboy and Lincoln, who was still suffering from his foot injury, went in search of food. With empty packs we descended 3000 metres in one day to a subsistence village called Hoga to buy whatever we could. That night in one of the open-sided huts, after a meal of boiled potatoes, I lay on a grass mat beside an open fire as rain pelted down and a miserable soaking looked inevitable. I wondered when the thatched roof would start to leak, but it was the last thought I had as the thick blanket of air at this low-altitude village made sleep come easily.

I woke gratefully dry, but the morning brought further rain. After a breakfast of more boiled potatoes I packed 15 litres of kerosene, topped up the remaining space in my pack with potatoes and tried hard not to think of the climb ahead—3 vertical kilometres of muddy trail back up to ABC. By 10.00 a.m. I was hungry. By midday I was ravenous and in rain that never seemed to end, I took from my pack a large raw potato. I ate it all except the last mouthful, which I spat out because it was mostly dirt. It was 6.00 p.m. before I climbed the grassy slope to ABC and made a bee-line to the kitchen tent. I sat exhausted, clouds of steam

rising from my sweating back, my hands trembling from
lack of food. Maila, our cook, patiently cooked whatever I
wanted, so long as it was rice and dahl. Tim, Greg and
Andy arrived in much the same condition.

It took two days to recover from our marathon food-
gathering effort before Greg and I went in search of a safer
route to the right of our original line on the rock band. The
others followed, rearranging and adding more pitons for
tie-off points for the rope. The low-angled slope leading to
C1 was dangerously overloaded with snow that had fallen
in the last week. Because of the likelihood of starting an
avalanche in the knee-deep snow, we climbed this slope one
at a time, while those behind sheltered under an overhanging ice cliff. C1 had disappeared beneath a metre of
fresh snow, so we scraped and poked gently with our ice
axes and snow shovels to find our tents and snow cave. One
tent was damaged beyond repair; the other two required
extensive repairs. The loss of one tent changed the sleeping
arrangements—Narayan and Tenzing moved to the kitchen
snow cave, Tim and Lincoln to the smaller tent, and I
bunked with Andy and Greg.

There wasn't much room in the tent that night with
three of us and all our belongings. The air was full of
climbing talk as Andy and Greg reminisced about past
adventures. They then started talking about food—their
preferences to the tiresome rice and dahl which had been
our standard menu for the last six or seven weeks. It was
self-inflicted torture. The real discomfort came later, however, when I needed to take a leak. I did not want to wake
the others, but finally in the early hours of the morning,

necessity overtook concern. I wriggled from my sleeping-bag trapped between Greg and Andy, who had both slid in towards the centre of the tent. I groped around in my sleeping-bag for one of the two bottles I always kept there at night. Making sure the bottle I found was not my water-bottle, I knelt in my sleeping-bag and began to pee into it, keeping one finger close to the top to warn against over-flow. My movements until then had not woken Andy or Greg, but the sound of the carefully regulated flow was like an alarm bell and they woke to follow my example.

On 30 September we stopped for a rest day having reached C2. I had been hoping for a chance to reach the summit, but as we prepared the supplies to be carried to C3, it became obvious that only four were going to the summit from C3 and I guessed that didn't include me. I asked Tim and he confirmed my suspicion, saying that only two pairs would be climbing above C3 and that an extra person would only slow things down. Although it was a blow I had anticipated right from the beginning of the expedition, it really didn't hit home until the next day when all seven of us, including the two Sherpas, Narayan and Tenzing, carried the first and final loads to C3. It was a spectacular day, made even more thrilling by a sense of discovery in covering new ground, and a change of scenery that unfolded as we climbed above the surrounding ridges which had for so long curtained our panorama.

To avoid wearing ourselves out with the tiresome load-carrying between the higher camps, the weight of our load to C3 was cut to a bare minimum. This meant sacrificing the tents in favour of building a snow cave. It was the preferred option, as Tim and Lincoln had learnt from our storm on Trisul that a snow cave couldn't rip open or blow away. To build a cave requires a slope with snow soft enough to tunnel into. At 7100 metres Greg found suitable conditions. Above us soared the remaining 800 metres of the steep and unrelenting South Ridge. Vast tracts of powder snow filled the fracture lines that lead to the summit. I wanted to continue on and in a half-hearted attempt to gain more height, I climbed another 50 metres to take a photo before returning to C3. There, the only sign of Greg was his two feet paddling in a flurry of snow. Like a dog burying a bone, he had tunnelled head first into the snow bank. Placing the supplies that I had carried up in a secure place, I shouldered my empty pack to begin my descent. Tenzing was also emptying his pack, while Narayan was involved in a lengthy conversation with Tim. Not wanting to prolong my disappointment, I wished the boys luck and left Narayan and Tenzing to make their own way down.

Ill-tempered, I stomped off down the slopes that had taken us five hard hours to ascend and reached C2 in fifty-five minutes. I was bitter because now I had fully acclimatised and felt confident I was capable of contributing much more to the climb, that I was indeed capable of making the summit. Tim thought otherwise and he was right. First I had to earn my stripes; the summits would follow. I had reacted with the immaturity of an inexperienced climber and had placed far too much emphasis on reaching the summit.

Tenzing and Narayan tried to catch up but gave up the chase. By the time they arrived at C2, I had made tea for them and we sat in the warm afternoon sun to drink it. The weather had been perfect and if it remained this way, the others would summit tomorrow or the next day. Narayan told me that at C3 he had been trying to persuade Tim to take me to the summit. I thanked him for his sincere support.

It was the calm before the storm. That night the weather broke and the wind punched its way through the narrow col of C2 in gusts emulating the same force as the storm on Trisul the year before. I had thought the Trisul storm was a normal Himalayan mountain storm until I was relieved to hear from Tim and Lincoln that we had survived the worst storm they had ever experienced. Now, twelve months later, I thought I was about to face another equally as bad. Narayan and Tenzing were in one tent; I was alone in the other. I sat on the windward side of the tent with my back pushed hard into its wall, but the gale-force wind just picked up the tent and tossed me to the other side. Concentrating intently on my own precarious position, I failed to think of the obvious solution. During a short lull in the storm, Narayan yelled, 'Mike, come to our tent or we'll all be blown away.' I hurriedly stuffed boots and gloves into my sleeping-bag as my tent threatened to break its tie-downs and release into the wind. As I crawled from my tent, I pulled out the poles to collapse it to the ground. If anything was left of it by morning, we could pack it then. Now the three of us battled to keep the remaining tent on the ground and in one piece by sitting our combined weight on the windward side. Even then we were pushed and shoved relentlessly in all directions as the fabric whipped and the poles shuddered. Finally at 2.00 a.m. the storm subsided and we more or less fell asleep still bracing ourselves against the tent wall.

Over the next three days, as the wind continued to blow violently, we built a wall of ice blocks to protect our tent. But even this needed constant repair as the wind blew large holes through the wall, which then threatened to collapse onto the tent.

By 4 October we were all expecting and hoping for a quick ascent of the mountain once C3 was in place. Tenzing, Narayan and I were to wait at C2 for the others to return, but the change in the weather made sure that it was going to be a drawn-out affair. On the occasional foray outside the tent, I scanned the wind-raked ridge for movement on the mountain. There had been none for days. On the afternoon of 4 October, however, Lincoln and Greg arrived at C2. I half-expected them to say they had given up, but I should have known better. They had come down to get more food and fuel. Handing over what little food we had left, I told Lincoln that we wouldn't be able to wait for them with the little supplies we had left. As soon as the weather cleared, we would head down to C1. I had desperately wanted to reach the summit, but at that point I was glad it was them trudging wearily back to C3 and not me. Once again I admired their determination.

On the morning of the third day, there was no breakfast as our food and fuel supplies were gone, except for a small stash that was meant for the four at C3 when they returned.

It would have been a mistake to use up the remaining supplies by waiting any longer for them. On the other hand I was reluctant to leave them behind in case they needed help. Tenzing and Narayan made the camp as secure as possible under the conditions, while I packed the excess of climbing hardware and equipment into our packs. Only one tent and the remaining food and fuel were left.

Our day started badly. Masking our faces against the sting of ice pellets blasting from the crest of the ridge, we leaned into the gale with heavy packs trying to make some headway. Once we had descended a short distance on the leeward side of the ridge, we were no longer bothered by the wind, but a more real danger emerged as we floundered in thigh-deep snow—avalanche.

For a moment I became confused. Were we inviting disaster by descending into an irreversible position? Should we return to the wind-battered tent at C2? An escape route tempted us just 60 metres ahead, if we could only get there without being swept away. A spur slightly higher than the surrounding slopes dropped 400 metres down to a glacier; from here we could descend the valley to a point where our ridge dropped to within 80 metres of the glacier. We could then climb directly back up to the ridge crest and along to C1. As we swam and dug our way to the spur, large cracks began to appear in the snow above, the trail collapsed behind us and the ground beneath our feet began to break up and slide towards the glacier. I stopped dead in my tracks. The hair on the back of my neck lifted. I was slipping towards the valley. Luckily the slope then ceased moving and we carefully continued, one at a time to avoid overloading the stressed slope. Once on the spur, we descended without any mishap to the glacier. The slope we had just crossed crumbled and tumbled past us in a foaming wave to our left before fanning out across the valley.

We arrived at C1 early in the night. Only a light breeze blew now as we wearily poked around with our ice axes near the bamboo wand that marked the buried entrance to the snow cave. We had to find it as we had no tents with us and the tent that had helped accommodate us with the snow cave at C1 had been moved up the mountain to C2. Once inside, the cosiness of our little cave unveiled itself with a couple of lit candles and the cold, black night was shut from our minds with one of our climbing packs shoved in the entrance.

As we sat in our sleeping-bags, Narayan complained that there was nothing to eat and no stove to make drinks, only a container of kero. Using part of my handkerchief, I fashioned a wick to place in one of the two old food tins that we found in our rubbish bag. Filling one tin with kerosene, I lit my handkerchief and we now had a crude form of stove. Unfortunately the second tin we used as a small pot still had the remnants of its previous filling and the melted snow produced a cold, oily scum. When you are thirsty, it doesn't matter. If only we had something to eat!

I poured abuse on my heavy and uncooperative rucksack the next morning as I forced it through the tunnel entrance of our snow cave. I emerged to a bright, sunny day. Two or three black dots could be seen standing around C3. I wondered if they would head for the summit today. I did not feel guilty leaving them behind, because again there were not the supplies here to allow us to wait. Considering the weather over the last couple of days, I knew that they would not have reached the summit. How long they were prepared to wait I did not know because we had no radio, a luxury we could ill-afford on our shoe-string budget.

While I waited for Tenzing and Narayan to scramble over some large blocks of ice, I once again stood at the top of the rock band with longing eyes on the comforts of ABC only an hour below. But this time I wanted to go further than ABC. I longed for home now that my summit aspirations were gone. With visions of Australia occupying my mind, the more recent surge of activity by the glacier above the rock band almost went unnoticed. The glacier was now breaking over a far wider front, including the new position for our fixed ropes. Tenzing and Narayan stayed close together some 30 metres behind me, while I checked the ropes and anchors. About halfway down our abseil, I was distracted by a sound similar to a rifle shot, and looking directly above me, I saw a block of ice break away from the glacier 100 metres above. Its sheer bulk, about the size of a small caravan, gave the impression that it was floating towards me, until some smaller blocks shattered around me. Still attached to the fixed rope by a karabiner, I dashed for a small overhang as the concrete-hard mass exploded only a few metres above. Although I was completely safe under the overhang, I had only just made it in time. I protected my ears from the noise of the explosion as powdered ice poured from above and the smell of crushed rock filled the air. I saw the look of disbelief on the faces of Narayan and Tenzing as they swung around the corner. At first they saw only the fixed rope dangling in space, then with a sigh of relief, they caught sight of me cowering behind the curtain of powdered ice.

Once the veil of snow had disappeared Narayan asked with a cheeky grin, 'Which way now, Mike Sahib?'

It was then that I took some notice of our descent route. A 1-metre-wide ramp of blue ice dropped for 6 metres at an angle of 45 degrees to easier ground, but to make things difficult, this glass-smooth ramp also sloped steeply across its width to a massive drop and the jumbled glacier 100 metres below. The frayed end of our fixed rope hung in space at the far end. Another rope would have been the answer but our spare ropes were at C3 for the summit climb. I had no choice but to down-climb this slippery section. I faced the ice and kicked the front points of my crampons hard into it, using the pick of my ice axe to maintain balance. Balance was the key to descending this section, as the points of my crampons and ice axe would penetrate the ice only a few millimetres. About halfway down I wished I had left my large, cumbersome pack at the top of the ramp for Narayan to lower, as it kept throwing me off balance by catching on the rock face. Under its weight my confidence rapidly faded, as did the strength of my calf muscles. At one point I hesitated as I thought I might fall. Should I climb back up or risk continuing down? Hesitation was costing me strength and rattling my nerve, so I quickly decided to continue down trying not to think of the consequences of a fall. It was a sobering and frightening experience so close to the safety of ABC at a time when my mind had switched off and

I was thinking of home. Once on safe ground, I was able to throw Narayan the end of the fixed rope. He wove an unrecognisable knot with the two frayed ends, then proceeded to abseil down to me. Tenzing followed.

––––––––

For two days we enjoyed the relaxation of ABC. Tenzing and Narayan complained of sunburn, only the paler circles around their eyes which had been protected by their sunglasses remained unscathed. This gave them a 'Teddy Bear' appearance. Despite our lethargy, we continued to scan the upper slopes for the others. Seeing nothing, I became increasingly concerned. During this time, avalanches regularly threatened our ropes on the rock band, making any attempt to return to the mountain far too risky. It came as no surprise one morning when Narayan told me that we would have to leave ABC the following morning and wait in a village down valley, as our supplies were almost gone. It had not bothered me to leave C2 while the rest of our party was still high on the mountain because I had no choice. Now, however, although the circumstances were the same, I felt guilty about deserting them because leaving ABC was like cutting the safety line.

We packed what little food and fuel there was left at ABC and stored it safely in the kitchen tent with a note to say we would be waiting for them at Siklis, a village two days' walk away.

From Siklis I sent Tomboy and Onche out to Kathmandu to advise our trekking agent that we would be another week. I was reluctant to say that I hadn't been in contact with Tim, Lincoln, Andy and Greg for the past week, as I didn't know how the information would be used. At Siklis Tenzing, Narayan, Maila and I slept around a small open fire in a dark and dingy attic. Lice soon invaded our sleeping-bags, and our room filled with smoke from the daily routine of cooking on a fire over which Tenzing juggled various pots to prepare whatever he had begged from the village folk. We were in no position to complain, for we had no money and we had to get by on the generosity of the locals.

I constantly worried about what I should do to help the others up on the mountain but found no real solution. Each morning, with homesickness and boredom now my enemy, I walked to the outskirts of the village with my only book, *Slow Boat to China*—appropriately titled considering the circumstances. Seeking out the same large, flat rock facing Annapurna II every day, I lay in the sun to read my daily ration of fifty pages. For hours I watched the trail heading up the valley to Annapurna II before wandering back to the village to an early dinner of boiled rice and a restless night.

Tenzing, Narayan and I became increasingly concerned as the days passed with no word from the others. My anxiety was temporarily broken when an Australian trekking group made camp just outside the village and I was invited by the trek leader, Judy Pyne, to join the dozen members for dinner. It was a welcoming distraction from my worries and a night of good conversation and plenty of food. The most interesting piece of news was that the Australians had won the America's Cup—a 130-year-old yacht race the

Aussies had been trying to win from the Americans for the last couple of decades. Although it was satisfying news, it seemed strange that after two months without contact with the outside world and in the middle of the Himalayas, this was the first news I should hear. I was sorry to see them move on the next day.

Although we could see most of the climbing route along the South Ridge of Annapurna II from the village, a great deal of snow had fallen and we were too far away to see any movement on the mountain. On the morning of the ninth day of waiting, it was time for me to make a decision. I figured if they were still coming down, then all we could do was meet them below ABC and assist with their heavy packs. If one or two were injured, then someone would be on his way down to get help, and then it would become a case of organising assistance from this village, or sending a message to Pokhara or Kathmandu. If they were dead, there would be nothing any of us could do. I felt the best thing was for me to wait at Siklis, while Narayan and Tenzing walked back towards ABC. We agreed that if by the end of the third day neither of them had returned, it meant they had not found the party below ABC and they would wait at ABC, using the provisions we had left there until they ran out. I was to head for Kathmandu on the morning of the fourth day to inform our trekking agent and the families of Tim, Lincoln, Andy and Greg via the Australian Embassy that they were missing. I would then return to ABC with money and more porters carrying more food and rope in case we had to go above the rock band again. It was mid-afternoon on the third day, as I lay

in my attic hideaway rehearsing the complicated story I
would have to tell when I returned to civilisation, when
heavy footsteps and the unmistakable Australian accents
drowned out the final words of my statement, 'Death by
misadventure'.

I rushed downstairs to my four friends as they dropped
their heavy packs to the ground. Their smiles said everything—they had made the summit. I was extremely glad to
see them but I also felt like a class dropout—I was not a
part of what they had just been through. I tried hard to
show some acknowledgement of their success, but the disappointment of not sharing the first ascent of the South
Ridge of Annapurna II accounted for wordless congratulations.

The milk tea came to a boil on our open fire amid excited
descriptions of their summit day. A small group of villagers
had gathered around. One of them translated to his eager
listeners as the events unfolded, and my imagination ran
wild with thoughts of the perfect summit day. But that was
the good part. As with any great adventure, there were
enormous hardships as they struggled down the mountain,
exhausted from their summit attempt, hungry and in
danger of avalanches, only to find C2, C1 and ABC abandoned. The camps may have been abandoned when they
needed help the most, but they knew Narayan, Tenzing
and I had had no choice.

———————

Twelve months later Tim, Lincoln, Andy and Greg went on
to climb Everest via a new route on the North Face. I

would have liked to be among them, but the road to Everest was longer and harder than I thought. On Everest, Andy suffered serious frostbite and would eventually have all his fingers amputated back to the middle joint.

During the flight home I had plenty of time to reflect on the climb and my performance. My disappointment had given way to satisfaction. I was lucky to have participated in such a climb and learn so much from the likes of Tim, Lincoln, Andy and Greg. It was one huge leap in experience to go from the Trisul climb to Annapurna II, leaving me in no doubt that I still had much to learn. In that huge leap, however, the possibility of climbing Everest had gone from a fragile dream to a possibility. In hindsight the climb was a turning point in my life—Himalayan climbing was what I wanted to do, there was no question about that now.

As I waited at the baggage carousel at the Brisbane airport to collect my two packs jammed with mouldy climbing equipment and unwashed clothing, I saw my mother approach. She was not smiling and seemed to look straight through me. She had failed to recognise me. Long-haired and bearded, I had lost 12 kilograms. To this day the South Ridge of Annapurna II remains one of the most difficult expeditions I have been on.

KANGCHENJUNGA, 1987

chapter four

Main Summit 8598m

C4 7900m

C3 7250m

C2 6650m

C1 6100m

'Attempts on this mountain by small parties are doomed to failure from their inception.'
 Erwin Schneider, climber, 1930 Kangchenjunga Expedition

After Annapurna II I knew my chances of joining another expedition were limited, unless I was prepared to make them happen by organising my own. Tim, Lincoln, Andy and Greg would do very little after their 1984 Everest expedition and there were only a few climbers from Australia venturing to the Himalayas on a regular basis. Between 1984 and 1985 I tried organising two expeditions to smaller peaks in Nepal. One was to Kantega at 6799 metres, which I planned for the spring season; the other was Thamserku at 6623 metres, which I would return to climb in the autumn. Both were relatively easy and safe climbs by their eastern slopes. They were also in the same valley as Mount Everest, the Khumbu, and I was keen to see Everest in real life.

I persisted with the letter-writing to a trekking agent, Nima, whom I had met in Kathmandu while we were preparing for the Annapurna II climb. Nima eventually became one of my dearest Nepalese friends and responsible for organising the Nepal content of just about every expedition of mine in the future. He was a valuable connection, often rescuing me from the masses of red tape and paperwork needed to mount an expedition in Nepal, and when disaster struck on the mountains, he would send in whatever assistance we needed.

Letter-writing is a very slow form of communication with Kathmandu and it usually took one month to receive a reply if it didn't go astray. As a result my two expeditions took shape at a snail's pace. With two months to go before we arrived in Nepal, Nima asked us to send money to purchase our climbing permit, equipment and supplies. Faced with a non-refundable financial commitment, half of my four-man team found reasons to pull out. On the verge of packing for the expedition, I had to cancel. I was extremely annoyed and felt betrayed. Their talk had been cheap; my time costly.

Finally in the latter half of 1985 I received a letter from a New Zealand climber, Peter Hillary, who had bought a permit for Kangchenjunga, the world's third highest mountain. For some reason he couldn't go and wanted to sell it for the price he'd paid: US$700. I had dismissed the notion of someone with my level of experience attempting it when, two weeks later, it occurred to me that it might take something like the world's third highest mountain to attract some committed climbers. Another month passed, by which time I had lost Peter's address, but I had since gained the interest of four other climbers: Shane Chemello, Jim Van Gelder, Chris Frost and James Strohfeldt.

Eventually I bought the permit from Peter and after three months of planning and organising, we arrived in Kathmandu. I had no false illusions that we would climb Kangchenjunga; in fact, I expected to fail because my level of experience dictated a degree of risk I was not prepared to test to reach the summit. By trusting in my own ability and by treading carefully on Kangchenjunga, I expected to gain a lot more experience. Although we did fail in our 1986 expedition, it gave me the confidence to try to climb Kangchenjunga again in 1987, this time with the summit firmly fixed in my sights.

It is usual for me to be a little nervous before leaving on an expedition, no matter how many times I have done it before, but in August 1987 it felt rather strange as I closed the door of my Brisbane home. For a few seconds I looked thoughtfully at the door I had just closed and wondered if I would be back to open it again. Leaving home is never easy, no matter how exciting the adventure ahead may seem and this time was even harder, as I knew very well just how committing this climb would be for John Coulton, who would accompany me, and myself. In fact, little did I dream just how taxing and life-threatening my second attempt on Kangchenjunga would be.

Just before I left home I had received some good news— I had been selected for the Australian Bicentennial Everest Expedition (ABEE), due to leave Australia in February 1988. Some people suggested that the expedition I was about to embark on was a training climb for Everest, but they could not have been further from the truth. John Coulton and I planned to climb Kangchenjunga, without bottled oxygen and (because of lack of funds) no Sherpas to carry our gear. The ABEE, on the other hand, was a large team of twenty or more, with oxygen, fixed ropes and money. Money for our climb was scarce, but we made up for the lack of it with our enthusiasm.

———————

As the plane approached Kathmandu I stared eagerly out the window, hoping to catch a glimpse of Kangchenjunga. It may be the third highest mountain, but separated by distance from the greater part of the Himalayan range it looked like an outcast, not big enough to be with the others further to the west. At 8598 metres, it was no dwarf and towered even higher than we were flying, but to my disappointment it was enveloped in cloud.

I settled back and recalled 12 May 1986, the day I had set out alone from C4 at 7750 metres on the South West Face of Kangchenjunga. When I left the camp that morning it seemed unlikely that my climbing partners, Jim Van Gelder and Shane Chemello, would be following me. Like me, they were mere shadows of their former selves. After two months spent edging our way closer to the summit, our spirit and strength were at a low ebb.

I was climbing at a pace that would become standard for me above 8000 metres: ten laborious steps followed by a two-minute rest. On occasions due to exhaustion, cold and lack of oxygen, I would fall asleep while leaning heavily on my ice axe. Although still feeling confident of my own ability, it was 2.30 p.m. when I reached 8400 metres and faced a further 200 vertical metres to the summit. Here I came to an imaginary line that told me to stop and consider the risk of continuing. Time was racing, within reach was the summit, but returning safely to C4 was the problem. It would be possible, but I would be taking a risk. If all went well now, I could be back at our last camp late that night. However, if things went wrong, I was on my own, and if I did summit without mishap, I would be returning to C4 on the limit of exhaustion. What sort of position would I be putting us in if I did that? I would have been placing Jim, Shane and myself on a deadly tightrope for our descent through a line of camps strung out down the mountain and, without assistance, there was no room for error or leeway for bad weather or bad luck. It seemed an eternity that I stood fixated by the lure of my summit chance, torn between going up or turning back. But I had stretched the safety line to the limit and, frustrated as I was, I gave up the attempt. A few metres lower, I stopped. Had I found a feeble excuse to give up? I turned again towards the summit but my indecision was short-lived and I continued the descent.

Now a little over a year later I was returning for another attempt. This time, instead of five climbers, there were two. John and I had lost contact with each other since we first met on the Changabang climb in 1982. A chance meeting with him in Mount Cook National Park in New Zealand gave us a chance to exchange our new addresses and from there we arranged to do some trekking peak climbing in Nepal in the early part of 1987. There are eighteen trekking peaks in Nepal, which range in height from 5700 metres to 6400 metres and require less time and consume far less money than the bigger expedition peaks. It was while climbing these peaks that we talked of another attempt at Kangchenjunga.

John was not due to arrive for another week, so I spent the time in Kathmandu purchasing food and equipment and channelling it to a small house that Nima had rented for me to cope with the volume of supplies and equipment. After a week of frenzied activity, bartering for goods and services, getting equipment through customs with under-the-table deals, I was exhausted and so was our budget. Nima came to my rescue again—he knew of five Americans who were heading for a climb in the same area as us. Both of our teams would be ready to leave in a couple of days' time when John arrived, so we arranged to share transport costs to the base of the mountain.

Early on the Sunday morning John and I and the Americans began to load the mountain of equipment onto our hired bus and a truck. The space that was left soon filled with bodies and an infectious atmosphere of excitement typical of the beginning of any great adventure. We left Kathmandu late in the afternoon on a journey that, although long, would only take us a little closer to our mountain. We progressed slowly overnight in the pouring rain across the plains of southern Nepal, the Terai, to the far eastern border. Sleep was difficult, and the excitement of our departure had given me a headache.

The light of dawn revealed the full extent of the excessive downpour. Rain had been falling continuously in the mountains for the last few days and the plains acted as a

major catchment area. The road was only just above a sea
of brown, dirty water and flooded villages. Dead cattle,
summer crops and the roofs of houses floated past us.

Our driver made many time-consuming and sometimes
dangerous detours. We seemed to have luck on our side
until late in the afternoon, when we started ascending the
foothills of the Himalayas. Here we were stopped by several landslides that had swept great sections of road into the
river. We had no choice but to unload the vehicles and
camp by the roadside. That night I couldn't sleep as I knew
how far we were from the roadhead where we were to start
walking. The rain continued to fall all night.

Next morning, due to inadequate protection against the
rising flood, most of our expedition food and equipment
was soaked. Despite the chaos, we hired porters from a
nearby village, believing the conditions couldn't get any
worse. Ninety porters, plus kitchen staff, started walking
along the road, making many tedious detours around more
landslides and washouts. And still it rained.

At first our ninety porters showed great spirit and made
an impressive sight marching stoically through the rain, but
their cheerfulness was quickly washed away as they became
drenched and muddied and their loads grew heavy with
water. This bedraggled cavalcade caused great amusement
in many villages along the way; they knew better than to be
out in such appalling conditions.

But the biggest laugh was reserved for me. Even without
a 30-kilogram load, I had the grace of a three-legged yak as
I followed clumsily in the mire, throwing verbal abuse at
anyone who so much as looked in my direction. It was only

while listening to our radio that evening as rain continued to fall that I heard we were in the middle of one of the worst natural disasters to hit Nepal in forty years. Hundreds of people were missing or dead and thousands homeless in widespread flooding and landslides across the country.

As the rain eased to regular showers after three days it gave us the false impression that it would now be a pleasant stroll to BC. Our group in excess of 110 people took on the appearance of an army manoeuvre as we ambled along the top of a rounded ridge at 2500 metres. Behind us we left the heat, flood waters and troubles of the last few days. But as we dropped off the end of the ridge, a journey not unlike a rollercoaster ride began. We plodded lethargically up to the crest of a hill, only to be confronted with a never-ending descent, or a skilful balancing act as we traversed above a torrent of white water. The discomforts continued to undermine our spirits, with the oppressive heat and humidity of the deep valleys and the armies of leeches that lay in ambush along rainforested ridges. On a crumbling trail above a steep drop into a gorge, a struggling porter lost his footing. A dull thud was followed by what sounded like a falling body and the sound of dislodged tins of food rattling down the steep side. I turned to see the porter tumbling headlong into the gorge. Fortunately his quick reactions allowed him to release his load, which continued its acrobatic descent into the river. The porter, visibly shaken but not injured, scrambled to the welcoming arms of his friends. His consolation was that he could now walk the remainder of the day without a load on his back.

The year before, after completing this very same section,

we had set up camp and a routine head count of the porters revealed that someone was missing. Armed with head-torches, three of us returned to the traverse above the gorge to look for the missing porter, but hours of searching and calling his name revealed nothing. To this day we have no idea if the porter fell into the gorge or decided to return home.

Fortunately only one bridge had been washed away in the upper reaches of the gorge, but it took a good part of the day to build a new one; time-wise it was a costly exercise. Here everyone worked tirelessly. Most of the porters worked in the forest cutting down two pine trees to use as the main spans for the bridge. Standing the poles on end, we tried lowering them across but, despite our manpower, they were too heavy without someone on the opposite bank to help. The only way across was via a log jam downstream. Coolay, our cook, did not hesitate to cross first, tossing his shoes to the opposite bank so he could use his toes to grip the slippery log. One slip and he would never have been seen again in the white torrent. I should have taken more notice of Coolay's sensible precaution and I began to regret this halfway up the slimy log leaning at 45 degrees to the opposite bank. No amount of grip could stop my slide into the river, when out of nowhere Coolay's hand appeared and hauled me to safety.

Disruptive as the monsoon was to our trek to BC, we managed to arrive there in twenty-three days, the last few days over the undulating glacial moraine of the Yalung Glacier. There was no trail and it was easy to become disoriented in the maze of hills and hollows on the glacier. Being familiar with the way from the year before, I led our

porters in the direction I knew. I was careful to leave a line
of rock cairns behind me for the porters to follow. I tried
to stay 100 metres or so in front in case I led them up a
dead end and had to backtrack. While I was putting the fin-
ishing touches to one of these rock cairns, a smooth round
rock caught my attention. It was brighter than the rest and
a great one to finish off the cairn, I thought. Picking it up,
I immediately noticed its light weight and I turned it over
to look underneath. Although by now I knew it wasn't a
rock, I was not prepared to find a human skull.

A closer inspection of the surrounding area revealed the
bleached and scattered remains of a human body and some
remnants of clothing that identified him as a porter from a
previous expedition. Our porters, who had worked tirelessly overcoming many hurdles to get us this far, were at
the limit of their tolerance and I feared they would be
unnerved by this grisly find. I quickly backtracked,
knocking down the cairns I had just made, and completed
a detour just as the lead porters appeared. Our dedicated
group walked on, oblivious to the remains lying across an
easier path just around the corner.

On our first rain-free day since leaving Kathmandu, I
arrived at BC a little ahead of the others, to find it still the
same as I had left it eighteen months before; no-one had
been there since. Finding a big, flat rock, I lay down and
gazed up at the summit. In full view, it seemed beyond reach
of mere mortals, and I began to imagine how satisfying it
would be to lie here having just climbed Kangchenjunga. My
dream was short-lived as John and the Americans arrived
with a group of porters and we began to clear platforms,

erect tents and store gear. Based on my knowledge of the area, the Americans chose this same site to stage their climb of Yalung Kang, a sister peak to Kangchenjunga. From here, John and I would be climbing alone.

We made our picturesque camp as comfortable as possible; it would be our home for the next six to eight weeks. For a while, only I was aware that we were, in effect, camping in the middle of a mountaineers' graveyard. The names of half a dozen climbers were crudely inscribed on rock headstones around the camp, from Alexis A Pache, who died in an avalanche in 1906 long before the mountain was first climbed by the British in 1955, to Afonso Medina in 1980.

We anticipated the need to place four camps above BC to be close enough to strike for the summit. C1 and C2 would be permanent tents, in case the weather forced us to return to these camps for safety. From C2 we would carry one tent, one stove, one rope and a small amount of food and fuel for C3 and C4, from which point we intended to go for the summit.

The bad weather returned quickly and prevented any climbing for the next week. This setback, slow acclimatisation and several days' preparation of an almost continuous line of ropes between BC and C1 meant a sluggish start to the climb. But at last we were ready to haul the many 15- to 18-kilogram loads to C1—everything we needed to reach the summit. The memories of the previous year's efforts flooded back, and I was consumed by such depression at the thought of the tremendous task ahead, that I felt like returning home. I forced myself to stop and think of the climb ahead. All I wanted was to reach the summit but to do that would require a calm and calculated approach, rather than a half-hearted attack.

In this respect, John Coulton was the perfect climbing partner. I could not help but be swept up in his unfailing enthusiasm and spirit. I also had great faith in his ability to look after himself in difficult situations and, always a good talker, he could be depended upon to strike up an interesting conversation at any time. Many restless hours were passed with idle chit-chat at the high camps, mainly at night while cooking, or as we lay in our sleeping-bags waiting for the weather to clear. His easy flow of conversation was a great remedy for homesickness, as it never allowed me time to dwell too long on places I'd rather be.

Great care was taken to weave a safe path up the avalanche-prone buttress of snow and rock to C1. It was not the small, powder-snow avalanche tickling our ankles that concerned us, but the bigger one that crushed, suffocated and buried its victims metres below the surface. One day, on a return load-carry to C2, a buttress collapsed over our path, littering it with tonnes of rock. Mindful of further collapse, we passed quickly. It was more likely, however, that we would be hit by one of the many small rocks that whizzed past with sufficient velocity to pierce our helmets. Fortunately nothing solid can travel through the air in excess of 100 kilometres per hour in silence and we could react to the unmistakable whirl long before they were upon us.

After an extended time on the hill, John and I decided to return to BC for a rest, having set up C2 and fixed ropes part of the way to C3. I dithered with chores of sorting, cleaning and rearranging at C1, but John, impatient to return to BC for lunch, was not prepared to linger. I promised to join him soon. With a line of ropes down to BC, we felt no need to travel together; in fact, it was preferred on this section because we could easily dislodge rocks and blocks of ice onto one other.

The steepest part of the climb so far was just below C1 and marked by a 70-metre section of green rope which we used to abseil. As always, I concentrated hard before the start of the abseil, double-checking everything, but once under way I slipped into a false sense of security, and daydreaming of the creature comforts I had long since forsaken. Just as I was imagining hopping into a steaming, hot bath, I felt myself falling and a bundle of green rope whipped violently towards me. The rope had snapped, severed by the sharp edge of a rock. The weight of my pack somersaulted me backwards on a descent that enabled me to keep my lunch-time appointment with John—dead on time. The fall was short—it could have been 600 metres— as the harness pulled tight around my waist and I swung from a strand of rope via a piton. A single blade of metal hammered 5 or 6 centimetres into a crack was all that was holding me. I remembered placing that piton on an impulse a few days earlier; it had jangled annoyingly from my harness and kept on catching on everything, so I got rid of it as an extra tie-off point for the green rope.

By the end of September we had been working on the mountain for four weeks and had placed 500 metres of fixed rope to C1 at 6100 metres, and shorter lengths between C2 at 6650 metres and C3 at 7250 metres, and all camps were stocked with supplies of food and fuel. A short rest at BC prepared us for the attempt on the summit, which we planned to reach in four days.

The weather foiled our first attempt. We made it to C3. John woke early, keen to get going but I felt terrible. An unexplainable fever and a bad headache left me in little doubt our timing was wrong. John wanted to wait another day at C3 to see if I would improve, but I felt I would recover better at a lower camp. As we descended, the weather deteriorated and forced us to go all the way to BC. Three days later we returned to the hill but were caught again by heavy snowfall and bleak conditions. This time C2 was as far as we could climb before backtracking to BC.

At BC we had some new neighbours, a three-man Belgian team. Pierre, Allain and Hubert had arrived to attempt the unclimbed South Peak of Kangchenjunga. We were only just getting to know them and admired their daring when it was time for us to leave again. As usual on the eve of our third attempt, I slept fitfully. My mind raced, checking this and that. Did we have enough food, fuel, rope? Would the weather hold? Each night I climbed the mountain; each morning I woke at the bottom. This would be my last time up Kangchenjunga, regardless of the out-come. I had no more motivation left.

Lighting the candle at 3.00 a.m. on 7 October revealed the untidy mess of my tent, half-read books, an unfinished packet of biscuits squashed by a frozen bottle of urine care-lessly discarded in the night, and half a dozen letters from family and friends that I re-read daily. Outside I found BC a hive of activity—our cook and kitchen boys were busily preparing breakfast. I found the over-reactive excitement of the boys amusing, for if our departure created this much excitement, how would they react if we came back successfully? I did know one thing: our BC staff had become our friends and when they shook our hands to wish us luck on our summit bid, we knew they meant it. I scribbled a note addressed to some bushwalking friends whom I expected to arrive at BC the day we intended to be heading for the summit, if all went well. I had helped Ron, Elaine, Stan and Bev organise this trek in Australia. They planned to be at BC when we returned from the summit. So far everything was going to plan.

Because the expedition was being run on such a tight budget, we could not afford a tent at each camp and so shuffled them between camps as we needed them. The tent from C1 was now permanently at C2, so this meant an early start, and beginning the climb at night also helped lower the risk of avalanches and rockfalls. We climbed by the light of a brilliant full moon. I felt the chill of winter arriving—the seasons were definitely changing and our time was running out. For the first hour I told myself that this was definitely our last attempt on the mountain before my mantra was lost in the concentration of the fixed ropes. Reaching C2 at 2.00 p.m., well ahead of schedule, was a sign that we were acclimatised and fit. We used this spare time to have plenty to eat and drink, for we suspected it would be a while before we could do so again. C2 was perched on a small, flat area, about the size of a large lounge room. Although it was spacious by mountaineering standards, we were careful to place the tent close to the overhanging ice cliff as protection against avalanches. Even though we didn't experience any at that camp, we could see the debris of previous falls that had shot over the top. From within the self-generated warmth of our tent, we prepared soup and crackers, and rehydrated a freeze-dried lamb stew with mashed potatoes, while a pot of steaming jelly set in the snow outside. Forever the perfectionist, I straightened the pot so the jelly didn't set lopsided.

The climb to C3 was short but steep and a slip from here would have been a deadly slide of 500 metres to C2. The view from the camp was breathtaking: to the south across the great sweeping plains of Nepal to the border of India; to the east the sun reflecting from windows in the Indian town of Darjeeling. I was glad to be up here, free from the stifling humidity of the lowlands and the view seemed to justify the risk in getting this far. C3 was also the windiest camp, with gale-force winds often flattening the tent onto our faces as we lay inside.

On 9 October we packed a small amount of food that was barely enough to feed one person at sea level for a day. With suppressed appetites due to the altitude, however, there would be enough for both of us for the next two days. From C3 we had to cross the Great Shelf, a 2-kilometre-wide plateau, before reaching the final summit pyramid. It seemed a waste of time and energy to spend so many hours barely gaining altitude, and taking only twenty to thirty steps between rests, each step sinking 30 centimetres into the snow, it became a long and gruelling haul.

My father first told me of Mount Everest as I posed for this photo before Mount Barney in Mount Barney National Park, south-east Queensland, when I was about six.

My father, Donn Groom, climbing in Tasmania in 1968.

(*left to right*) Lincoln Hall, Tim Macartney-Snape and Andy Henderson on the roof of the bus going to Pokhara to start the 1983 Annapurna II climb in Nepal.

Jumarring the fixed ropes on the rock band on the Annapurna II climb. The tents of Advance Base Camp can just be seen on the grassy slopes below me.

The easiest section of the Annapurna II climb between Camps I and 2. Camp I can be seen in the shadows to the right.

The first attempt of Kangchenjunga, Nepal, May 1986, as seen from the second day of our walk to Base Camp. It took another twenty-four days to reach the camp due to heavy snowfall.

Shane Chemello and James Van Gelder crossing the Great Shelf on Kangchenjunga on our way to Camp 4 at 7900 metres. The large blocks of ice are recent avalanche debris from the summit slopes.

John Coulton and I on the summit of a 6000-metre peak in Nepal in early 1987 as part of the preparation for my second attempt on Kangchenjunga a few months later. Dominating the skyline is Mount Everest and to the far right, Makalu.

The day we left Kangchenjunga Base Camp. I was loaded into a cane basket as I was unable to continue due to frostbite on my feet, hands and nose. A helicopter later succeeded in a high-altitude rescue of John Coulton and me. *(Photo: Ron Quickenden)*

Sheltering from a storm while trying to reach the helicopter site below Kangchenjunga Base Camp.

Frostbite to my feet after the successful 1987 climb of Kangchenjunga.

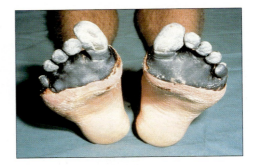

After surgery.

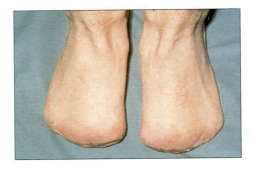

Ama Dablam, Nepal, 1989. Our route comes in along the sunlit ridge on the right.

Back at Base Camp celebrating the successful summiting of Cho Oyu.
(*left to right*) Jane and Rick White, me, Steve McDowell and Tony Dignan.

Steep rockclimbing on the North Ridge of Ama Dablam, which we eventually abandoned when Chris Hawthorne and Shane Chemello returned home early.

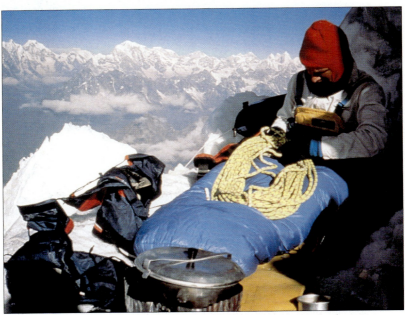

At Camp 3 on the South West Ridge of Ama Dablam. We slept on ledges too small for a tent. (*Photo: Stan Pickering*)

On the broad expanse of the summit of Cho Oyu, 10 May 1990 at 9.05 a.m. Everest (*centre*) and Lhotse (*right*) are the mountains dominating the background.

The Western Cwm on Everest leads to Camp 2, among the rocks in the bottom left corner. Lhotse is at the head of the Cwm and Camp 3 is one-third of the way up this face tucked in under one of the ice cliffs. The South Col is the low point between Everest on the right and Lhotse on the left. Just below the small, square, shiny patch in the centre of the face is where I was hit by the avalanche in September 1991 during my second attempt of Everest. The fall-line was straight to the bottom, which is out of sight behind a rise in the Cwm.

A broken nose and a few suspected cracked ribs was all that I suffered after the 900-metre fall down the Lhotse Face in September 1991 while attempting Everest.

At Everest Base Camp, May 1993. Lobsang Bhutia (*right*) was the nephew of the legendary Tenzing Norgay who accompanied Sir Edmund Hillary on the first successful climb of Everest in May 1953.

To meet this demand, we had purposely stripped the weight of our packs to 15 kilograms each, comprising a tent, sleeping-bags, a 50-metre rope, stove, one pot, three fuel canisters, food and extra clothing needed for the summit attempt.

It was a test of our perseverance to dig a platform for C4 at 7900 metres; not much care was taken in making sure it was level—rough enough was good enough. We had spent most of the day crossing the Great Shelf, so in the last half hour of daylight I tied the guy ropes of our tent to our ice axes buried in the snow, while John prepared soup and crackers as the temperature inside the tent fell to minus 25°C. The real test came the next morning. Still tired from the day before, I cursed miserably at the walls of the tent that showered me with ice while I wrestled with my boots. They were frozen stiff because I had forgotten to warm them in my sleeping-bag overnight. Stopping to draw breath while doing up the laces, it took twenty-five minutes to get them on. Such are the effects of the thin air at 8000 metres that it is common to stop and catch your breath even in mid-sentence. Despite our best efforts to depart before sunrise, we struggled to leave before 7.30 a.m. In the confines of a cold, ice-encrusted tent, the simple tasks had become troublesome, the difficult near impossible.

We started by traversing right across a slope that increased in steepness to the base of a 45- to 55-degree gully known as the Gangway, which would take us to 8400 metres. Beyond this was the short West Ridge to the summit. To make any upward progress we had to share the debilitating task of breaking trail through the knee-deep snow. As I followed immediately behind John, the spikes from his crampons broke the snow alarmingly close to my eyes. Hardly a word was said despite regular rests, and we contemplated little beyond achieving the next twenty or thirty steps. The morning drifted into afternoon and our pace decreased to one breath per step and ten steps before a rest. Gasping after such little gain, I could only continue once the dizziness had disappeared.

For a while I tried to amuse myself by pretending that people back home were paying me a dollar for every step upwards. The list of contributors was long and my high-altitude bank account substantial as I convinced myself that I must not let them down. Having completed my share of trail-breaking for the time being, I waited for John and guessed the time to be mid-afternoon. It took a couple of minutes for him to gain enough breath to gasp that he had had enough and it was time to head down. Checking my watch, I saw it was only 2.30 p.m. but I was really looking for an excuse to end this torture. I wanted to agree as my motivation and energy had long since disappeared and John's suggestion weighed heavily on my already confused mind.

Staring miserably at the snow, I focused on nothing else but facing defeat on this mountain for the second time. Then suddenly I had a sense of *déjà vu* as I realised that I was in exactly the same spot where I had turned around on 12 May 1986, 200 metres from the summit. Without saying a word to John, I removed my pack, threw it down and started climbing again, my spirit renewed with a new-found determination. I was not going to fail on this mountain again. After struggling upwards for half an hour I turned and was happy to see that John had changed his mind and was following.

From the crest of the West Col, the West Ridge stepped in rocky buttresses to the summit. I felt overwhelmed by the exposure. It seemed as if all the world lay beneath me. Now, for the first time in a long day, I dared to think that I might actually get there. A bitterly cold wind blew from the northern side of the mountain and I could only afford a quick look, even though I longed to sit and take in a pilot's view of the earth. What lay ahead of me was what I had come back to do—the last 200 metres.

Pulling my scarf over my face against the sting of the icy wind, I climbed just below the crest of the ridge to avoid its full force. Searching for foot and handholds to climb the short, steep rock sections helped to take my mind off my exhaustion. At one stage I thought I saw a climber sitting in the snow, perhaps one of the last three to climb Kangchenjunga, who disappeared without a trace. As I climbed closer, it became obvious that it was just another rock. A short time later, a high point appeared along the ridge. Surely this could not be the summit, I thought, but I could not help feeling a little elated. I climbed up the last rocky knoll to discover that it was, in fact, a false summit. Ahead, about 80 metres away, stood my goal. To get there I would have to drop down a little to traverse under the summit itself, then struggle up a short gully of mixed rock and ice to reach it.

Although I was dizzy from hypoxia, nothing could stop
me now. With only another 8 metres to go, I stopped,
recalling the meeting with the Ministry of Tourism officials
in Kathmandu. If we were lucky enough to reach the
summit of Kangchenjunga, we were requested not to stand
on the highest point as the summit was believed to be the
sacred place of local Nepalese gods. It felt like the conversation had taken place years ago. There was no temptation
to climb a little further, there was no elation, no sense of
achievement. It was 6.15 p.m. I could see no sign of John;
perhaps he was hidden behind the false summit. I stood
long enough to take some photos in the direction of the
four points of the compass. All the wind in China seemed
to be roaring across the top and it was impossible to stand
still. Frightened by the power of the wind and its equally
deadly partner, the cold, I backed down from the summit
to the more sheltered South West Face, feeling disappointed that after reaching the third highest point in the
world, I felt so flat. Perhaps subconsciously I had already
told myself that the game was not over; I was only halfway
there, I still had to get down. Not even the sun setting
behind the curve of the earth, or the dark silhouette of
Everest some 100 kilometres away, could distract me now.
It was already night-time in the valleys and the dark shadow
of night was approaching fast. Moving slowly and carefully
I climbed down into the night of 10 October.

I was now terrified by the thought that I had stepped
beyond the point of safe return and I would never see the
light of day again. With fading hope I arrived at the false
summit, where I noticed a snowy ramp running diagonally

down to the left—all the way, it seemed, to the Gangway. I was sure that this was the route the British had climbed on the first ascent in 1955 and it offered a quick and easier path down than the ridge. There was still no sign of John, so I assumed he had turned back and was making his way down the ridge. My descent of the ramp was quick, although for a moment I did hesitate, thinking of my father's advice many years ago: 'Always descend the same way you came up, unless you know the descent route.'

I had learnt this lesson the hard way while climbing with him in Alaska, but now mentally and physically weakened, I was easily tempted by the easier path I was now on. One hundred metres lower I heard my father again: 'I told you so.'

I was standing on top of a 12-metre-high cliff beneath which was a sloping rock slab that shot steeply over a 400- to 500-metre drop—a fall from here would be fatal. Almost in tears because of my stupidity and in a state of exhaustion, I looked back up to the ridge. There was only one escape route and that was down.

At this altitude it is normal to wear at least three pairs of gloves and double boots (one inside the other). Negotiating the first half of the cliff was extremely difficult: the small, widely spaced holds were only just within reach of my boxing-gloved hands and cumbersome boots. The second half seemed near impossible. At last with no confidence in down-climbing any further, I returned wearily to the cliff top, where I sat in the snow, longing to be anywhere else but there.

For a few minutes I regretted bitterly that I had ever become involved in mountaineering. The sight of the sickening drop below me disappeared quickly with the coming of night.

Standing, I allowed some time to compose myself as best I could before facing the cliff again. This time it would have to be down-climbed in complete darkness. Shaking with fear, I searched for handholds while my feet trembled on small rock edges and even when I did find something to hold on to, I was unsure of my grip because of my bulky gloves. Only by good fortune and not by good climbing did I reach the rock slabs and slide on my backside to the safety of the snow gully below.

I knew that I had found our ascent path when I tripped over the pack that I had abandoned hours earlier. It was like finding a needle in a haystack and once again it was sheer luck. From here I could see the beam from John's head-torch high up on the ridge. Eager to keep moving, I waited impatiently. Staring dumbly at the flashes of light from his torch, it suddenly occurred to me that I was having trouble judging the distance. Although it was pitch black, my vision was not unlike looking at car headlights through a frosted window. Puzzled and disbelieving, I shook my head and was relieved to hear John's crampons scraping on rock just a couple of metres away. It had been three or four hours since I had last seen him and I was having difficulty pin-pointing his exact position. Little was said, except to enquire after each other's well-being. Not wanting to cause alarm, I foolishly did not tell John of my sudden troubled sight and suggested we keep moving. John began the descent and I tried to follow close behind, but it was the blind leading the blind. John's eyes were as bad as mine.

Later when we had a chance to talk, John, who is a doctor, suspected it was retinal haemorrhage, when the tiny blood vessels in the eye burst due to the high altitude. A common problem for climbers, it rarely causes complete loss of sight and is only a temporary condition. Alternatively he thought it could have been the start of cerebral oedema, during which there is a movement in fluid balance of the brain due to lack of oxygen, causing the brain to swell and push against the optic nerve, causing impaired vision.

We zig-zagged back and forth, vainly trying to find our ascent tracks and no doubt we crossed them many times. At some stage there was an increase in light, which I guessed to be the full moon; it didn't help us find our position on the mountain but it did help distinguish the rock features in the snow and eventually the bottom of the Gangway. This gave us a reference point on the mountain. With renewed confidence that we would find C4 soon, I took the lead and began to traverse the steep snow slopes. John lagged behind in what was becoming a familiar pattern as we unintentionally swapped responsibility for finding our way home.

A dark line appeared in the snow in front of me which I took to be a crevasse. Taking particular care, I knelt down to peer at it; this did not help to identify the mark, but I came to the conclusion that it was the same crevasse we had so easily stepped across that morning just above C4. The excitement of the thought that the comfort of our little tent was only a few metres away overrode the precaution of probing the suspect area with my ice axe. I stepped over the narrow crevasse with confidence. But it was a step into the unknown.

I fell into the depths of a black void. Bouncing off the walls of the crevasse, I came to a sudden stop, my face buried in the snow. Stunned by the impact of what was an 8- to 10-metre fall, I could easily have lain there forever, any hope of survival fading as I drifted towards unconsciousness. It seemed like the easiest thing to do, but the warm blood running from my nose and the freezing snow stuck to my face helped bring me to my senses. I had obviously stepped over the wrong crevasse and my first thought was that I had broken my left leg, which was hanging awkwardly beneath me. There was no pain; that would come soon enough. But I hadn't broken my leg, nor had I landed safely on the bottom of the crevasse. My fall had been stopped by a small ledge, leaving both legs dangling uselessly off the end. I could feel myself balancing on the brink of another fall as I began to slide towards the unknown. Luckily my ice axe was still strapped to my right hand and I used it to claw my way back onto the ledge. It then took several frantic strikes before the axe stuck in the ice above me and, using both hands, I hung desperately to it for fear of the ledge collapsing. Fortunately the downhill wall of the crevasse was not quite vertical, and I began to climb, chopping out holds for my hands and feet. After bridging up an ice wall, I reached a short, steep section and beyond that I managed to crawl on to easier ground. All this took about twenty minutes and I was lucky to emerge from a potentially fatal mistake with only a broken nose and a couple of broken ribs.

Sitting in the snow at 8000 metres in the middle of the night, inert with fatigue and shock, it was strange that I should feel so embarrassed by my clumsiness. John knew nothing of my near-death detour as the light from his head-torch shone on me from the other side of the crevasse. Unbeknown to me, he had lagged some distance behind, even stopping for a rest, while I searched for the tent. He could have easily climbed straight past me if I had still been in the crevasse. Even if he had been right behind me when I fell, he was in no condition, nor did he have a rope, to execute a rescue. As he edged his way blindly towards the edge of the crevasse, he stopped, sensing that something was between him and me. I suggested he try another route to his left. Twenty minutes later he found a way around the crevasse.

Too tired to give details of my fall or to ask why he had fallen so far behind, I set off in search of the tent, leaving John sitting in the snow. Despite the brilliance of the full moon I stared into nothing. My eyes refused to focus. Once again I was left climbing mostly by feel and luck, neither of which had been much help an hour before. Some 30 metres below John, I stopped in my tracks, sure that the tent was around here somewhere. I could sense it—it could have been just a few metres in front of me. I was consumed by frustration and helplessness, but the thought of falling into another crevasse terrified me, as I knew I wouldn't be so lucky a second time. The only safe thing to do was to stay where we were until daylight, so I returned to John. As we dug out a seat in the ice, John complained of his failing eyesight.

It soon became a cold hell. The wind picked up from the south-east and pelted us with snow and ice. We had to stay awake because falling asleep at this altitude means death. We stumbled into what seemed to be a small hollow for more shelter and here we spoke the only words for the remainder of the night.

'Did you make the summit?'

'Yeah,' I replied flatly. 'You?'

'Not quite. I turned around 40 metres below it.'

Removing his boots to improve circulation to his feet, John placed his feet in his pack while I willed for some magic hands to do the same for me. None came and there was no energy left to do it myself.

I sat on my pack, stamping my feet, my hands tucked deep into my armpits as snow and ice stung my face. It had been minus 25°C in our tent the night before and calm; now it was easily that, most likely lower. It didn't take me long to start shivering violently now that we had stopped moving and there came a moment during the night when I stopped shivering and became drowsy from the intense cold. The occasional glance towards John gave me the impression that he was coping with the cold reasonably well; in fact, he looked comfortably warm. This only filled me with envy and I stamped my feet and swung my arms even more vigorously. We were beyond the reasonable logic of combining body heat by huddling together. It would have been so easy to drift off to sleep, never to wake again, but I fought the temptation by keeping my mind busy with memories from the past, interrupted only by standing to gaze blindly down the slope for the tent and in it our warm, cosy sleeping-bags. It was the coldest I had ever experienced; if we survived the night, we would certainly pay. Then it started. It began as a slow monotonous tap in the back of my head. At first I thought it was my heartbeat but I realised it was the tiresome melody of boredom. I shook my head to see if it would disappear, however it would stay with me for the rest of the night. I refused to look at my watch. The temptation to sleep remained a deadly invitation.

On 11 October John stood up from his humble seat and I heard the sheets of ice fall from his frozen climbing-suit. I knew it was morning because I could see the blurred red outline of John a couple of metres away and also, unbelievably, the yellow smudge of our tent less than 100 metres below us. Leaving John to put on his boots, I shuffled slowly towards our tent, too tired to feel any emotion about our discovery. A miss is as good as a mile I told myself. Opening the tent door, I fell inside and crawled into my ice-encrusted sleeping-bag. I don't know why but it represented safety.

Several hours passed before I woke. It was about 9.30 a.m. and John had not arrived. With squinting eyes I anxiously peered outside, but the only detail visible in a sea of white was a dark line in the snow that seemed to continue down the mountain. It was no doubt a trail made by John. I don't know why I rushed to pack but I did and I made the mistake of trying to carry all that John and I had brought up. I wobbled feebly down, my only guide being the shadow-line left by the deep trail carved in the snow by John. Keeping it in front of me at all times was my first priority, for if I deviated from it I would be hopelessly lost again. But then what if John was still as blind as me? Was he leading me straight over the edge? I had no choice—it was my only link to safety and I followed it blindly. Every 20 or 30 metres I fell backwards into the snow with little motivation to get back up, hacking away with a worsening cough that I thought was most probably the start of pulmonary oedema—a potentially fatal condition as the lungs slowly fill with fluid.

It was a marathon ordeal of exhaustion and incredible thirst, shared only by my shadow that was an excellent imitator of my weak and clumsy movements. Eating snow was not a solution for thirst. My only consolation was the gradual return of my sight. By late afternoon I reached the abandoned platform of C3, but there was no sign of John except a line of tracks continuing downwards. For an hour I poured abuse on my tent and clumsy hands as I tried to erect it before finally winning the wrestling match and collapsing inside, breathless, due to the suffocating effect of my cough. At the end of my strength, I felt defeated. I had been on the move and exposed to the elements for thirty-six hours with one litre of water, nothing to eat and three hours' sleep at C4. As I crawled back into my sleeping-bag it occurred to me that this could be my last resting place. It did not alarm me and I was comfortable with this thought. Even while lying completely still, my laboured breathing was rapid and shallow. Day turned to night before I knew it and the wind began to erode what little confidence I had left in getting off this mountain alive. It blew with such force that the tent began to slide off the ledge, leaving one end over the edge. Perhaps the only thing holding me there was the single guy rope I had just managed to tie to my ice axe buried in the snow. I was powerless to do anything to help myself.

Some time later I thought I was dreaming when I felt the presence of someone in the tent next to me. He knelt close by my right side, placed a firm hand in the middle of my back and lifted me into an upright position. My breathing now became easier as I rested my dizzy head between my knees but I still felt the presence of someone watching over me. I knew that I was not dreaming as showers of ice from the tent wall annoyed me by falling down the back of my neck and the tent continued to box me around the ears with the occasional knock to the floor by extra strong gusts. When I became aware that it was morning, I was still sitting in an upright position but alone.

Abandoning all the gear was easy and would go a long way towards giving me a chance to survive this climb. I left C3. My first steps were weak and clumsy, even though I was carrying very little. Shuffling my way to the edge I stood for a moment's hesitation; the 500-metre ice slope that stretched between me and C2 looked steep and unforgiving. It had taken such an effort to climb when I was fit and healthy; now it looked like an accident waiting to happen if I dared to step onto it. Behind me was the clouded memory of my life close to the point of no return and the help of a friend with no recognisable face. I had nothing to offer my companion and no amount of thanks would be adequate for the someone I was deserting at C3, but a searching glance showed no more than the yellow blur of the tent. Making up my mind not to delay any longer, I threw caution to the wind and holding little regard for the consequences, I descended to C2. My fingers on both hands were frozen, single claws and refused to cooperate with the security our fixed ropes offered. Our efforts to create this safety line on the ascent were now almost useless to me.

I tentatively approached the back of our C2 tent. It was surrounded by a deathly silence, which I was hesitant to break. As I walked around to the front I was enormously relieved to see John's huge feet protruding from the door and wriggling happily in the sun. We were ecstatic and relieved to see each other and John instinctively offered me a cup of tea. It was my first drink in forty-eight hours and I sipped it appreciatively as John told me how hallucinations had led him to believe that everything was OK. They started the morning after the icy bivouac at 8000 metres when I walked off to find our tent. John followed, arriving at C4 a few minutes later but he was now starting to hallucinate. Here he saw several tents where there was only one and, assuming they belonged to someone else, continued down the mountain. During his descent he turned around regularly to see me following some 20 metres behind and would ask how I was going.

'Fine,' I would reply.

At C3 he asked me the same question to which he got the same answer. His hallucinations continued all the way to C2 where, after spending the night at a lower altitude, he came to his senses and realised I was still up on the hill. It was a remarkable story and we both knew the final chapter must read that we made it to BC today if we wanted to live to tell the tale. We did not hesitate to abandon more gear at C2.

I slowly whittled away the distance between C2 and BC but in doing so I had let John fall some distance behind. He seemed to have his own pace and so long as he continued down I was not concerned. It was mid-afternoon on 12 October. I now progressed in a painfully weak shuffle; it was all I could manage to stay on my feet and move along the flat glacier above BC. My eyes were slowly returning to normal, and I could just make out a crowd gathering at BC—trekking friends, BC staff and porters, maybe twenty-five to thirty people. There was only one obstacle remaining between them and me—a 30-metre abseil off the glacier into BC and the last chance for something to go wrong. Hooking the rope with my arm I placed the rope in my mouth and with the palms of my hand and the occasional poke with frozen fingers, I managed to attach the abseil device to my harness. With my usual double-checking of buckles and hardware on my harness, I accidentally tugged on the rope and pulled out the ice screw securing the rope. I was left teetering off balance on the edge, the spikes of my crampons the only thing stopping me from falling onto the large boulders below that lay waiting to break my back and spirit. As I fumbled to replace the ice screw, a fear similar to my first abseil more than twenty years before overcame me. Finally, wiping my sweaty brow and biting my trembling lip, I abseiled into BC.

With shaky legs and a deceptive balance I stood at last on firm ground, like an ocean sailor coming ashore after a long sea journey, my outstretched arms finding support on the shoulder of Pierre Soele, the doctor from the three-man Belgian expedition. With great concern he enquired after my well-being.

'I'm OK.'

'Did you make it?' he asked.

Overjoyed by the sudden sense of security and expected comfort, I could only nod my answer to Pierre and he raised his arm in a victory wave to the distant but lingering crowd. Some approached with eager anticipation, while others stood indecisively. The first to arrive were Ron and Elaine, followed closely by Stan and Bev. Months ago, when we had sat in the comfort of my mother's lounge room discussing the possibility of the walk into BC to meet John and me, I had purposely avoided giving an accurate description of the trek because I wanted them there as moral support. Now Elaine was after my hide. She had found the trek to be more like a nightmare than an adventure. Thankfully her initial intentions quickly changed and instead I was welcomed with a big hug. I was escorted by a group of excited porters and BC staff to the mess tent, where I drained several cups of tea before removing gloves and boots to reveal the true cost of climbing to the summit of Kangchenjunga. The black rot of frostbite had invaded all my fingers and thumbs to midway between the first and second joints; my feet were black back to the arch.

Dr Pierre, who was keen to assess the real damage, had me carried off to my tent, where he washed the blackened extremities in disinfectant, bandaged them and set up an IV drip with some pain relief. His diagnosis was that I might lose from behind the toe nail of two or three toes; the rest should heal with care and time. A short time later I was woken by the welcome John was receiving and through the nylon wall of the tent I enquired how he was feeling. I only remember our conversation was short and I drifted back to sleep.

John's frostbite was confined to a few toes, thanks mainly to his removing his boots during the night in the open, thus allowing better circulation, but his hands were far worse than mine. John could walk, but neither of us wanted to walk for the fifteen days it would take to return to the roadhead. So we instructed Rinzie, our mail runner, to return to the nearest village, six days away. He assured us he would do it in three, contact Kathmandu by radio and arrange a helicopter pick-up for John and me. Our only problem was that BC was too high for a helicopter to land and we would have to reach a more suitable site at Ramche, a good day's walk down from BC.

BC was busy again as the dozen porters we had sent for arrived to carry out our gear; they were busy sorting loads and scrounging from our kitchen staff, who were always cooking up something. Meanwhile John and I lay in our tents suffering the agonising pain that occurs when circulation begins to return to frostbite injuries. Over the next couple of days my only relief from the interior of my tent was when Ron would carry me rather awkwardly on his back to the toilet rock for my daily constitutional. It was during one of these escapes that I found the big flat rock I had lain on when I first arrived at BC all those weeks ago and I asked Ron to put me down for a while. This time I knew what it was like to lie gazing up towards the summit of Kangchenjunga knowing that I had stood there. Strangely enough, despite the importance we had placed on reaching the summit, it proved to be no more important than any other aspect of our climb: the teamwork and mateship, the struggle and the hardship were just as important.

On the morning of 17 October a modified cane basket arrived at my tent door, its creators standing proudly on either side. With a bit of padding added to the bottom, I was lifted with the utmost care into the basket and, facing the opposite way to our direction of travel, the basket and I were hung from the shoulders of Coolay, our cook, and I waved goodbye to the crowd as we left BC. The path taken out of BC led us past a couple of grave sites that prompted me to think for a moment that we were indeed lucky to be leaving this mountain where others have been less fortunate. John hobbled painfully along behind.

The walk to Ramche would normally have been one long, strenuous day but we expected to be slow and we allowed three days. My feet swung aimlessly near Coolay's backside and I wished they could be of some use in our tedious progress. They were taking great care in carrying me and it was no-one's fault that I was sent tumbling from the basket on a number of occasions. Apologies were profuse as I was stuffed back into my basket, but by early afternoon we decided to make camp on the rocky Yalung Glacier. With some urgency in their actions, our porters quickly placed John and me in a tent as the afternoon cold began to seep into our blackened hands and feet that were still agonisingly painful. It was a long night for both of us without pain relief, and to make things worse it had started to snow.

We waited until midday to see what the weather would do; then the decision was made to move. John and our dozen porters broke trail for Coolay or Rinzie, who were taking it in turns to carry me. Stan and Ron followed closely behind to support Rinzie or Coolay when they stumbled. Behind them came Elaine and Bev. The afternoon passed miserably, the weather deteriorating rapidly and snow gathering knee-deep on the glacier. Coolay and Rinzie stumbled into the snow-covered holes that lay between the glacier boulders with increasing regularity and I winced in expectation of a bone-splintering noise if one of my fingers or toes should snap off. They cursed as they struggled to extract themselves from a hole that had just claimed a foot. I was beginning to take their anger personally and it all became too much when one stumble sent me flying from the basket and I thought Coolay had broken his leg. Our present position, in the middle of nowhere in this blizzard, was the direct result of my injuries and if I didn't do something about it, we could all be in danger of dying from exposure, not to mention the serious injury that Coolay or Rinzie could sustain in their fight to support my post-expedition weight of 58 kilograms.

I took some satisfaction in throwing the basket to the wind and I started to walk in a pair of camp boots which were nothing more than heavy-duty slippers—nothing else would fit my swollen, bandaged feet. Almost immediately I felt the cold penetrating to my feet and I knew that it would exacerbate my frostbite. But my conscience was finally at ease as I was now contributing to getting us out of this mess. By 3.00 p.m. the blizzard was so fierce that I thought we were heading for disaster if we didn't find shelter soon. A large rock offered a small overhang for

Elaine, Bev, John and me, while everyone else erected the three two-man tents for the six Westerners to use. I felt miserably selfish, knowing that our small mess tent would have to accommodate the remaining eighteen members of our team. But, although it would be cramped, body heat would help keep them alive far more efficiently than wet, torn blankets.

John and I lay silently, our damp sleeping-bags offering little warmth in our tent that became a black hole of misery. After all that John and I had endured up on Kangchenjunga, we were not going to be released willingly from the clutches of what had become a very hostile mountain. Over the deafening roar of the gale-force winds that buffeted our tent, we only just heard the zip of the door open slightly. Through the narrow slit appeared two hands, back-lit by a torch and a voice that said, 'Michael Sahib, soup ready!' Under normal circumstances we would have tossed the bowls of cold, kerosene-flavoured soup back the way they had come, but the boys had overcome enormous difficulties to prepare it. It was the last thing we expected and the only thing we had had to eat or drink since break-fast that morning.

───────────

I woke to an eerie silence. The claustrophobic feeling caused by the thin, stale air indicated that our airflow had been cut off. I pushed against the door, the walls, then the roof but in all directions I met with solid resistance. Our 1.5-metre-high tent had been completely buried by snow for some time. John woke with my efforts to push the snow off the tent using the back of my hand as my fingers were bent and frozen, but the snow was too deep. I fell back into the hollow over which our tent had been pitched and waited for outside help. Half an hour later I began the search for my pocket knife to cut our way out as our breathing had become more rapid. My sticklike fingers were useless, refusing to extract the blade, so I punched the wall of the tent with frustration which brought a muffled shout from outside. A few minutes later a shaft of light shone through the top of our tent and then our door was opened. At least two pairs of hands were thrust towards us with shouts of, 'John Sahib! Michael Sahib!'

I was grabbed by the wrists and pulled up through the narrow opening of our tent as though my life depended on it.

It was a brilliantly clear, sunny day. The storm had passed during the night, leaving an unrecognisable landscape. Dunes of snow had buried all tents except the mess tent, and Stan, Bev, Ron and Elaine appeared like rabbits from holes in the ground. The weather may have been perfect but there was no food or fuel left, and without fuel there could be no water. We were already terribly dehydrated and hungry, not having had anything substantial to eat or drink since leaving BC. From the surrounding mountains I picked up a bearing from which I judged our position to be less than a third of the way to Ramche. It was 20 October, the day the helicopter was to pick us up from Ramche.

The morning started with some enthusiasm, for we held a little hope of reaching Ramche that day, where the trekking team had left a supply of food and fuel. The thought of this alone was enough to drive us on, not to mention the helicopter ride for John and me, but our enthusiasm quickly dissipated as we became bogged down in deep snow. Speaking little, we battled on, each in their own little world of misery. Some tried eating snow in a desperate attempt to relieve their hunger and dehydration, but I had long since learnt it caused painful stomach cramps and increasing thirst. I tried not to think of the damage I was doing to my frostbitten toes as the pain throbbed deep into my feet.

When sunset was only about thirty minutes away I called to the boys to find a suitable campsite for the night and in doing so broke off my moustache of ice. There had been no sight nor sound of the helicopter that day and now John and I were even more discouraged by the thought of walking the remaining twelve to fifteen days to the roadhead. As long as the weather remained settled, death was not a threat, but the longer we went without medical treatment, the greater the danger of irreparable damage to our frostbitten hands and feet became. In the privacy of our tent John and I discussed the one remote chance we thought we had left—that the helicopter had been delayed by the storm. But if it had not arrived today with good weather, tomorrow offered only faint hope—the only hope we had. Before retreating despondently for the night, we resolved to give it our best try, but we were yet a long way from Ramche.

It was a still night camped on the glacier and I struggled to draw some warmth from my damp sleeping-bag. Shivering for most of the night seemed almost normal now. I thought of Ron, Elaine, Stan and Bev who, unused to such environmental hardships, had borne the brunt of these tough days courageously and without complaint. Tomorrow they, and perhaps John and I, would be below the snowline and would reach the stash of food and fuel. Once they hit the roadhead it was an eighteen-hour bus trip back to Kathmandu. If the helicopter came, we knew it could only take two of us—its limit at this altitude. I asked if they wanted us to send the helicopter back in the next day, but they assured us that once they reached their stash they would be okay to continue. If the helicopter failed to arrive, then I would have to seriously consider being carried the rest of the way.

At 5.30 a.m. on 21 October, we said goodbye to Ron, Elaine, Stan and Bev. I felt guilty because they had endured much in their short relationship with Kangchenjunga and we were leaving them in the middle of nowhere without food or water. By now we hadn't eaten in four days and there had been little to drink. John and I left with five or six of our strongest porters who were to break trail, but by 9.00 a.m. they, like us, were exhausted from thirst and hunger. John and I were driven beyond our normal limits by the knowledge we had more to lose of our fingers and toes and the hope of the helicopter ride. A smile was all I could offer in appreciation as John and I passed them sitting in the snow, their faces full of regret. Sheer exhaustion limited us to twenty to thirty steps between rests and nothing was said as we concentrated all our energy into keeping going until 11.30 a.m. Suddenly we heard a noise that did not belong to nature. At first I could hear the helicopter but couldn't see it. I suppressed my excitement, for this could be the final disappointment in our nightmare expedition. We stood in our tracks straining to see it.

After a long thirty seconds the helicopter appeared from behind a ridge and proceeded to fly directly over us without giving any sign of recognition. We both stared after it in disbelief as it flew in increasing circles a day's walk back towards BC. We knew then that we had just one more chance to catch the attention of the pilot when he returned. John pointed to the only flat area near us about 100 metres away. With our frozen feet we ran through the deep snow. It surprised me that we had the energy to do so, but we had never been so desperate. On several occasions we were sent sprawling by large, hidden rocks and by the time we got to the flat area we were covered in snow and exhausted. But we could not rest: a wordless glance at each other and we both knew what had to be done next. We proceeded to stamp out a big H in the snow. John asked me if I had anything bright to display and I placed my red down jacket in the middle of the H. The helicopter was giving up its search further up the valley and was now heading back towards us, so we grabbed whatever we could to use as a flag and started waving. For some stupid reason we were yelling at the top of our voices. This time the helicopter was returning at great speed and again I thought that the pilot would not see us as it passed about 200 metres directly above us. I was just about to release a torrent of abuse, when I began to congratulate the pilot on his extraordinary aviation skills as he swung in a tight arc to land on our helipad.

John and I sheltered behind a rock from the icy down-draft. From a cloud of snow and ice the co-pilot emerged, dressed in a military flying suit; the pilot remained behind the controls, an oxygen mask covering his face. Above the roar of the rotor blades the co-pilot asked if I was Australian, to which I replied, 'Yes, I am.'

'Are you Michael Groom?'

'Yes.'

With that he showed us the door, pushing us into a crouching position to enter the helicopter.

It was warm and cosy in the back seat of the helicopter, but I sensed all was not well: the helicopter seemed to be shaking itself to pieces in its efforts to lift off. The co-pilot, struggling to don his oxygen mask, ordered us to toss out our packs. As we did so, I noticed the pilot tapping a gauge to see if it was reading correctly. Were we too high for a helicopter to land and take off safely? I hesitated to think of the consequences.

I watched my pack fall into the deep snow knowing that my passport, cameras, exposed film and wallet with all my money were in the pack. Then all eyes were glued to the instruments on the control panel. I sat on my hands to hide any sign of nerves. I was frightened because for the first time in a long while a dangerous situation was out of my control. Dying in a helicopter crash suddenly seemed a real possibility. After all John and I had endured to get this far! For long seconds we held our breath as the helicopter laboriously gained enough height to skim across the surrounding terrain. In less than a minute I watched three days' walking pass below us as we zoomed down the valley to the village of Ghunsa where we stopped to refuel. The pilot introduced himself as a close friend of our trekking agent, Nima, and I wondered if Nima had pulled some strings to get the pilot to fly here.

As I eased myself into the back seat of the helicopter for the second time, we were up and away with much more ease than before. We flew well below the height of the surrounding ridges following the twists and turns in the valley, but once again there was cause for alarm as we rounded a corner and flew point-blank into a thick, engulfing cloud. The pilot banked back the way we had come, a tight manoeuvre to avoid colliding with the valley walls and in doing so lost his direction in the thickening cloud.

As we slowly spiralled downwards to the base of the cloud cover, I was not sure if the co-pilot was looking for an emergency landing site or trying to get his bearings on a landmark. Then quite unexpectedly the cloud thinned and our pilot got a bearing on the pass that led us from this mountain range. The clouds quickly closed in again but the pilot held true to his original bearing, knowing only too well that in most of the cloud around us lay steep mountain slopes.

At last we fell through the cloud on the other side of the pass and beneath us lay the hot, dry plains of the Terai, with not another cloud in sight. We landed at Biratnagar for more fuel. John hobbled over to the airport shop to buy us a Coke with the few rupees he had in his pocket. Soon, however, the fumes from the refuelling forced me from the cabin into the thick, warm air of Biratnagar. As I stepped down, my foot missed the rail and I fell heavily onto the tarmac. My climbing-suit, designed for temperatures below zero, stuck to the melted bitumen. I didn't care. I had fallen in the shadow of the helicopter and, for the first time in a long while, felt warmth seep into my body. I lay waiting patiently for John to bring me a drink.

It was late in the afternoon when we arrived back in Kathmandu and Nima was there to greet us as we stepped clumsily from the helicopter. We must have looked a curious sight in our climbing clothes, with our crazy gait, long, matted hair and sunken eyes and cheeks. Nima urged us to go to a hospital immediately and directed us towards a waiting taxi. John, a doctor, decided it would be in our best interest to get back to the modern medical facilities in Australia as quickly as possible, so we asked Nima to find us a hotel room for the night instead. It was no simple task: we had arrived back in Kathmandu during the peak tourist season. As Nima ran into the reception office of each hotel, we were carefully scrutinised in the rear vision mirror by our taxi driver. Finally, at the sixth hotel, we found a place to sleep the night.

We began to cut our climbing clothes from our arms and legs, not having the strength or movement in our damaged fingers to carefully undress over swollen hands and feet. As these were the only clothes we had, I was careful not to destroy everything, and fashioned a rough pair of shorts and T-shirt from my long underwear, while John enjoyed his first hot shower in three months. The door to our room remained open and Nima came and went with food, drinks and the medical supplies John had sent for. We began to disinfect and bandage our injuries. With the open door came unwanted visitors: some just came for a sticky-beak; others were climbers returning prematurely due to the same storm we had experienced during the walk to the helicopter. All of them left shaking their heads: the storm, it seems, was the worst ever experienced in the month of October and stopped the progress of all expeditions.

The first beds we had slept in for nine weeks looked inviting, but the local rock 'n' roll band practising just across the street and the relentless pain from the thawing out of our frostbite allowed us no sleep that night.

Nima arrived early next morning with some clean clothes. I found myself in a pair of bright green pants, four sizes too large, complemented by a fluoro pink T-shirt that shouted, 'I love Nepal'. My big, red moon boots were all that I could get on my swollen feet. John struggled to hide his laughter when Nima asked if I was happy in my new clothes. John is much taller than me and at least fitted into his clothes. It would have been funny if I hadn't felt so pathetic. In these outfits we went to the Australian Embassy, which Nima had persuaded to open, so I could get a new passport. I suspect the ambassador had prior warning of our condition as she greeted us warmly without remarking on our appearance. After less than the usual formalities I was graciously granted a temporary passport.

In the taxi on our way back to the hotel Nima handed me some mail from home. One letter was from my father. I had purposely not told him I was returning to Kangchenjunga as he, being a climber, would know more than most what

I was in for. He had obviously found out via the grapevine and did not hide his concern. He wrote that a return to Kangchenjunga was like 'pulling the tiger's tail twice'. While I dwelt on what he would say when he found out the true extent of the tiger's bite, Nima asked me for my plane ticket. After thumbing through the pages he handed it back, saying that my plane was leaving in an hour and a half. John, who was booked on another flight, did not have to rush. We parted with mutual hopes for each other's swift recovery.

MINUS 10

chapter five

At just over 9000 metres we were flying only a fraction higher than the summit of Kangchenjunga, but the shaft of soft light that filtered through my window hid the unforgiving harshness of the world that I knew was outside—a hazardous world that had challenged my body and soul and from which I was lucky to escape. Now I was paying the price. On reflection the climb seemed total stupidity and I had no desire to return to the Himalayas. In all likelihood, even if I had wanted to, I would probably be physically incapable of doing so. As strong as my feelings were against returning, there seemed to be a hidden message in this ray of light that one day I would return.

My flight home was full. To make matters worse I was stuck in the smoking section and by now, with no form of pain relief, I was in so much distress that I did not care if I lived or died. Wriggling in agony only drew the attention of my fellow passengers, none of whom offered any help or sympathy, instead staring and whispering at my misery. I could only find minor relief by sitting on the toilet with my throbbing feet propped up against the door. Here I passed most of the nine-hour flight back to Brisbane, despite continual harassment from people knocking and banging on the locked door.

With no possessions left from the expedition, I shouldered my carry-bag containing only borrowed essentials and shuffled painfully to the far side of the closed customs door at Brisbane airport where, hopefully, someone would be waiting. A large gathering of family and friends greeted me, holding a white bed sheet displaying the words, 'Congratulations to the Kangchenjunga Kid'. A little embarrassed by the fuss, I was very happy that they had taken the time to welcome me home, but I could see their smiles fade as they saw the cheap Chinese slippers fastened to my bandaged feet. Everyone congratulated me on what they said was an outstanding effort of achievement, but I had yet to convince myself of the same. Sore feet and dizziness made idle talk difficult, so I was quickly bundled into my mother's car and taken off to the hospital.

Lying in the emergency room I counted ceiling tiles while I waited for some attention. Even though I had slept in a rock-hard bed in Kathmandu this was, in comparison with the last three months, luxury. Suddenly the curtain of my small cubicle was flung open.

'And what do we have here?'

'Frostbite,' I replied, shoving my right hand towards the doctor.

He pulled and squeezed my defunct digits with the curious wonder of someone who had never seen frostbite before. It was the case for most of the medical staff who had anything to do with me and I learnt to keep my explanations short. He finished his brief examination and with a careless stroke of his finger through the middle of the arch of my foot he said, 'We'll have you up in the theatre in an hour or two to operate on the frostbite to your feet and all of the fingers on your right hand. Most of what is already black and perhaps a little more will have to be removed.'

It was a vague and frightening prescription. The assisting nurse sensed my devastation and placed a box of tissues next to the bed before she left with the doctor. I looked down at the invisible line that had been drawn across the sole of my foot. Half of both feet would be amputated and the fingers and thumb on my right hand down to the middle joint. This was heartbreaking news because up till now I had believed that I would lose very little, based on what Pierre Soele had told me at BC. But worst of all, my mother had to leave for the long drive home, believing that the next time she saw me I would have very little left of my feet and my right hand.

I was transferred to the burns unit where I waited for a decision to be made about my operation. Here I had plenty of time to regret my decision to walk in the blizzard during our trek to the helicopter—it seemed it would cost me dearly. I did not see my original doctor again as more specialised doctors came to squeeze and poke at my toes and fingers. Fifteen-centimetre-long needles were speared into each toe in an attempt to draw blood. None was drawn and by the time they had finished, my feet looked more like the target at an archery range. Many phone calls were made to seek the advice of other doctors and finally the decision was made not to operate immediately.

With the news of my return and hospitalisation, many family and friends visited me during my long stay in hospital.

Andy Henderson from Annapurna II was one of the first to ring. He had lost all his fingers down to the middle joint due to frostbite on Everest three years earlier and he was very sympathetic and understanding. His advice was not to let them operate for at least two months. Greg and Lincoln also called with congratulations and encouragement.

Every morning for the first week a hospital administrator came to my bed to enquire if I would be willing to speak to the media who were calling daily. However, the media, judging by the questions they asked my mother, seemed more interested in the number of fingers and toes I would lose, than the achievement of being the first Australians to climb unassisted the world's third highest mountain. Each day I sent her away with the answer, 'No'. I was reluctant to advertise our achievements via the media—self-satisfaction was all that I needed and with time that would come. I also saw it from a different angle: we may have been the first Australians to climb Kangchenjunga, but the big picture showed me it had been climbed before.

After three weeks in hospital I was sent home to play a waiting game and see how much flesh would regenerate. The media persisted and I continued to deny them an interview. My gangrenous toes and parts of my feet were mummified into pencil-thin, jet black sticks and my right thumb was heading the same way. Most people in the medical profession hinted that a wheelchair or walking-sticks would become my mode of transport, and the social workers suggested I return to school to retrain for a career behind a desk. A few were more optimistic but the quality of recovery remained unknown. In the meantime my mother sought quotes from builders and plumbers to modify my Brisbane home for wheelchair access. The cost of climbing Kangchenjunga was beginning to mount. With haunting regularity I would wake in the mornings with the hope that the last three months were nothing more than a repeating nightmare, only to peek at the end of the bed sheets to see that it was very real.

John had avoided entering hospital on his return but finally had to admit himself when he realised that parts of his fingers and toes must be amputated: half of both big toes, half of the two toes either side on both feet, and on his right hand the tips of the index and middle fingers and half of the little finger.

I forfeited my position on the Australian Bicentennial Everest Expedition.

In the heat of the Brisbane summer my toes began to rot and the stench was unbearable and embarrassing. A definite demarcation line formed across the width of my foot leaving a sizeable gap between the pink, healthy tissue and the solid black mass. Through this ever-widening crack, I could see, in the suppurating mess, the vestiges of what were once the moving parts of my foot. The rot became so bad I was frightened of snapping off part of my feet with an accidental knock.

Once the doctors determined that time would heal me no further, I returned to hospital for surgery. Some toes were almost prematurely removed when an absent-minded nurse walked into my feet that were protruding from the end of the bed for the doctor's examination. The searing pain with the speed of an electric shock shot straight to my

brain, forcing me to sit bolt upright. I searched the floor.
How many would it be?

———————

Two weeks after the operation to remove all my toes and
half of the ball of each foot, I took my first tentative steps.
It became immediately obvious, with the throbbing pain
of the blood rushing to my feet, that it was not going to
be an easy task to walk again. I had expected a neat,
rounded amputation line but instead it looked more like
a lamb chop, bone and all. I was confined to a wheelchair
and manoeuvring around the hospital corridors and lifts
was often hazardous. My hands remained intact, except
for the loss of a great deal of padding, the flexibility from
the thumb and the tip of my little finger on my right
hand.

While in hospital I was injected every four hours for pain
relief. At home, however, I had to rely on comparatively
ineffective tablets. It was never enough even to take the
edge off the pain and the next dose always seemed too far
away. The dosage was increased, but this soon led to a desperate dependence. Because I had to visit the hospital every
second day I lived alone at my Brisbane home rather than
at my mother's place in the country. Most of the time I sat
in an apathetic state in front of the television, my feet
propped up on a chair. Even this drew a considerable
amount of pain and if I wanted anything I had to either do
without or crawl to get it. Once I had made myself comfortable in the morning, that was more or less where I
stayed for the remainder of the day. Life could not have

been more frustrating and depressing as I watched so many of my friends lead an active life outdoors.

Living with a fair amount of risk had only increased my desire to live a full and rewarding life, yet it was only now, with that freedom gone, that I realised how much it meant to me. Unfortunately at this stage of my recovery I tended to dwell too much on the past—what I could or should have done—instead of looking at ways to cope with the future. If I did gain anything from all of this, it was a far greater respect for the true value of time—it is something not to be wasted. Hidden among these months of mixed emotions there grew a faint glimmer of hope that one day I might get back on my feet. There was never any thought of climbing again; the ability to walk a straight line without falling over was goal enough. It was an enormous challenge and that would take many years.

So bad was my sense of balance that if I closed my eyes while standing unsupported, I fell over. So in the early days it was easier and less painful if I crawled around the house on my hands and knees. One weekend, to escape the lone-liness of home, I stayed with some friends. Getting up early in the morning I went to the bathroom to wash my face, without the assistance of a walking-stick. Leaning forward over the basin without support to splash water over my face, I lost balance, my head cracking sharply on the bottom of the basin. I also quickly discovered I no longer had perfect aim at the toilet bowl and after unsteadily spraying the walls and floor, found it was safer sitting down. Likewise in the shower. At least these activities could be practised behind closed doors and weren't nearly as humiliating as tripping or losing my balance in public. This was often greeted with disgust by strangers who thought I was either drunk or drugged. Public outings were embarrassing and difficult and therefore rare. If I could have crawled to an edge I would have pushed myself over.

I received a get well card from Narayan. It was a heartfelt message that only he could write in a combination of broken English and Australian slang learnt from years of climbing with Tim and Lincoln.

That same week I received a phone call from Ongch. Narayan, he said, was dead. He was killed in an avalanche on Everest on 21 September 1988.

Six months later, a friend, Bernie Kelly, wanted me to meet an acquaintance who was looking for a speaker at a national business conference. What drew me to this meeting was my need to take on another kind of challenge other than my physical health—I was deeply depressed and desperately needed a goal to pull myself together. I was, however, literally terrified by public speaking—since childhood I had been a listener, not a talker. But I agreed to meet John Smart to give a preview of my slides and story before he engaged me. Waving aside my fear, John handed me his address and the time, pointing out that this was a golden opportunity not to be missed. I didn't see the gold in his opportunity but I was taken aback when I saw his address: Everest Street.

Despite a lot of rehearsal, the big night at Everest Street came far too soon for my liking. I couldn't help but think that if I was so nervous about showing slides in someone's house, how would I cope with 250 people? To make things worse, John had invited a dozen friends along as an audience. This caused a sudden need to go to the toilet. Being in someone else's house I could not crawl, so I hobbled painfully from the room.

Sitting on the toilet I searched for courage to survive this ordeal. On the back of the toilet door hung a poster of a snow-covered mountain. For a moment I forgot my worries and started to plot a climbing route via the jagged ridges to the summit. In the blue sky to the right of the summit was a simple sentence: 'Tough times don't last, but tough people do.'

Here was the invitation to the real challenge I had been avoiding during the previous six months because it seemed too hard and unachievable—accepting the responsibility for learning to walk again was mine, instead of waiting for some medical miracle to save me from the desk-bound life I seemed destined for. The Himalayan mountains had always overwhelmed me with their sheer height and technical difficulty, until I took the time to break the mountain down into smaller, more achievable stages. Now I saw that was the way to get back on my feet, even if it was only by a few extra steps a day.

My time in the toilet was time well spent and although I faced my small audience with no more confidence than before, I did find some relief and benefit in talking about the ordeal on Kangchenjunga for the first time and it left me with a more positive attitude towards the future.

It occurred to me during the drive home that the golden

opportunity John had mentioned had presented itself, perhaps not in the form he had intended, and I was about to embark on a totally new life. John liked my slide presentation, and the invitation to speak at his conference was the beginning of what is now full-time work around Australia and overseas. But the real bonus that night came from the motivation and inspiration gained from the words on the back of the toilet door—to tackle something that I thought was near impossible, to learn how to walk again.

CHO OYU, 1990

chapter six

C2 7100m

C1 6440m

BC 5600m

Climbing route
Climbing route hidden from view

I was now determined as ever to become mobile again and the answer seemed to be practise, practise, practise in as short a time as possible. Torrential rain fell for most of the week after the meeting at Everest Street and by the following Sunday afternoon I was driven from the house by cabin fever and the urge to start walking again. After carefully bandaging my feet, the bones of both big toes still visible in the wound, I stuffed newspaper into the ends of my shoes and drove cautiously to a level concrete path by the Brisbane River that I had set my sights on conquering. It immediately became obvious this was not a good day to be out as I ran the gauntlet of overflowing gutters, stalled cars and dead traffic lights. I knew driving was a risk as my feet had little sensitivity or control. I would have been disappointed, however, if I had turned back and found some satisfaction in just getting out of the house and seeing the real world.

By the time I reached the path the rain had eased and I selected my objective—a post 500 metres away. I was confident I could achieve this distance that I used to run in a minute or two. Shortly after starting, the deluge returned with a stiff winter breeze blowing up the river. I hadn't brought a raincoat and soon became depressed by the miserable cold and my slow, pathetic shuffle. The newspaper in my shoes turned to paper mush and formed uncomfortable lumps under my feet. Fifty-five minutes later I returned to the car, water-logged and demoralised by the pain and difficulty of this very short walk. That night my feet hurt so much I could not cook dinner and no amount of pain relief could ease my suffering—I thought I had caused irreparable damage to my feet.

———————

The struggle to walk again and returning to work consumed the next three years and I grew thoroughly sick of my slow and frustrating progress. My footwear advanced from bandages and cotton wool to wrapping thin layers of foam rubber around the stumps of my feet and stuffing the ends of normal shoes with newspaper. It took a dedicated podiatrist two years of trial and error to perfect a suitable pair of orthotics. By then, although I had recovered enough to hold a secret urge to climb again, I was constantly but politely told that it would not be possible. In an effort to find out for myself, in 1989 I organised a climb on Nepal's 6856-metre Ama Dablam with John Coulton and four others. Disappointment from failure was always on the cards, so I resigned myself to being BC manager and running the climb from there. It did not take long, however, to be lured by the summit, and I attempted venturing upwards.

This expedition achieved two things. First it forced me to kick the eighteen-month habit of taking pain killers—I intentionally took too little to last the expedition. Second it gave me some hope for the future.

The climb went well. John and I enjoyed good weather and spectacular climbing up a narrow and steepening ridge but ran out of time around 70 metres from the summit. We ignored the temptation to finish the climb, having no desire to test our luck with the nightmare descent and injuries from Kangchenjunga still fresh in our minds.

Struggling up Ama Dablam also proved that climbing in the future was going to be extremely painful on shortened feet—so acute at times, I felt it wasn't worth the effort.

———————

Mountain Designs is a manufacturer and distributor of outdoor clothing in Australia and they had supplied some of the specialised high-altitude clothing I needed for Kangchenjunga. In November 1989 I had to deliver some long-overdue photos to their office for a new catalogue when Rick White, the managing director, asked me if I wanted to join his expedition to attempt the unclimbed North Ridge of Cho Oyu. The world's sixth highest mountain at 8201 metres, its summit ridges hug the border between Nepal and China. The thought of China captured my imagination for a moment before I dismissed his offer—it was too much too soon. But two weeks later, although still indecisive, I was back in Rick's office to ask how much and when. I had spent the last three years pulling myself out of deep depression and now I needed more direction, something to aim for. The discouraging and painful climbing I had suffered on Ama Dablam six

months earlier told me to leave climbing for good and find
something else. On the other hand I felt I owed it to myself
to give mountaineering just one more try. The offer of Cho
Oyu, although more than I wanted to tackle, began to prey
on my mind.

It wasn't until the end of January 1990 that I accepted
the invitation to join the Cho Oyu expedition due to leave
in early April. I had made it clear that I was still having
trouble with my feet and that I couldn't be counted upon
as a strong, contributing climber. Rick understood this, and
speaking on behalf of the other climbers, none of whom I
knew, said they were happy to have me along to make up
the numbers. The team comprised Steve McDowell, Tony
Dignan, Tim Balla and Rick's wife, Jane. It was Tim's and
Tony's first time in the Himalayas and they came with a
record as strong technical climbers. In 1981 Rick and his
team had been successful on a long, demanding technical
climb of Shivling's East Ridge in India. It was the type of
climbing Rick enjoyed and the unclimbed North Ridge of
Cho Oyu, with its intimidating rock formations, was an
inviting challenge. Steve, Rick and Jane were old climbing
partners and had also enjoyed an expedition to Mutagh Ata
at 7545 metres in far western China.

In the short time we had left I prepared for the expedition
by cycling short, repetitive sprints around a planned street
circuit to build up my weakened leg muscles. With inadequate use since the operation they had practically dissolved,
particularly my calf muscles. I modified the pedals and toe
clips of my bike to allow the arch of my foot to sit over the
top of the pedals so I could push down. On weekends I went

on longer 30- to 40-kilometre rides. This was all that my feet could tolerate—running or walking up steep hills with a heavy pack was out of the question. Another battle was the financial one: my share of the expedition cost around $8000; to replace the equipment abandoned on Kangchenjunga, an additional $3000.

I had been working as a plumber on a casual arrangement of four hours every second day. If my feet were too sore, I need only call and say so. It was always my intention to increase the work load gradually, but to raise money for this climb, I had to work full time immediately.

———————

On 11 April 1990 we began the walk to BC. I regretted every painful step as I trudged over the Tibetan plateau. I began to wonder if I would make it into camp before dark, and to add insult to my difficulties, I had to watch the yaks carrying our expedition gear amble effortlessly past.

If it hadn't been so painful I might have found some humour in the scene. Mixed emotions about my future as a mountaineer occupied my thoughts for most of the night, until I finally resolved during the early hours of the morning to find the answer to this dilemma in the new day. The morning brought a better and more appealing view of Cho Oyu and the promise from our yak men that today's walk would be shorter. Although suspecting that I was being fooled, I struggled on. I wasn't the only one having problems. Tim was worried. He was constantly being propositioned by the Tibetan yak herders who thought he was actually a she. His blond Shirley Temple locks and fair complexion certainly made him attractive to some of the younger yak herders who had obviously been on the move all summer moving their grazing yaks from one area to another. It became so bad that Tim was threatening to expose himself to the admiring yak herders if they didn't stop their amorous advances.

Aiming for the North Ridge, we established two camps, reaching 6900 metres before we deemed the rockfall on the ridge too dangerous to continue. We turned our attention to the North West Face instead. Steve, Tony, Tim, Rick and I salvaged our gear from the high camp on the North Ridge, some of which had been lost in a storm when a tent blew away. We still had enough time and supplies to continue up the North West Face. Jane had had trouble acclimatising and had missed much of the climbing. Facing our next option of a fast alpine-style ascent of the North West Ridge, she felt it wise to stay at BC. This kind of ascent involved carrying everything on our backs in a continuous push to the summit with no fixed camps or ropes. For an attempt like this we needed to rest first, then move up the mountain when a favourable spell of weather came through.

Thapa, our cook, had no-one to help him prepare our meals, so I would sometimes slip into the kitchen tent to help. After one such occasion I emerged from the tent with no desire for lunch and retired to my tent. By mid-afternoon I had an increasingly painful ache in the middle of my chest. I climbed out of my tent to have a pee and on my return fainted. Fortunately I was talking to Steve and Tim at the time and they rushed to my assistance. A Japanese doctor from another team diagnosed a stomach ulcer and I was placed in Rick's tent on pain relief and a drip which Rick had to replace every four hours. I watched my summit chances drain away with each drip and by morning they were all but gone. However, the boys, who were ready to head up the mountain, were prepared to wait a couple of extra days in the hope that I might improve. That I did, just, but I was warned of the consequences if it recurred high on the mountain. On 8 May all of us left BC for C1.

I overdressed for the start of the new day and after climbing only 100 metres above C1 I had to shed a layer. Rick and Steve had also stopped and were deep in conversation. Steve climbed up to me to say that both of them were heading back to BC, too exhausted to continue. It came as a complete surprise to me, as we were all showing signs of the debilitating effects of the altitude. I was disappointed for their sake and mine, but it was their decision. For a few minutes I watched them descend, hoping they might change their minds, but it was clear by their slow, cumbersome movements they had made the right decision. Meanwhile Tony had got away to an early start and Tim was close behind. I caught up to them thanks to the 30-centimetre-deep trail Tony had ploughed through the snow. Now it was my turn to break trail but I couldn't go straight up as we had entered a maze of crevasses. Some of them were marked by bamboo wands left by a Japanese team the season before, but most remained hidden. At one point we encountered a steep, 40-metre headwall of ice that would have taken hours of difficult climbing to negotiate. Having climbed about 15 to 20 metres up the face we found the entrance to a cave and eventually wormed our

way through it to emerge at the top of the headwall. Once
we were beyond another section of crevasses I became
absorbed by my immediate challenge of the next twenty
steps and I unintentionally pulled ahead of Tony and Tim.

By the time I was aware that there was 100 metres
between us I decided to keep up the momentum and break
trail until I found a safe site to make C2. It was 4.00 p.m.
when I found it—a small, wind-sheltered notch on a buttress of rock at 7100 metres. Because I had hurriedly
snatched the group gear from Steve and Rick when they had
turned around and later divided this between Tony, Tim
and myself, I had ended up with ropes, food and fuel, but
no stove. There was nothing I could do to prepare camp, no
tent to put up and no way to start melting snow. Every few
minutes I glanced down the slope for Tony and Tim. If they
didn't arrive it would be a very cold and thirsty night.

As time passed it looked increasingly likely that I might
have to spend the night in the open with my sleeping-bag.
This didn't overly concern me as I felt in no real danger
unless the weather turned, but I was concerned for the
others. Had they fallen? Had the slope avalanched behind
me taking them with it? Should I go down and look for
them? Three-quarters of an hour passed and I glanced
down the North West Face once more. The slopes were
turning a light shade of pink and there was still no sign of
the others—it would be completely dark within half an
hour. I stepped back from the edge. My mind was made
up. I pulled on my head-torch to descend in search of the
others, when from the edge I could just see a small dot had
appeared on the slopes a long way below. No arms or legs

could be seen moving; only occasionally did the dot move slowly towards me. It was almost dark by the time I reached Tony. Tim, he said, had turned around long before, so I shouldered his pack and we climbed together to C2.

We pitched our tent in the dark making do with whatever uneven ground we had placed it over. We weren't hungry, and neither of us wanted to broach the subject of tomorrow's climbing plans. One hour later hot drinks had brought some warmth to our aching bodies, and I tentatively asked Tony about tomorrow. We both knew that for the best chance of reaching the summit we needed to put in another camp between us and the summit. This would mean carrying 15-kilogram packs and wasting another valuable day in this unpredictable weather, which could change overnight. Should we chance it and waste more time for better odds on the summit or should we try to reach the summit from here? The latter meant a 1100-metre summit day—a long day even by Everest standards—but Tony and I considered it our best option. We planned a 3.00 a.m. departure and the alarm was set for 1.00 a.m.

It was a calm night and for once I slept well at this altitude—unusually well. When the alarm woke me I felt tired and sore from the previous day and was reluctant to move. For twenty minutes I questioned my desire and ability to face more hardship, particularly the cold, which I knew was waiting for me outside. Eventually guilt got the better of me—I had worked so hard to get this far; there was the temptation to give up, but could I live with that decision later? I removed a gloved hand from my sleeping-bag and scratched around the tent floor for my head-torch. In preparation the night before I had already filled the cooking pot with snow and ice. Lighting the gas stove brought some welcome life to our cold tent. Tony hadn't stirred and he could afford to sleep for as long as it took to bring the melted ice to boil. This would be at least half an hour. I woke Tony with a shove and a cup of coffee and biscuits. I continued to melt more ice for our water-bottles and tried to warm up the insides of my boots by holding them over the flame lapping from the sides of the pot. Setting my boots alight was not my intention, but after igniting the inside of one boot I settled for the safer option of warming them up in my sleeping-bag. By the time Tony and I had breakfasted on coffee and biscuits and filled our water-bottles, it was after 3.00 a.m.

There seemed to be as many stars buried in the snow as there were in the night sky, the full moon sparkling off individual ice crystals all around us. It was a wonderful feeling to be in such surroundings. This surreal setting was one of mountaineering's great pleasures. Despite having left the tent feeling warm, within half an hour I was so miserably cold I considered turning around. I was breaking trail through deep snow that made my feet feel like blocks of ice. I considered my options carefully. Only warmth would solve my problem and our tent, not yet 100 metres away, tempted me back. While I waited for Tony, I made my decision. My feet, although throbbing, had not yet gone numb, so I figured that as long as I kept moving and my feet continued to hurt, I could proceed upwards with caution. I told Tony this; he understood my reasoning and we slowly lost sight of each other.

Climbing by the full moon reminded me of my early days on Mount Barney under the same light conditions and the watchful eye of my father, although the terrain and temperature were completely different. For the next hour or so to help fight the penetrating cold, I lost myself in thoughts of the past. When an unclimbable rock face appeared in front of me I took a gamble that I would find a weakness if I traversed right. A couple of dangerous options presented themselves but I found one that I was prepared to climb unroped. I became so engrossed in the climbing that it was only when I reached the top of the rock band that I realised the cold grey of dawn had arrived. From here I looked out across Tibet. There was no sign of Tony below me so I assumed he had turned back. I guessed I was at 8000 metres but I was on the wrong side of the mountain to receive any benefit from the sun for a couple more hours.

This was my sixth expedition to the Himalayas and I still hadn't got into the habit of keeping a diary. I had tried on an earlier expedition but found it difficult and opted for keeping a photographic record of events instead. Normally I take dozens of rolls of film, but as the years and the expeditions go by the memories of each climb become lost in a whole mountain range worth of expeditions. Now I wished I had kept a diary of my feelings and events. Alone on Cho Oyu I continued with my photographic record, but I would have liked someone to be included in my photos.

The monotony of breaking steps 30 centimetres deep into the snow caused time to pass slowly in a hypnotic trance: 28, 29, 30 steps and rest for twenty breaths before continuing again 1, 2, 3. From BC, Cho Oyu shows a pointy summit and it suddenly appeared 100 metres away above low-angled slopes. I rested at the base of this final summit pyramid, preparing my camera for the summit photos I anticipated taking. Once on top I had to subdue my elation for a little longer as I looked out over a plateau the size of a couple of football fields, and across the other side were more lumps and bumps that were as high, if not higher than where I was standing. I am glad that I forced myself to go over there as the view on the Chinese side of the mountain had become all too familiar, and as I plodded south across the broad expanse of the summit plateau, the most dramatic panoramic view I have ever seen unfolded. It brought me to the edge of the South Face of Cho Oyu, the true summit. The southern edge of the summit plateau came to an abrupt end and beneath me lay most of Nepal; across the valley lay Everest, Lhotse and Kangchenjunga. It was 9.05 a.m. on 10 May.

It was a perfect day, not a cloud in the sky, not a breath of wind—the type of day all climbers dream about for a summit attempt. For the first time that day I was feeling warm. A few metres away a mound of snow about the area of a large bedroom looked like the highest point, and once I was on top, it felt only just higher than everything else. I laid out my water-bottle, chocolate and camera gear with no fear of losing them over the edge and sat down on the broad summit. I was captivated by the view with Mount Everest dominating the skyline. At the exact time that I was on the summit, Tim Macartney-Snape reached the summit of Everest for the second time in his Sea to Summit marathon. Three-quarters of an hour and many photos later I got up to collect my belongings and leave.

Everest has always dominated the skyline from this position, but now it was dominating my thoughts, for in the last three years I had all but given up hope of climbing it. Now I had climbed Cho Oyu, it seemed remotely imaginable. As I ambled off the summit plateau a spring of confidence returned to my step, a confidence that in the previous three years I thought had gone forever. Everest seemed possible now, but no-one in their wildest imagination could have foreseen the consequences of this very day three years later.

I had to put the feeling of great personal satisfaction out of my mind and concentrate on the job of descending. I had forgotten about Tony, believing he had gone back long ago but at around 300 to 400 metres below the summit he came into view after cresting a steep rise. He was moving slowly upwards, still intent on reaching the summit. I felt he was going too slowly to reach the summit before night but no amount of persuasion on my part could sway his stubborn determination, so I wished him luck and promised to wait for him at our high camp. It was 12.00 midday when I reached C2 and the nicely warmed tent was a welcome place to be. I filled the pot with snow and lit the stove only to fall fast asleep. Half an hour later I was woken by the sound of the lid bouncing on top of the cooking pot. For the remainder of the afternoon this routine of drinking and sleeping continued.

By 6.30 p.m. I was becoming increasingly concerned for Tony. I put on my boots and plodded sluggishly back up the slope for 100 metres, fully aware of just how much the summit climb had drained my energy. Like the evening before the slopes were turning a light shade of pink and there was no sign of Tony, but then I couldn't see the entire length of the face. I stood for a few minutes wondering what to do next. It would be dark shortly and then would come the cold. I returned to the tent for more clothing and my head-torch with the intention of climbing higher in search of him. There was still some water in the pot, so I decided to reheat it and take it with me, as it would most likely be the first thing he would want if I found him. It was just before 8.00 p.m. when Tony crashed through the door as I was filling the water-bottle. Slack-jawed and motionless he lay at my feet. Only heavy breathing answered my many questions and I felt for a minute or two that he was in serious trouble, but as I prepared him a drink he slowly roused and within a few minutes told me he had turned back 100 metres below the summit because it was too late in the day to go higher.

Neither of us felt like eating but I continued to melt snow for hot drinks late into the night. I could tell that Tony was bitterly disappointed that he had not reached the summit so I did not gloat about my success. To the non-climber it's difficult to understand why you would turn back so close to the summit. To the mountaineer though, 100 metres represents an hour or two of exhausting climbing. Despite this, it is still very hard to make the decision to turn around so close to the summit and in many ways more difficult than completing the climb. For Tony, though, the risk had become unacceptable and it was better to live to climb another day.

Nursing weary bodies and dizzy heads we did not manage to leave C2 until after 9.00 a.m. and we figured that if we descended to the base of the climb we could leave the long trudge back over the rocky glacial moraine to BC until the next day. Fortunately there was a welcome sight at C1. Tim had climbed back up to help us carry down the gear and he said Steve and Rick were waiting below to help with the rest of the equipment. Cho Oyu was not the most pleasant of Base Camps but when Tony and I staggered in late in the afternoon, it felt like home. That night Thapa baked the traditional summit cake for us to celebrate the success of our expedition and more importantly everyone returning safely.

The day after reaching BC, I walked with great difficulty on my badly bruised and battered feet and was once again struck down by my stomach ulcer. When we returned to Kathmandu a week later, I elatedly submitted an application to the Ministry of Tourism for an Everest permit, even though I expected to wait for several years. I was back in business!

EVEREST, SPRING 1991

chapter seven

Everest   Lhotse   Nuptse

C4 8000m

C3 7300m

C2 6450m

C1 6150m

BC 5500m

Everest 1991 Australian Expedition

Two years earlier I had spent all the money I had—$1500—on two second-hand slide projectors. There were times when I wished I had not spent my money so unwisely, but now I was making my investment pay—I had since given up much of my plumbing work to present slide shows at business conferences. Often during the long drives home in the early hours, I questioned my motives. But it had helped me overcome my fear of public speaking, it was an alternative source of income, and it was at one of these conferences that I was lucky enough to meet Judi Kilroe, my future wife.

It was the second weekend of November 1990 and I was still coasting along on a high from my ascent of Cho Oyu earlier that year. I could not have been enjoying this high in a more contrasting place than a five-star resort on Australia's Gold Coast. However, I was not here for a holiday. I had been asked to speak at the Bank of Queenland's annual managers' conference. By now I had become a little more comfortable speaking in public, at least the butterflies were flying in formation.

The bank had asked Matthew Brannelly to introduce me,

as he knew my life story as well as anyone, a result of listening to my countless presentations to the Australian Youth Development Program for which he was a founding member. Matthew was to bring his girlfriend Judi Kilroe with him. Judi was not averse to hearing an interesting story but had no desire to listen to a mountain climber for one hour when the beach was a more attractive alternative.

Matthew's introduction was great. After my presentation I mingled with members of the bank at morning tea and it was here that I bumped into Judi. For someone who had no interest in mountaineering she suddenly had quite a few questions. For a while I was spellbound by the flirtatious style of this woman. 'What sort of training are you doing for your Everest climb?' she asked. I had just recently started swimming to give my feet a rest but I had had no proper training and I was finding it extremely hard and tiring. Judi had done a lot of swimming, having been coached by Laurie Lawrence, and she offered to help me.

We made no formal arrangement to meet and I soon forgot about her offer. Two weeks later I received a phone call from Judi asking me if I wanted to go swimming. I suggested we met at 5 in the morning as it was the only time I could do so with my work and other training commitments. For a moment there was long silence on the other end of the phone. I could almost hear her thinking carefully about the prospect of getting up at 4.30 a.m. to go swimming. I didn't know it at the time but she dislikes getting out of bed before 8 a.m. at the best of times.

Judi swam effortless lengths of the pool time after time while I just about drowned on each lap. I'm sure I tested her patience, and it must have been frustrating to try and teach someone that had such an incompetent swimming style as myself. But I stuck with it and in time I was swimming a couple of kilometres. With the exception of being away on expeditions we have been constant partners ever since.

Mountaineering expeditions are renowned for their extraordinary physical and mental hardships. Close teamwork and a good understanding between the expedition members are therefore imperative if the climb is to be safe and successful, let alone enjoyable. Needless to say, such unrelenting conditions can create potentially soul-destroying conflicts, in which egos and petty dramas can destroy the goodwill of any team.

Fortunately only one of my expeditions fits into this category. My first encounter with Everest in the spring of 1991 was an interpersonal nightmare.

I desperately wanted to climb Mount Everest, but it was unlikely that I would receive a golden invitation to join somebody else's expedition—I would have to take the initiative myself. Organising an expedition was not foreign to me, but Everest is the world's highest mountain and attracts higher overall costs. On my income this ruled out climbing it the way I preferred—with one or two other climbers, no Sherpas, no oxygen. There would have to be a team of six, maybe eight climbers, and to do this we would eventually add a team of nineteen trekkers to help fund the high expedition costs. The permit for the South

Col route had already been issued, so it was either the more difficult West Ridge or nothing.

Chris Hawthorne and I worked on the general organisation of both the climbing team and the trekking team, which would walk into BC with us and return to Kathmandu after a couple of nights there. I found working full time, training for the climb and trying to organise both teams was more than I could handle, and the end result was that I did none of them well. I am sure in hindsight that we were all in the same boat and as a result we did not get off to a good start.

It felt strange that nearly twenty-five years after my father had pointed me towards Mount Barney and told me about Mount Everest, he should be accompanying me to the Base Camp of this very mountain. Despite bad knees, he accomplished the trek with a walking-stick. More mountains than he had ever seen rose around him and I often caught him looking up in admiration. No doubt he felt disappointment that he was no longer capable of attempting them. He admitted that he had recognised it was time to quit mountaineering the day he stood on the summit of a snow-capped peak in New Zealand and felt unsafe. He realised then it had become too risky and if he continued to play the game, sooner or later he could be faced with his own life-or-death situation. Tentatively he suggested that after I climbed Everest I might feel the same way.

John Coulton had returned for this expedition. Frostbite amputations had no visible effect as he strode along the trail to BC with his usual brisk pace. He was always keen to see what was over the next hill and was even in the habit of doing a little extra walking after getting into camp in the evenings. It served as a depressing reminder of what we used to be able to do together. John carried with him his usual meticulous medical kit for the expedition.

Tony Dignan and Rick White from the Cho Oyu expedition and Stan Pickering from the 1989 Ama Dablam climb made up the six-man team. In the comfort of our lounge rooms during pre-expedition meetings it felt like a harmonious team; I knew that better than anyone as I had climbed with every one of them.

It was an unusually hot afternoon the day we arrived at BC but it quickly turned cold in the late afternoon as we hurried to erect our tents. Tony took time to thank me for the work I had done as we watched the rapid transformation of our BC. Unfortunately the next day Rick received a hand-delivered letter from Kathmandu—it required him to return home to Australia as soon as possible and he left with my father and the rest of the trekkers. We had all had many great times together and I was sad to see them go. Now that I was relieved of the responsibility of the trekking group, I could focus on what we had come here to do. From that point it was a downhill slide for our expedition.

You can practise mountaineering techniques in any mountain range in the world, but it will never prepare you for the Khumbu Icefall, a unique landmark on Everest on the Nepal side. A slow-moving waterfall of ice with a vertical gain of 800 metres over a distance of 2 kilometres requires an almost continuous line of rope to be fixed either in the horizontal or vertical position as the route zig-zags its way from the bottom to the top of the Icefall. Spread out along this route are aluminium ladders, tied end to end with ropes to bridge bottomless crevasses and overcome ice walls. It becomes a dangerous game of Snakes and Ladders—if you lose, you pay for it with your life, as nineteen climbers already have.

Pre-dawn starts and speed are essential to climb the Icefall before rising daytime temperatures cause melting and expansion of the ice. My shortened feet made balance on the horizontal bridges extremely difficult and I found the easiest way to cross them was to crawl on my hands and knees. I was poised halfway across the widest span of 6 to 8 metres, my head-torch cutting through the blackness of a particularly evil-looking crevasse, when an uneasy wobble began in the ladder. I didn't know whether to inch my way forwards or backwards. If the ladder collapsed under me from the movement in the Icefall, I doubted whether the anchors on the safety rope would hold. After a moment's hesitation I decided to continue but no sooner had I done so, than the ladder dropped away to one side. The more I moved in either direction, the more the ladder shook, threatening to flip over. There seemed only one escape: straight ahead with all possible care.

As I neared the end of the ladder my head-torch picked up the cause of the problem: only one side of the ladder was embedded in the ice on the edge of the crevasse. We had crossed this crevasse on our way down the afternoon before and a good metre or more had overlapped each end of the ladder. Crevasses were opening and closing at an alarming rate and the lesson I learnt that day was always allow someone else to be the first through the Icefall at the beginning of a new day.

C1 was perched on a long, narrow block of ice that ran the width of the top of the Icefall. A deep crevasse on the uphill side of our camp meant that the block we were camped on would be the next to topple into the Icefall, and we counted on it holding for the duration of our climb. C1 was moated on nearly all sides and I felt this was far more important as it protected us from the avalanches that tumbled off Nuptse and the Western Shoulder of Everest. The camp also gave us access to the Western Cwm, a 4- to 5-kilometre-long valley that led to the base of the South West Face where we wanted to place C2. It was a distance of over 3 kilometres for a meagre height gain of 450 metres, but from C2 onwards height gain was unrelenting.

Shortly after trudging wearily up to C2 at 6500 metres, the morale of our team steadily declined. A combination of events, none of which seemed insurmountable at the time, drove a wedge through our team. Losing Rick before he had stepped onto the mountain was an immediate drain on our manpower and a violent spell of weather not only slowed progress but ripped a tent from its tie-down points at C2. The tent and its valuable equipment were never seen again. Hidden behind our early setbacks, and continuing to rear its ugly head, was personal ambition. Tony and John were accusing Chris and, to a lesser degree, Stan of not doing their share of load-carrying and thereby jeopardising the success of the climb. I tried to remain neutral as I knew that within each expedition there are always strong and weak climbers and the balance of strength can easily change from day to day. I was confident that, given more time, Chris and Stan would acclimatise better and would become more involved in the climb.

The good rapport that I usually enjoyed with team members had deteriorated and I found myself very much on the outer, particularly with John and Tony, probably for not taking control of the situation. It was a vast pity because we had endured many great climbing adventures and hardships together. I wrongly believed that a group of friends could happily manage an expedition without an appointed leader. Uncomfortable giving orders and delegating responsibility, I failed to give the group proper direction. It was no way to operate a party of climbers on the world's highest mountain.

A heated argument broke out among the five remaining members at C2, and as a result we returned to BC to cool down. Chris saw no reason to prolong his disappointment in the expedition and decided to go home. This left four of us to continue, but only Tony considered us strong or fast enough as individual climbers or as a team to push the limits of the West Ridge. Fortunately both John and I, who had suffered more frostbite injuries than anyone else on the team, knew the limits of our capabilities, particularly above 8000 metres, and realised the West Ridge was no longer a safe or viable proposition.

The alternative was to change to the easier South Col route but to do this we would have to get permission from the Ministry of Tourism in Kathmandu. It would take about two weeks to get a written reply and with the window of opportunity for the spring weather approaching, the four of us decided to push our camps through to the South Col in the hope that permission would arrive just as we were about to make the final push to the summit. Pushing on to the summit without permission would mean a hefty fine and long term suspension from Nepal.

We progressed to the South Col route, managing temporarily to ignore the ill-feeling in the group. I suspect Stan also fell prey to the depression of our dysfunctional team with a noticeable drop in his motivation at C2. He decided to go no further and returned to BC to wait out the remainder of the climb.

Tony, John and I reached the South Col some time during the first few days of May. We had left BC 4 days earlier and maintained radio contact with BC each evening to ask if our permission had been granted. Our final call from C4 failed to make contact with BC so we decided to take a gamble on the summit. That evening cyclonic winds battered our tents and we were lucky to make it through the night with our tents still intact. The morning brought no relief, and with my summit hopes gone, I battled down the mountain, leaving John and Tony to gamble with their summit chances for another day. Twenty-four hours later, however, they were forced down by the appalling wind that continued to blow across the South Col. It was rumoured at BC that we had been forced down by the effects of a Bangladesh cyclone centred some 500 kilometres away, but I believe we were, in fact, experiencing the very real threat of the jet-stream winds that constantly blast the upper slopes of Mount Everest at speeds in excess of 200 kilometres per hour. I had felt the strength of such winds just briefly on the summit ridge of Kangchenjunga, but fortunately was able to escape their full force by climbing on the lee side of the ridge.

The final blow to this miserable expedition was the letter from the Ministry of Tourism that awaited me at BC. It stated that under no circumstances was the Australian expedition on the West Ridge of Everest to transfer their intentions to the South Col route. Without this permission we could go nowhere, and the difficult and long West Ridge was not an option under the present circumstances. Our expedition ground to a halt and disbanded.

My first encounter with Mount Everest had not been a pleasant one, nor had it been the mountaineering challenge I had hoped for. Despite the good intentions of all six climbers, the expedition had turned into a battle of human relationships. For this I accept part of the blame and I took the failure of the expedition personally, for it had been mounted in friendship and had ended in disharmony. The lesson I learnt was that if I initiated another expedition, I must assume full leadership responsibility. But as I had organised and led most of the previous seven, I was happy for the time being to let someone else take on that time-consuming and responsible position.

EVEREST, AUTUMN 1991

chapter eight

Am I in heaven? Or have I checked into hell?

I was only fooled for a few seconds as I looked up into the pale blue light, panic quickly overwhelming my momentary relief as the suffocating feeling returned. I struggled with my left arm to crack the 30 centimetres of snow and ice that trapped me from the outside world, simultaneously removing the packed snow from my mouth with my finger.

Beaten into submission, dizzy and confused I tried to stand up but fell over immediately. Warm streams of blood trickled over my face and ran into my eyes, making it difficult to see. All around me lay dark objects; I could only guess that they were pieces of climbing equipment scattered in the snow. My hands caught the ragged edges of my torn climbing-suit as I tried to find the source of the blood. With no obvious wounds it seemed the blood was dripping from damaged fingers freed from their three pairs of gloves by the fall.

The three Sherpas had escaped the full force of the avalanche but assumed that I was dead as they surveyed the scene from 900 metres above. It was only a short distance back to C2, so I started to walk—I knew there was a trail somewhere in front of me with bamboo marker wands meandering through the crevasses. My vision was blurred and my head dizzy and I kept losing my sense of direction. No doubt I was wandering dangerously close to crevasses. It did not occur to me to stop and rest. I needed to pee but my hands were too cramped and frozen to negotiate the fly. I was tempted to go in my climbing-suit but I wanted to see if I was bleeding internally, so I made myself hold on until I could get some help undressing. Somehow, I managed to stagger down to C2.

At camp everyone was amazed that I had come down in the avalanche, as they had watched it from C2. I was half-carried to the large kitchen tent of a Basque expedition where the doctor tended me. By now I was hypothermic and shaking uncontrollably—snow and ice had penetrated my one-piece climbing-suit and my underclothes were saturated. I was very anxious about my frozen fingers as I could not bear the thought of losing them to frostbite. There were many hands helping to strip off my soaked clothing and I was wrapped up in two sleeping-bags and given hot tea, but my eyes, badly grazed by the ice, refused to focus on the cup, so I had to be fed like a baby. Dry clothes were brought from my tent and when unfolding a pair of socks, a handwritten note from my girlfriend, Judi, dropped out. I could not prevent its contents from becoming public and it was translated into many languages to the accompaniment of wolf whistles and howls of laughter.

All this time someone was holding my hand and it brought back memories of my lone experience in the tent at C3 on Kangchenjunga. When my sight was eventually restored a little later, I found the person holding my hand was Takolo from the Basque expedition. I had passed him many times on the Icefall but there was never any acknowledgement of my greeting; now he seemed to be my best friend. He stayed with me for hours until one of my team members took over for the night shift when I was carried to one of our own tents.

Working for the Basque team were Tenzing from my Annapurna II climb and Mingma from Kangchenjunga. Although they were supposed to carry loads for the Basque team the next day, they arranged to escort me down to BC allowing my three climbing partners to continue climbing.

—————

We had an unusual combination of climbers on this expedition. I had not known Andrew Lock, Mark Squires and Ian Collins long enough to become friends, let alone embark on an Everest climb with them. I had recently met them when passing through Sydney. With an Everest permit in my hand but bitter memories of the dismal failure of my first expedition to Everest earlier that year, we talked about teaming up for another attempt. None from the former expedition could join us: some could not afford another two months off work, and I had lost contact with the others. Because of the scarcity of Himalayan climbers in Australia, it was inevitable that one day I would have to team up with climbers I scarcely knew. So for my prospective Sydney climbing partners and me it was a two-way gamble, but once we overcame some initial hurdles we worked better as a team than my first group to Everest.

During my week's rest at BC, while facing the possibility
of returning home early, some mail arrived including a few
letters from Judi and a large envelope containing a copy of
Playboy magazine. When I went to thumb through it, I
found some of the pages were stuck together; a closer
inspection revealed that *all* pages had been glued together.
I didn't have to guess who had done this. Luckily with a
day to kill I managed to separate most of the pages with a
sharp pocket knife, much to the amusement of everyone at
BC.

Andrew, Mark and Ian arrived wearily back some days
later and I am sure they were expecting to find me packing
for home, but instead I announced that I would be
returning to the hill with them after their rest.

————————

I set a leisurely pace up the mountain, as cracked ribs and a
broken nose inhibited my breathing. I couldn't help the
occasional glance up to the Lhotse Face where the scar of
my avalanche was etched deep into the Face. It gave me
many moments of doubt. When the time came to cross the
avalanche slope I hesitated. The broken ends of the yellow
rope that I was once tied to hung down the Face and
another had been put in its place.

Only Andrew, Ian and I made it to C4. Mark, exhausted,
turned around 200 metres below. It was going to be a tight
squeeze for the three of us in our two-man tent, until
I remembered the Basques' offer to use their tent at
C4. Moving to the unoccupied Basque tent would give
everyone the best chance of resting and getting away early

for our summit attempt. The night passed with little sleep as my lungs rattled with the sound of fluid and I had a hacking cough. Although I was not suffering from cerebral or pulmonary oedema, I put it down to a side-effect from the avalanche and with the gale-force winds buffeting our tents in the morning, my decision to descend was easy. I passed by Andrew and Ian's tent to tell them I was heading down. They had some bottled oxygen and were prepared to wait one more day to see if the wind would die down. Their summit chance came the following day but, after a gain of a couple of hundred metres, the intense cold got the better of them and they wisely returned.

Ours was a happy expedition and my only regret was that I did not let my guard down enough to become more friendly with Mark, Ian and Andrew—I still had the bitter taste of disappointment from my earlier Everest expedition. We had done amazingly well, considering the expedition had been put together in six to seven weeks after the withdrawal of another team had left a vacant permit. Being in the right place at the right time meant that I was offered this permit, but it was Ian, Mark and Andrew who did the back-breaking work in those short weeks to bring the expedition together.

EVEREST, SPRING 1993

chapter nine

'The reflection I find fascinating is that Everest is exactly the right height to provide the perfect physical challenge to the climber's strength and endurance. Were it 1000 feet lower it would have been climbed in 1924. Were it 1000 feet higher it would have been an engineering problem.'

Peter Lloyd, 1984

1992 was a bad year. I could not find suitable orthotics for my feet. Nothing worked and they ached after a short walk or standing in one spot too long. I avoided any sort of social gathering that required standing. There were no mountaineering plans for that year and very little rock-climbing, as I had destroyed several pairs of expensive rock-climbing shoes trying to invent a design that might work on the rock. Frustration and disappointment followed. I also hated work and it all led to deep depression. I tried with little conviction to tell myself that I was expecting too much too soon. The painful result was that Judi could no longer cope. I couldn't expect her to understand and we went our separate ways after living together for two years.

I eventually found a podiatrist, Peter Quinn, who was

willing to persevere with my problem. Over a ten-month period he moulded plastic and foam together to form orthotics that would run the full length of my shoes and fill the space where my toes once were. I could not wear the first pair he made for more than a few minutes, despite my efforts to adjust my feet to them gradually. The next pair lasted for an hour or two each day and after a month some more plastic and foam were either added or taken off, depending on where my feet had settled into the orthotic. Another problem was that most of the metatarsal pads had been removed when my toes were amputated. Peter was able to source some 3-millimetre-thick, soft-compression, silicone-type material from the USA that provided some cushioning effect to the bottom of my feet. At US$100 a square foot it was expensive material, but I gladly paid it. Later that year X-rays showed that the bones at the end of my feet were elongating due to the unusual stress I was placing on them by the shock absorption of walking. I have been told that no matter what material I use to help absorb the pressure, the damage is done. The bones will continue to elongate and in time stress fractures will occur, making it impossible to lead my usual active life. I have not been given a time frame, so I have chosen to live for today; in the meantime I continue to experiment and search for ways to halt the process.

Throughout 1992 I had been speaking to a group of people about returning to Everest in the spring of 1993. Feeling positive that the climb would go ahead, I went the extra step and contributed $5000 to the cost of a permit worth US$10 000—money that was non-refundable. The expedition never got off the ground and the huge financial loss left me powerless to contribute to the running costs of any other expedition that came my way. I had long since accepted that I was not going to attempt Everest that year. It was yet another terrible blow for 1992.

By early 1993 things started to change for the better. I had made some great progress with my orthotics, thanks to Peter, and more importantly with Judi; we had sorted out our differences, and although I was still depressed and frustrated, she was confident I would come out of it sooner or later with the progress I was making with my feet.

One night in early March 1993 Judi and I were discussing our wedding plans for the coming Saturday over dinner when the phone rang. I was reluctant to answer it, but quickly changed my tune when I discovered it was Tashi Tenzing. We talked for a while but all that I remember was that he invited me to climb Everest with his team; we were to leave on Friday week! Tashi Tenzing is the grandson of Tenzing Norgay who along with Sir Edmund Hillary were the first to summit Everest on 29 May 1953. Tashi was organising an expedition to Everest to celebrate the fortieth anniversary of his grandfather's ascent. Unfortunately his grandfather would not be there to appreciate the occasion as he had died in 1985. Tashi had wasted no time in getting to the point of his call. 'Do you want to leave for Everest next Friday?'

This was not a phone call out of the blue; Tashi and I had spoken on a couple of occasions about this expedition, but I had been already financially committed to another Everest expedition. When he heard the expedition had fallen through, he tentatively offered me a position on the climb, subject to the agreement from the rest of his team. The problem was that all the hard work in planning and organising had been done. A number of major sponsors, Lipton Teas, and Clark, manufacturers of stainless steel products, had come up with the cash to run the expedition and Thai Airways International was supplying the plane tickets. It was an understandable concern, considering there was a great deal of money involved and the hard work that had been done to get it. Tonight Tashi had just come from a team meeting where it was decided to invite me to be the eighth member of the team. 'See you Friday week at Sydney airport,' said Tashi.

I returned to the table where Judi was still waiting to finalise our wedding plans. 'You're going to Everest aren't you?'

'Yes, that was Tashi confirming my position on the team. We're leaving Friday week.'

'I thought you were! You haven't smiled like that in twelve months. I'm glad you're able to go at last.'

Judi and I were married on the highest available point in Brisbane, Mount Coot-tha, and after the wedding Judi, instead of going on a honeymoon, watched me pack for Everest. I was fortunate, however, that my new wife not only understood my situation but was my main support in this expedition. I promised we would go on a honeymoon when I returned.

I was facing again the risky proposition of climbing with people I didn't know. Andrew Lock, who had been a member of the 1991 autumn Everest trip, was the only one I knew in this expedition, and even then I didn't know him well. Mike Wood, whom I'd met a couple of times while in Perth speaking at various conferences, was a white-water kayaking specialist and it surprised me that he was on the expedition until I found out that his role was BC manager. This stemmed from his years as a trekking and rafting guide in Nepal, plus his organisational skills as owner and manager of the Mountain Designs outdoor equipment store in Perth. Mike also intended to do some load-carries up the mountain as far as his experience and stamina would take him. Alex Aleksov and Dimitar Todorovski were two stone and marble masons who specialised in the bathrooms and foyers of Sydney's high-rise buildings. Both were originally from Macedonia with extensive climbing experience in the European Alps and an expedition to the world's eighth highest mountain, Manaslu. They lived in Sydney but remained fiercely proud of their origins. My first introduction to Alex and Dimitar in Sydney just before we flew out was brief and uncommunicative—they seemed more engrossed in some last-minute packing problems. David Hume was also unknown to me, although he took the time to introduce himself over the phone in a pre-expedition chat. I did not meet him until we boarded the plane in Sydney bound for Bangkok. During the flight I got to know him a little better. He has a big frame for a mountaineer and was hoping to trim down to a post-expedition weight of below 100 kilograms. To the non-climber he might fit the mould expected of a mountaineer—bearded and tall, strongly built with pack-bearing shoulders. His jovial nature and his interest in electronics and computers meant it was going to be fun and interesting having him around. The final member to make up the eight-man team was Lobsang Bhutia, Tashi's mountaineering uncle and nephew of the famous Tenzing Norgay.

———————

As we shopped for expedition supplies in Kathmandu we discovered the presence of fifteen other expeditions due to go to the Nepalese side of the mountain. This was an overwhelming number but it did not surprise me as the Nepalese government was due to put up the peak fee for Everest from US$10,000 to US$50,000 next season and everyone was trying to get in before the massive price rise.

———————

An early spring snowfall prevented us from reaching BC. For three days we did not feel the sun's warmth and warmed ourselves by the heat of yak dung fires. Our enforced delay extended our eight-day walk into BC to eleven. We shared this delay in the village of Lobuche with two other Everest teams, one of which was an all-women Indian team. When at last the weather cleared, everyone was eager to make the final days' walk to BC, but Lobsang and I lingered. BC could wait. We preferred to warm our hands and shuffle our cold feet in the sun.

   We talked about our previous attempts on Everest.

'I guess it's important for you to summit this year so you can really celebrate your uncle's ascent.'

'No, there is no pressure on me to climb Everest because my uncle did. It's more because it's something I have wanted to do ever since I can remember.'

There was an air of confidence in his manner and I nodded agreement. I recognised his dream.

———————

By 28 March there was deep snow at BC and the continuous roar of the jet-stream winds was unsettling, even though we were sheltering in an amphitheatre of ridges. The occasional rogue gust of wind that sneaked past this defence flattened some of our tents. To make things more unpleasant, the yaks carrying most of our cold weather clothing and anti-boredom weapons such as books, portable cassette players, cards and games could not reach BC because of the deep snow. For the next two days we lay silently in our tents trying to stay warm. Talking all day is hard work for an introvert like me, so the hours passed slowly.

By now David had the alarming ability to look as if he had just come back from an expedition before he had even started. He had a distinct dislike of soap and water, and became the brunt of our jokes, in a likeable sort of way, as the source of the bad odour around BC. Mealtimes in the mess tent were the only escape from the boredom, but they remained brief as we were exposed to the cold with insufficient clothing.

With the opening of the trail to BC came the remainder of our equipment and the largest gathering of teams ever to attempt Everest in the same season, all fifteen wanting to settle into an area not much bigger than a couple of football fields. BC soon resembled a tent city as our neighbours from a vast array of nationalities caused quite a social scene, if you had any energy left after coming down off the hill.

The Korean team had already fixed 2000 metres of rope and twenty-five to thirty ladders in the Khumbu Icefall and we paid our share of the cost of establishing this route. The Icefall opened to traffic on 1 April and at 5.00 a.m. we started carrying loads up to C1 at 6100 metres.

Not everyone in our team was acclimatising at the same rate. Alex, Andrew and Dimitar were suffering severe headaches and nausea, while Mike stayed at BC to sort through supplies recently brought in by the yaks. In the meantime, David, Tashi, Lobsang and I each carried 15 kilograms of tents, food, fuel, stoves, pots and pans to C1.

The Icefall is like a giant mousetrap ready to snap shut at any time on an unsuspecting climber. For the climbers who pass at night or in the early hours of the morning, the chances of being caught are minimal, but those who linger with little respect for the dangers may well find their names added to the list of nineteen who have been killed in the Icefall. This year it was the worst I had experienced. Our path meandered through it to avoid teetering towers of ice and bottomless pits. We made hard work of our first journey through the Icefall due to slow acclimatisation and unfamiliarity with the new route. Once on top of the Icefall we searched for a place safe from avalanches and crevasses to make camp and stash away our gear. We could see avalanches sweeping off the western shoulder of Everest and Nuptse on opposite sides of the Cwm. Despite the broad expanse of the Western Cwm, the only suitable place was a small, confined area capable of accommodating the tents of just a couple of expeditions. The site had already been claimed, so we had to move further up the Cwm to share another site with the Indian group. This was also protected on three sides by deep crevasses with the access into the camp marked by bamboo wands. The size and depth of these crevasses was unnerving; there were many that remained hidden, covered by a thin layer of snow, and this was a deterrent to anyone wishing to take a shortcut on the zig-zag trail in and out of camp.

We continued to carry loads for the next two days with the other team members who had been ill from the altitude when they had recovered enough to help carry the equipment and supplies we would need in our four camps above BC. The twenty oxygen bottles, masks and regulators were the heaviest items and could only be moved in small quantities.

A windy first night at C2 had brought 15 centimetres of snow and it looked like settling in for some time so it came as a complete surprise on the morning of 8 April when the weather cleared. Lobsang and I dropped down to C1 to help David, Andrew and Tashi bring up more loads to C2, but Alex and Dimitar had to descend to BC suffering further altitude problems. With most of our climbers now at C2, we erected three two-man tents on small, rocky platforms and tied them down securely with ropes as gale-force winds were known to spring up in the middle of the night. I had already lost a couple of tents here on earlier expeditions. Tashi had purchased military-style ration packs left over from the British expedition that had attempted Everest a couple of months earlier during winter. Some of the food was passable, but years of eating freeze-dried meals has left me with little appreciation for them. They had rather noisy side-effects and loud blasts of wind from neighbouring tents reverberated all night.

On 9 April David, Lobsang and I were given the job of establishing C3. Tashi and Andrew were feeling ill and had a rest day. The morning cold quickly seeped into our hands and feet. I wanted to turn back but Lobsang was setting a cracking pace, determined to reach C3 despite the cold. Thirty minutes later our suffering eased as we reached the sunshine and we stopped to soak up its warmth. To maintain body heat we still had to keep moving and within three hours we had climbed to 7300 metres and found a suitable site for C3. There was a noticeable attrition rate of climbers moving up the mountain to the higher camps—Lobsang, David and I were the only ones up there. This certainly suited me. David was unable to keep our pace and was still about 600 metres below, jumarring up the safety of the ropes that hung down from C3. It was hard, blue ice where we were standing, so we tied ourselves and our packs to an ice screw and shared a thermos of tea before hacking out a ledge for our tent. We sent a shower of snow and ice down on David but we knew it would cause him no harm.

While Lobsang and I dug in short bursts, I told him of a strange experience I had had during one of my previous attempts on Everest. It was at this very site in 1991 that I found myself having to sleep alone in an abandoned snow cave. It had been an exhausting day, so I fell asleep easily until 1.00 a.m., when I was woken by the familiar sound of heavy boots and crampons scraping the ice near the entrance of the snow cave. I sat up in my sleeping-bag and started to make room for my visitor, whom I expected to come crawling through the entrance at any moment. Instead they seemed to walk in circles in front of the snow cave. A break in the commotion outside allowed me to call out, 'Hello!' There was no reply, and almost as quickly as they came, the footsteps faded into the night.

Crawling from the cave the next morning I was quick to look for any sign of footprints or a climber moving on the ropes either above or below C3, but there was nothing.

Lobsang was not surprised by my story and had a ready explanation.

'The *Chockidar*,' he replied.

He explained *Chockidar* means 'watchman' in the Sherpa language, and is the ghost or spirit of those who have died near the exposed and dangerous C3. It would seem, according to Lobsang, that the night watchman of C3 had paid me a visit.

It had taken us three-and-a-half hours to climb up to C3 and almost as long to dig a platform that was just big enough to accommodate our tent and secure it in such a fashion that it would still be there when we came back. David arrived just as we were leaving, and although suffering from slow acclimatisation, exhaustion and a heavy pack, he was still able to manage a smile. I was impressed by his cheerfulness, despite his torment. We offered to wait but David insisted we did not.

Lobsang and I were back at C2 by 4.00 p.m. David called on his radio to say he was about halfway down the fixed ropes from C3 and, because he would arrive late, was happy to spend the night at C2 with Andrew. It was time for those who had been load carrying to take a break and Lobsang and I decided to continue on to BC that afternoon so we wouldn't use up more food and fuel at C2. We had just enough time. Entering the Icefall just on sunset we emerged at the bottom with our head-torch beams criss-crossing each other in search of our path to BC. It was 7.30 p.m. by the time we stumbled in and those who were at BC congratulated us on our efforts. It had been a long day.

David and Andrew returned to BC the following day, but our good progress ground to a halt during the next week and we were left idle in our tents owing to the onset of bad weather.

A rather happy and social event took place on 17 April. David washed his face and hair for the first time since leaving Kathmandu.

By 19 April everyone, including Dimitar, who had been having great difficulty acclimatising, was ready to carry more supplies up to C2 and from there hopefully push on to establish C4. More supplies of everything were needed at C3 before a carry could be undertaken to C4. I did a quick calculation of the weight of equipment we needed to haul up to C4—four 10- to 12-kilogram loads, with the remainder to be carried up during the summit attempt. Lobsang, Dimitar and I were given a reprieve from this carry. It was during these final days of setting up our four camps in preparation for a summit attempt that I noticed the pressure of being the expedition leader bearing down heavily on Tashi's shoulders. Coping no less admirably than at the beginning of the expedition, I sensed, however, that he was no longer enjoying the task. It is never an enviable position and I could sympathise with his burden of responsibility. Yet the climb was going along reasonably well compared to others I had been on, and I told him so.

It was on 22 April that one of the other expeditions got into trouble. A Nepalese mountaineer, Pasang Lhamu, was hoping to be the first woman from her country to climb Everest for which she would receive great recognition. She had attempted Everest about three times without success and it was on one of these earlier climbs that I had met her. But this season the stakes were raised when another Nepalese woman stepped onto the mountain and the race to be the first to the top began. I don't know if any shortcuts were taken in their preparation because of this, but Pasang Lhamu was making a rather early season summit attempt. Our team had called a rest day at C2 and some of us, including Lobsang and I, were lounging around outside our tents, the stove purring away for our next cup of tea, when Tashi appeared looking very worried. We didn't have to ask before he told us that Pasang Lhamu and her team of five Sherpas had reached the summit late in the day but on the descent most of them had run out of oxygen near the South Summit which is barely 100 metres below the main summit. Running out of oxygen had had a crippling effect on Pasang and she was unable to descend past the

South Summit without it. Tashi knew all of this having visited their team's tent at C2 just when the frantic radio calls were coming down from the South Summit. Now sipping our tea in the afternoon sun at C2 we spoke openly about what we knew would inevitably happen to those who stayed on the South Summit—they would be dead by morning. We also knew we were powerless to help as we were two fixed camps and over two vertical kilometres below them. The night of their deaths I remember gale-force winds forced an Arctic cold through the walls of our C2 tents. I lay snugly in my sleeping-bag, thankful of our small comforts and aware of the desperate fight for life thousands of metres above. The fact that we couldn't do anything to help preyed on my mind for many hours.

During the night of 23 April three of the five Sherpas miraculously made it down to their C4, but Sonam Tshring, Pemba Nuru and Pasang were forced to spend the night on the South Summit. In the morning only Pemba Nuru descended with remarkably little frostbite considering his exposure. He was lucky to survive while his companions died. These two deaths had a demoralising effect on our motivation, and with our four camps almost set up we agreed to return to BC for a rest and to wait for the 200-kilometre-per-hour jet-stream winds that were now gusting across the summit to die down.

Back at BC by 27 April, we each had the luxury of our own tent. It was a comfort we all looked forward to, considering our cramped living arrangements on the hill. Every day Lobsang would crawl into my tent around mid-afternoon for a chat. If I was preoccupied with writing letters or my diary he would not disturb me and being familiar with the layout of my tent would fossick for my food stash, read a book or use my compact stereo with headphones without so much as a word. If we were lucky, one of the kitchen boys would bring us tea and biscuits, and this became the afternoon ritual for BC. But this afternoon Lobsang interrupted my reading. He was concerned about my announcement to the team at lunch-time that I had decided to try to climb Everest without the use of bottled oxygen. I was not throwing a spanner into the works, as everyone knew I had been toying with this idea since the beginning of the climb. My decision would not affect anyone else's chances, only mine, and would leave more bottles of oxygen available for the others.

Lobsang asked why, after two failed expeditions to Everest, I was reducing my third attempt to less than a 10 per cent chance of success by not using oxygen. I knew the risks were high and my chances slim: only about forty climbers had succeeded without oxygen, one a year since the mountain was first climbed in 1953. Having studied these facts, I also knew that five climbers hadn't made it back down, and others had suffered serious frostbite for their efforts. It was not an easy decision to make and I had agonised over it for weeks. However, I was comfortable with the thought of failure if I took on Everest on its terms, rather than bringing the summit down to my level by resorting to the use of oxygen. Lobsang nodded agreement to my explanation but we both knew that it meant the end of our partnership, for once we set out for the summit from C4, we would be travelling at different speeds.

At dinner that evening we heard a favourable weather report for a summit attempt on our short-wave radio. It was only a very brief opening of the weather window, however, when the jet-stream winds would die down for a twenty-four-hour period beginning on 10 May. There was a lot of discussion about the weather and what it might or might not do. I aired my point of view by saying that during any given season there might only be one or two days in which a summit attempt could be made, so if this was our first we should take it. Some questioned the accuracy of the weather report, but I argued that any other option was only a guess anyway. If we were to take advantage of this opportunity, which might be our only one, then we had to move quickly up to C4 over the next two days. There was one more option—11 May might be calm also and this would give us an extra day to reach C4. Although David and I were the only ones in complete favour of 10 May, the evening ended with a general consensus that the next day we would all climb to C2 and review the situation from there. That night I went to bed feeling comfortable with the thought that a decision was made for a summit attempt. I was beginning to feel homesick and missing Judi terribly.

On 8 May light snow was falling at BC. Everyone left at different intervals with doubts about the weather. Lobsang and I teamed up for the climb and the weather improved the higher we climbed, but Dimitar still struggled with the altitude and wisely decided he would not go past C2. In between rising waves of nausea caused by the altitude and the thought of the unpalatable food packs, I was tempted to eat a little, but at the height of the nausea I would have vomited it all back up. A dangerous downward spiral would have developed every time I ate or drank something only to bring it up. The loss of fluids would have meant the end of the climb. I sipped lukewarm tea and nibbled tentatively at a crumbled muesli bar. I needed food for energy, yet over the next few days I would be crawling along on an intake of two or three muesli bars each day. During a final sorting of equipment for our climb to C4, I changed my socks before getting into my sleeping-bag and noticed deep, red, fleshy splits in the callused skin on the stumps of my feet. I had been wondering why they had been hurting so much during the climb back up from BC this morning. Now I could see. Normally I try to keep the callus build-up to a minimum by regularly carving it off with a scalpel, but this time the injuries were caused by the cold. All that I could do was rub skin moisturiser into the stumps and put up with the pain that I knew would become a lot worse.

I was woken on 9 May by the alarm at 2.00 a.m. and I immediately recognised the sound of snow falling on the tent. I looked outside my tent only to come face to face with Lobsang doing the same from the tent he shared with Tashi. We elected to wait and see. However, by 3.30 a.m. things looked more promising and David, Alex, Andrew, Tashi, Lobsang and I set off for C3 and C4 with the hope that the weather would continue to improve. Our team plan was to continue to C4 that day—a long day, but it had to be done if we were to catch the predicted forecast for 10 May—so at C3 I wasted no time waiting for the others as my hands and feet ached with the cold. It was mid-afternoon when I arrived at the South Col which possessed an eerie calm and I wondered if it might be the calm before a storm. All the other times I had been here there had been gale-force winds. There were a few other tents already set up on the Col, and their bent and twisted poles showed the effects of the menacing wind that I knew belonged here. From one such tent emerged a climber in a bright yellow climbing-suit with a thermos in hand. Although he was only 10 flat metres away, he was breathing heavily by the time he reached me.

'Hi! I'm Harry. I hear you are going to try to climb without Os.'

'Yes, that's my plan,' I replied, wondering how he knew.

'Would you be interested in teaming up with me as I want to do the same?' he asked.

Sipping the cup of tea he had just given me gave me time to consider his question carefully. I felt as if I would be abandoning the rest of my team-mates if I went with Harry, but I was essentially on my own anyway. I would be leaving C4 before them to start the summit day and most likely arriving back at C4 after the others had returned. I could not see anything wrong with Harry's proposition; if any-thing it would give a much-needed boost to my motivation to climb with someone who was prepared to take on Everest by its own terms, not that I have any less respect for those who use oxygen.

I agreed to team up with Harry and we set our departure time for the summit at 11.00 p.m. that night. It gave me barely a few hours to rest, but before that I had to make camp. From under a pile of rocks I found a tent among the food, oxygen bottles and other equipment that the others had carried up earlier. As Harry helped me erect the tent I wondered on what information he had judged me a suitable partner for this next and most difficult stage on Everest. I was taking the same chance with him.

Shortly after the tent was up Tashi and Lobsang arrived and I quizzed them on the whereabouts of the others. There had been a change of plans, Tashi said. David, Alex and Andrew were staying at C3, as they didn't think they could have made it to C4 today. They would come up tomorrow. Weary as we were from our extended effort that day from C2, we did our best to melt snow for drinking and to eat something. But it wasn't enough; barely two cups of tea each and half a muesli bar was all I could stomach for the second night in a row. Foolish as it was, I was faced with the same problem of nausea that I had had at C2 and I worried about vomiting. It was late in the afternoon by the time the three of us had settled into the tent. There wasn't much room as we juggled oxygen bottles dangerously close to our ignited stove and untangled oxygen hoses from around the stove and boots. I pointed out to Tashi, 'If one of these bloody oxygen bottles of yours ignites, we could be blown to the summit.'

'Yes, but would it count as an oxygenless ascent?' Tashi said. We fell about laughing at Tashi's quick response and it seemed to ease the nervous anticipation that had a stranglehold on our thoughts. With preparations complete for our big day, tiredness and anxiety kept me awake for the remaining few hours.

I felt as if I had only just settled down when my alarm sounded at 10.30 p.m. In the confines of our small tent I tried not to disturb Tashi and Lobsang, who were not starting for another two hours. There was no room to light the stove for something to drink and again I felt unable to force food down. I knew it would seriously hinder my summit chances, but I could do nothing about it. Eleven p.m. came quickly, as did Harry; his arrival at my tent door put me under even more stress, for I still had to force the second of two boots onto my left foot, and despite my effort to keep them warm in the tent during the last few hours, they were frozen. The air is thin at the South Col but at 11.00 p.m. that night it was thick with abuse directed at my uncooperative frozen boots as I sensed Harry's urgency to be moving. Tashi and Lobsang had remained deathly still throughout my rumblings and when it came time to leave, I chose not to wake them and slipped silently away, regretting a few minutes later that I had not wished them luck.

I was pleased to see the full moon lighting the South East Ridge; it has been a lucky sign for me as most of my summit attempts have been conducted under a full moon. One of the benefits of not using oxygen was that we didn't have to carry a pack and Harry and I stuffed water-bottles, cameras and something to eat into our climbing-suits. Harry set the pace and a pattern of a rest every ten steps. It was one I was all too familiar with, but tonight I could not maintain it. Harry edged further in front. It's normal for me to be slow and struggle for the first twenty minutes until I find my rhythm, but after an hour I was still struggling to find it. I blamed this on not eating or drinking enough during the last couple of days. Fortunately the snow was not deep, but I gained no satisfaction in having to follow Harry.

Three hundred metres higher I saw several lights from head-torches appear from the tents on the South Col. This suggested that it was already 1.00 a.m. and I hoped that two of the lights belonged to Tashi and Lobsang.

A couple of hours later, while climbing in the dark shadows of a couloir where the climbing wasn't difficult but breathing was, I reluctantly gave in to failure. I had been concentrating more on trying to keep warm than finding a suitable climbing rhythm, but did neither well. Any feeling that remained in my hands and feet had long since gone and they now felt like aching blocks of ice. Harry, who was only a few metres in front, was unaware of my internal battle and his distressed figure leaning heavily on his axe gasping for breath did little for my confidence. I started to descend. For a while I felt emotionally shattered and too exhausted to yell to Harry. Quietly I started to descend. Now that I had made up my mind I would descend until I had caught my breath then give Harry a shout to say that it was all over for me. Five metres lower I paused; Harry was still bent over and unaware of my descent. When I compared my actions to Harry's determination, I was ashamed of my cowardly retreat. I returned to the uphill slope.

After wading through more hours of anguish before dawn I finally succumbed to the terrifying cold. It brought more intolerable pain to my tortured hands and feet and again I began to accept failure. Turning to head down in the cold, grey light of dawn I paused—the beginning of a new day could not go unadmired. Silhouetted against the eastern horizon 100 kilometres away was the unmistakable mass of Kangchenjunga. With this came memories of the far greater hardships I had overcome during the years between Kangchenjunga and Everest and the question I had to ask myself was why was I giving in so easily when I had overcome more difficult hurdles to get where I was standing today? To give in now would mean a decision that I would most likely regret for the rest of my life.

The sun on the crest of the South East Ridge about 40 metres away was enormous motivation: it represented desperately needed warmth. Behind us were six climbers on oxygen, climbing faster than Harry and me and I wondered if we could beat them to it. We didn't, but once in the sun we stopped to enjoy it. During this time I drank my litre of water and ate my chocolate, glad to be rid of the extra weight. Harry was especially relieved when the six climbers passed us—none of whom we could recognise because of their oxygen masks—as we now had someone else's tracks to follow. However, with the slope increasing in angle to the South Summit, there was little need to kick steps in the hard-packed snow.

I was never going to be warm climbing Everest without oxygen—another benefit of using it—but thankfully the sun was taking the edge off the agonising cold as we neared the South Summit. Now, with the fear of more frostbite fading, I was able to convert some of my nervous energy into finding my old form as well as a role reversal with Harry, as the morning's effort began to take its toll on him.

Climbing on top of the South Summit gave me a clear view up the remaining ridge. The true summit could not be seen. The ridge, although undulating with jagged cornices, did not look as intimidating or as long as the photos I had studied suggested, but somewhere along this ridge was the Hillary Step, a 20-metre-high buttress of rock and ice and the last obstacle before reaching the summit. I had recovered from the morning's depression when I had crossed the line between success and failure many times.

Just on the other side of the South Summit I saw Pasang Lhamu's frozen and twisted body, half-sitting, half-lying in the snow. I remembered how sad I had felt for her the night she died. When I bumped into her at BC she had always been willing to have a chat and, as she was sponsored by a beer manufacturer, I was invited on a number of occasions to sample her sponsor's product. Now, I callously sidestepped around her body to get to the Main Summit another 100 metres higher.

The lure of the summit drew me away from Harry and I left him behind; this was not intentional as the caution needed on the narrow ridge leading to the Hillary Step demanded my full concentration; it was only when I reached the base of the step that I saw Harry still standing on top of the South Summit. He looked defeated, but I knew he was still internally strong. I was forced to wait precious minutes as the six climbers who had so effortlessly passed us earlier were doing battle with the Step, a battle they didn't seem to be winning convincingly. It felt like half an hour before I was able to start, about the time Harry left the South Summit to follow.

I was careful not to catch the spikes of my crampons on the old, tattered fixed ropes left hanging on the Hillary Step by expeditions years before, nor did I use them for support for fear they would break. A fall from here would have meant a tumble into Nepal on my left or China on my right. Once on top of the Step I felt a strange sense of guilt or even disappointment that I was now climbing so easily. You're supposed to be on your hands and knees by now, I thought. I continued on a little further, being careful to stay well below the fracture line of the huge cornices that hung over China on my right. I expected this ridge to be unrelenting in its quest for altitude, but over one rise I saw, just 50 metres away, the six climbers standing together on top of the ridge. They seemed to be happily striking poses reserved only for summits, so I guessed they were there and I was keen to join them.

The ease with which I climbed above the South Summit could have been contributed to by the excitement I felt in nearing the summit of my childhood dreams. Suddenly it all came down to a moment of disbelief and one more step. It seemed that everything that I had aimed for and had dreamt about since I was a small boy came down to this final step. Many thoughts flashed through my mind and I made this step last a little longer than the others. It was 10.20 a.m. During those first few moments I wondered if perhaps I was dreaming. It was too much for me to believe that I had actually reached this long-hallowed, small piece of frozen earth. I don't remember whether I actually punched myself to see if it were true, but some action was necessary to test the moment. I felt extremely lucky to be

there and the sense of pleasure and achievement overwhelmed the disappointment of having to share the
bathtub-sized summit with six others. They introduced
themselves as the first three Korean women to climb
Everest and their three climbing Sherpas. One Sherpa
offered to take my photo, but a couple of weeks later when
the film was developed I only had a photo of the Sherpa's
foot for my efforts. Their stay on the summit was short.
Within five minutes of my arrival they were leaving and I
watched them disappear down the way they had come. To
the non-mountaineer it might seem that Mount Everest is
climbed every day of the year. However, with teams poised
on both the Chinese and Nepalese sides of the mountain
waiting for that perfect day, it is likely that the weather
allows maybe half a dozen summit days in any given year.

Now that I was alone I tried to take it all in. There wasn't
much of a view as the cloud level was low but a lot of peaks
were poking through but it certainly made you realise that
you were on top of the world. The frustration of my camera
being jammed frozen would not bother me until much
later.

I saw Harry appear on the crest of the ridge, perhaps half
an hour away. I had been on the summit for twenty minutes now and wanted to stay longer, at least until Harry
arrived, but I was overcome with a sudden urgency to
descend with the realisation that I still had to get down.
Long ago I had learnt that the majority of mountaineering
accidents happen while descending and it's only the foolish
or the inexperienced who think they have made it when
standing on the summit. With one last look around I

started down. A few metres below the summit I stopped to pick up some small rocks and then continued down to Harry. At close range he looked to be coping much better than he had from a distance. He immediately apologised for being slow and congratulated me on the summit. I offered to wait but he said he was going well and wouldn't be too far behind me. For Harry the summit was twenty minutes away and he wasted no more time talking about it and continued.

At the top of the Hillary Step I was forced to wait again as someone climbed up. Staring down and around the side of the Kangshung Face I saw the profile of the Step and Lobsang's brightly coloured suit could not be mistaken. I suddenly didn't mind waiting. It would have made a great photo if my camera had been working. But as the minutes ticked by I was becoming increasingly more irritated by Lobsang's slow progress up the Hillary Step. After all he was on 2 litres of oxygen per minute and should be climbing it easily, but if the truth be known my ascent of the Step would have been much slower. For a while I was distracted from my hurry to escape this dreamlike world as I became absorbed in a possible future climb—the West Pillar of Makalu dominating the eastern skyline. Lobsang grabbed my knee and shook me from my daydream as he topped the Hillary Step; it was just the start of many handshakes and back slaps. He knew I had made it; my smile told him so. His voice was muffled by the hiss from the oxygen flowing into his mask and the oxygen bottles clanged together in his pack as he sat down beside me. My curiosity nearly tempted me to ask him for a sniff to feel the effect it had. If I hadn't felt so tired, I might have started a conversation but neither of us talked, preferring instead to stare in wonder over Nepal. Finally Lobsang tapped my glove. He wanted my goggles in return for his sunglasses. As we swapped eye protection I offered to wait, but Lobsang shook his head and pointed down to C4. This gesture I understood to mean, wait for me at C4. Perhaps he and Harry would come down together. In my state of forgetfulness I had forgotten to ask about Tashi and had to shout back up to Lobsang for the answer. Talking from the side of his oxygen mask he yelled, 'Gone down.' I felt sad for Tashi but his actions were those of a mountaineer who knew his limits.

We went our separate ways. Just below the South Summit I was overcome by a wave of fatigue as the slope steepened and my legs weakened. I could only just manage to maintain a pace that was slightly faster than going up. There was no sign of Harry or Lobsang along the summit ridge, but they should be able to catch me up at this pace, I thought. Descending the South East Ridge I located the gully that we had ascended during the darkness of the predawn hours. Here I simply sat on my backside and started sliding, using my ice axe to steer and as a brake when I picked up too much speed. I had to be careful as there were a number of rock bands that needed careful downclimbing. Nevertheless it took just a few minutes to descend 200 or 300 metres and I was back at C4 by mid-afternoon. David, Alex and Andrew were there to meet me with cups of tea. I wanted to keep going to C3, but Everest's summit had clouded in, and with no sign of Lobsang or Harry, I prepared myself to stay another night at C4. It started off as an anxious night of waiting, but I soon fell asleep from exhaustion. Much later that night Harry emerged from the darkness and the wind. He had summited but was now in bad shape: exhausted, a partial loss of vision had slowed him down and he had suffered exposure to the cold as a result. Fortunately a couple of his team-mates had moved into position at C4 and were able to take care of him.

It was only in the morning, speaking to David from the other tent, that I found out that throughout the night the wind had threatened to flatten our tents. I had expected to see Lobsang lying snug in his sleeping-bag next to me.

'Is Lobsang in your tent, Dave?'

'I'm afraid, Mike, he hasn't turned up. I spoke with Harry a few minutes ago and he said he last saw Lobsang about 50 metres below the summit, still climbing. Last night there was nothing we could do in these conditions and I think it's getting worse. I'll speak to you later,' and with that he zipped the door closed as my tent was filling with wind-driven snow. As my head spun with thoughts for Lobsang, I saw his sunglasses that he had given me at the top of the Hillary Step lying neatly on top of his sleeping-bag covered in a thick layer of snow and ice. The wind picked up to gale force and the temperature dropped into the minus 30s or 40s. I knew that no-one could survive these conditions outside and any hope of seeing Lobsang again faded. I didn't dare go outside to see David, Alex or Andrew in our other tent or to see how Harry was going. We were confined to our tents with no chance of move-ment, despite my anxiety to get down as quickly as possible for fear of being overcome by the debilitating effects of the altitude if I stayed there any longer. David, Alex and Andrew had supplies of oxygen that would last forty-eight hours and were prepared to wait in the most unlikely chance that Lobsang would turn up. I could not imagine that Lobsang was dead and instead favoured the idea that in the darkness he was unable to find C4 and had continued down to C3. I looked forward to seeing him there.

By mid-morning I tried to leave but no sooner had I crawled from the entrance of the tent, than a gust of wind blew me back in. It delivered a sharp, stinging sensation to the end of my nose and my right ear lobe. Instant frostbite.

I was forced to wait a couple more hours in the solitude of my tent before getting the break in the wind that I needed to escape. Harry, with the support of his British team-mates, would follow. I did not find Lobsang at the lower camps, only Tashi at C2, distraught with grief over the disappearance of his uncle. We stayed at C2 that night, but confusing and conflicting radio reports from C4 only gave false hope that Lobsang was still alive. Grief, fatigue and the roar of the wind prevented the sleep I sorely needed and I tossed fitfully.

———————

During a lull in the unsettled weather on 12 May, Alex turned up the flow rate on an oxygen bottle and set out in search of Lobsang. He spent hours criss-crossing the slopes above C4 before finally locating Lobsang's body just 200 metres above the camp at the bottom of the same gully I had slid down. It was clear that he had fallen from near the South Summit. It was generally thought that he had run out of oxygen, become confused and disoriented, and simply walked over the edge. But Lobsang was too strong a climber to be affected like that and I thought back to the moment on top of the Hillary Step when he had asked me for my goggles to replace his inadequate sunglasses. Had he recognised the irritating itch of snow-blindness setting in, caused by inadequate eye protection? It takes only a few minutes at that altitude. No-one will ever know. His smashed wrist watch revealed he died at 2.55 p.m. on 10 May.

———————

The expedition came to an end the day Lobsang's body was found. No more summit attempts would be made, and David and Andrew left for home. I could have gone too, but I stayed at BC to support Tashi, if only in appearance, as did Mike, Dimitar and Alex. I had a small amount of frostbite to the stumps of my feet, my right ear lobe and the tip of my nose. Tashi's only concern now was giving his uncle the final rites and cremation that are so important to Buddhists. This required getting Lobsang's body off the mountain. Alex, Dimitar and some members from other teams under the supervision of Tashi were able to drag Lobsang's body down to BC. From here it was carried to the village of Pangbouche.

It was perfect weather the morning of the cremation and it started early with the collection of wood for a site that allowed a clear view up the valley to Everest. The ceremony was a drawn-out affair, taking up most of the day. During this time the atmosphere around the funeral pyre changed dramatically as the clear, blue sky was replaced with a low, grey cloud that poured into the valley, filtering the sun's rays to an eerie light. The cold cloud enveloped everything, except one mountain, which seemed to draw the sun's rays like a magnet—it was, of course, Everest.

I flew home alone. Mike, Dimitar and Alex had different flights, while Tashi had the unenviable task of returning Lobsang's ashes to his wife and son in Darjeeling. It was not the best way to end an expedition with everyone going their separate ways so unexpectedly. It had been a roller-coaster climb of great personal emotions, first to the top of the world and the fulfilment of both Lobsang's and my childhood fascination, and then to the helpless despair when Lobsang died on the descent. Although we guessed he had summited, a film from the camera I had lent him was developed showing him standing on the summit—a fitting memorial. I dealt with Lobsang's death by understanding just how elated he would have been the moment he stepped onto the summit. I was also comforted by the Buddhist belief that he would return to earth one day, reincarnated.

Harry, on the other hand, had suffered frostbite to a couple of toes and was taken by helicopter out of BC and straight onto a plane for London. The transition from BC to London could not have been done more quickly, so that when he landed at Heathrow to face the media interest in his becoming only the second British climber to climb Everest without oxygen, he looked as if he had just stepped off the mountain. Harry was a worthy candidate for all the attention he received from the newspapers, radio and TV talkback shows.

I also returned to a great deal of attention, not so much from the media, but from family and friends: Judi, Mum, my grandmother, aunts, uncles and many friends were at the airport to meet me. Dad had also flown in from New Zealand. I soaked up the attention thankfully, but there came a time a few days later when enough was enough. Everest had consumed too much of my life already and it was time to put it behind me.

MAKALU, AUTUMN 1993

chapter ten

Makalu

West Ridge

Makalu La
High Point 7200m

High Point 6800m

Bivouac 6800m

C2 6500m

C1 5900m

C1 6100m

CHASE

Kukuczka Route

The Chase Manhattan
Makalu Expedition 1993

BC 5420m

Mount Everest at 8848 metres rises head and shoulders above K2 and Kangchenjunga, the world's second and third highest peaks. Ascents of the latter two hills are generally done today without bottled oxygen, but Everest still dictates that 99 per cent of its summit climbers use oxygen.

There are fourteen peaks in the world that exceed 8000 metres, but instead of investing huge amounts of time and money trying to climb them all, I set my sights on the Big Five: Everest, K2, Kangchenjunga, Lhotse and Makalu. All, except K2, which is in the Karakoram Range in Pakistan, are in Nepal. The biggest drop in height of 262 metres is between Makalu and the sixth highest, Cho Oyu—Makalu stands at 8463 metres, Cho Oyu at 8201 metres. A gain of 262 metres would be considered insignificant at sea level, but at over 8000 metres represents hours of climbing and the physiological value of about another 2.5 kilometres to be climbed. This, in my opinion, differentiates the Big Five from the remaining nine.

After the autumn Everest expedition of 1991 Ian Collins and Mark Squires put into operation their plan of attempting the West Ridge of Makalu. Ian had been considering the idea for years, and after our attempt on Everest in 1991 had extended a tentative invitation to me to join the climb. It became an on-again, off-again project with the team size and structure changing several times. Finally, while I was on Everest, the Chase Manhattan Bank offered a large cash sponsorship that got the expedition up and running and allowed Ian and Mark to put together a team comprising Warwick Payten, Wil King, Warwick Baird, Jonathan Leicester and me. Each member had some expertise in either high-grade technical rockclimbing or high-altitude mountaineering. On paper we looked like a strong team worthy of attempting the very difficult and intimidating West Ridge of Makalu. Ten climbers had already climbed the ridge; not all of them came down.

I returned home from Everest at the end of May. Judi and I had only been married for six days before I left, and now the preparation time before returning to Nepal was less than eight weeks. It was hardly fair on Judi, but I had made the commitment to the Makalu expedition before we were married. In her supportive way she helped me recover from Everest and prepare myself. While I had been away on the Big Hill there had been a great deal of development in the organisation of the Makalu climb; in fact most of it was done and I was slightly embarrassed by my free-loading position as I had been on Everest. Playing on my mind even more was leaving Judi for another eight weeks. I again promised a honeymoon when I returned, but it was a trip we would never take.

The ten-day walk into Makalu BC starting on 25 August had much of the same discomforts as the trek into Kangchenjunga BC—high humidity, rain, leeches and mud. I never really got to know everyone in the group; they were all Ian's and Mark's friends and in my usual way I didn't help the situation by being quiet and was happy to take an attentive back seat. We gained some lasting value at Ian's expense and took every opportunity to remind him of an interview he had given to a business magazine about the up-and-coming Makalu climb. When asked what their chances of success were, Ian responded that he believed the team had a high chance of success—the team was as fit in the mind as it was in the body because we were intellectuals. Whether Ian was misquoted or not I never found out but a group of intellectuals sounded like an unusual description for a team of climbers. We were, though, a mixed bag of professions: Ian was a banker, Warwick Baird a solicitor, Warwick Payten an engineer/scientist, Jonathan a neurologist, Wil a mountain guide, Mark a conference producer and me. In the last couple of years I had given away plumbing and had been earning a living as a speaker on the conference circuit.

After three weeks on Makalu we had made good progress up the West Ridge and by 2 October had established C1 and C2 with about 3500 to 4000 metres of fixed rope in place up and along the narrow and exposed ridge. This was good progress, considering there had not been a spell of good weather lasting any more than three days. The ridge was long and undulating and even though we were replacing the front teams with fresh climbers, it was taking the fresh team three days to climb from BC up to our high point before being able to begin any further upward progress. Our high point was at 6800 metres where Warwick Payten, Mark and I had enjoyed a good day's climbing and had fixed 1200 metres of rope to reach the base of the real technical difficulties. Again the weather turned against us, strong winds and a snowfall preventing us climbing any higher and the relieving team coming up to replace us. In the past, the relieving team, myself included, arrived at the high camps looking as tired as those who were descending for a rest, such were the difficulties and the length of the route. By mid-morning there was a lull and we escaped to BC, having spent the last four nights at the high camps. It was time for a change of lead climbers. Radio communication with BC had been patchy but it did not concern us that a plan to send up fresh climbers was not in place when we descended as it would most likely take a couple of days for the weather to settle again.

With weary minds only just having control over our tired bodies, it took us most of the day to descend to BC. During the last hour we saw someone plodding towards us under the burden of a heavy pack. It was Ian, and following him Warwick Baird and Wil, all intending to make their way up to C1 that night and then on to C2 the next day in anticipation of the weather clearing. We dropped our packs and found seats on the rocks. For the second time during this expedition the subject of whether we should continue with the West Ridge was broached. A week before some had challenged how we could entertain the thought of abandoning the climb without first giving it our best shot. It was a valid point. It wasn't a matter of whether we could continue to make upward progress, but whether, coupled with dwindling motivation and energy, we could make enough progress before the winter conditions made climbing more difficult and dangerous. With half of our team resting at BC at any given time, and with the real difficulties still above us, the most likely outcome was that we could continue to fix ropes and camps up the mountain only to run out of time and manpower. This was an acceptable risk to take, but what concerned me most of all was the tremendous amount of gear in the form of dollars and potential rubbish that we would have to abandon due to our state of exhaustion after getting it there. My experience from a dozen expeditions told me it would completely drain our energy to get it there, leaving none to take it down, regardless of whether we reached the summit or not. If we tried to bring all the equipment down, it would be an open opportunity for a tired climber to make a mistake that could result in serious injury or loss of life. It was the practice many years ago for the big-budget expeditions to leave all their ropes and camps in place once the summit had been reached or the expedition called off. These days it is considered bad climbing and environmentally unethical. I worried about this a lot. However, in a life-and-death situation you have no choice but to abandon gear. It was this type of situation that we were all trying to avoid.

The discussion we had among the rocks ended agreeably with Ian, Warwick Baird and Wil deciding to climb up to our high point over the next couple of days and take a look at the route from there. Warwick Payten, Mark and I would wait at BC.

On 5 October we could just see with the naked eye from BC Warwick Baird and Ian climb to the top of the fixed ropes. Here they stopped for some time, obviously contemplating moving upwards, but those of us at BC knew their chances of continuing were getting slimmer by the minute. We waited half an hour for the fellows to relay their decision by radio and we could sense their disappointment. The West Ridge climb was over. During the next four days we cleared all of our equipment and rope from the mountain.

We had a few days up our sleeves before the porters arrived to take us out, so an attempt on the mountain via a less technical route seemed a worthwhile consolation prize. The two Warwicks, Ian, Mark and I packed four to five days' worth of food and fuel and headed up the Kukuczka route, a moderately steep variant on the original ascent route. It would involve no fixed camps or the fixing of rope.

On our second day out we were forced to return to our previous campsite and remain there for the rest of the day because of strong winds higher up. The winds subsided overnight, allowing us to ascend the next morning, but shortly after setting out Warwick Baird abandoned the climb owing to a sudden attack of bronchitis.

The ascent of the Kukuczka spur was exhilarating and

interesting climbing because it felt as if we were gaining plenty of height at last compared with the tediously slow progress of the West Ridge. Just on sunset, at around 6800 metres, we found two ledges in the ice. The ledges were big enough for two climbers on each ledge but not for the careless placement of gear or big enough for our tents. Mark and I were on the upper ledge and by luck of being the first there I took the more secure position in against the ridge, while Mark was on the outer limits of the ledge. He placed a couple of ice axes to mark the edge of the 1100-metre drop below us, so he knew how far he could roll during the night. By the time we laid out our sleeping-bags on the ledge it was nearly dark and becoming exceptionally cold, but thankfully it remained calm.

We stopped our fidgeting to watch the sun set behind Everest and Lhotse, but no camera could adequately capture this magic, perched high on the mountain overlooking the Himalayas from east to west. Despite the night air being miserably cold, we were extremely warm and comfortable in our good quality sleeping-bags and clothing. Any action to top up the pot on the stove with more snow was quick; when it came time to drink our cups of milky, sweet coffee, we balanced them delicately inside our sleeping-bags. Although we were in a dangerous, exposed position, a sudden change in the weather looked unlikely and we relished the comparative comfort and carefreeness. Mark and I talked about the expedition, future climbing plans and life after the Makalu climb was over. I suspect we both knew that from this position the expedition was not going to succeed in reaching the summit. Nevertheless we both felt lucky to be here and the satisfaction with the climbing we had done was worth it. More importantly, so far there had been no accidents. This particular night was, for me, the most memorable moment of the expedition.

The price we paid for our westerly-facing ledge the next morning when the sun's rays did not reach us until 9.30 a.m. This made it hard to motivate ourselves into action, as aching fingers and our awkward position prevented any movement until the sun warmed our ledge. I suspected Ian had made the surprise decision to turn around during the night, because shortly after leaving our ledge that morning he stopped us and apologised for going so slowly, and descended. It was sad to see him finish in such a demoralised frame of mind, for he had put a great deal of time and effort into this expedition. He had seen Makalu for the first time ten years earlier and decided then that it was a mountain he wanted to climb.

Shortly after Ian had left us we hit deep, loose snow and my crampons scraped across the top of the rock slab that lay underneath. I worried whether the snow slope would avalanche. I continued on to safer ground above. Hours passed and I became tired of searching for hope around every corner or at the top of every rise. As I neared the Makalu La at 7200 metres I was up to my knees in deep snow; below me I could see another person heading back to BC. It could have been Mark or Warwick, or it could have been both as I could not see every metre of slope that lay between me and the antlike figure 1000 metres below.

I felt terribly lonely standing there in the knee-deep

snow; the summit seemed an impossible distance above and my climbing partners a long way below. The decision to abandon the climb was easy. Below the slope that I thought might avalanche I met Mark who was still climbing up. We were both tired with little motivation left and Mark easily accepted my report on the conditions above us and we headed down together.

K2, 1994

chapter eleven

High Camp 7800m

C3 7400m

C2 7300m

C2 6700m

C1 6400m

C1 6100m

South
Spur

Abruzzi Ridge

BC 4900m

'You've climbed the highest mountain in the world. What's left? It's all down hill from there. You've got to set your sights on something higher than Everest.'

Willi Unsoeld, 1963 American Everest Expedition

K2 may be the second highest mountain but it has the reputation of being the most difficult and dangerous of the fourteen peaks over 8000 metres. Unlike Everest, K2 does not compete with its neighbouring peaks and soars imposingly above everything else. Even to the trained eye it leaves one doubting whether it could ever be climbed.

Shortly after a speaking engagement at a five-star hotel on Queensland's Gold Coast I received an urgent message from Steve Untch, the leader of the American K2 Expedition, living in California. The expedition was due to get underway in early June and as it was already late March, things had to move quickly if I was going to join it. Harry Taylor had told me about it in some correspondence after our Everest climb. He was supposed to be going too.

The message from Steve Untch was in response to my letter enquiring if I could join the team. My first conversation with

Steve was brief but encouraging: understandably he wanted
to see my climbing résumé, which I promised to fax to him
immediately. When I asked if there was anything else I
could do, he said that Harry had given me high recom-
mendations and that was good enough for him. The
climbing résumé was more for the Ministry of Tourism in
Pakistan as part of their pre-expedition paperwork. Steve
promised to reply soon to confirm whether I could fit into
the team at this late stage. True to his word he called the
next day to tell me I had been accepted. I was very disappointed to hear, though, that Harry couldn't go. In the
short but intense time we had climbed together on Everest
I never really got to know him and was looking forward to
a better opportunity on K2.

A week later I received a call from a member of the K2
team, David Bridges, who informed me that he was now
the leader of the expedition—Steve had become bogged
down in the organisation which finally ground to a halt.
Hardly a great start to the climb, I thought, but at least
David sounded enthusiastic. He assured me that despite
Steve's lack of enthusiasm for the organisation of the trip,
he remained a keen and reliable climber. For once I enjoyed
a leisurely couple of months' lead-up to my departure and
Judi and I spent as much time together as possible. As a
result, when it came time to leave I had the feeling I was
going on a holiday rather than to climb the world's second
highest mountain. There was no hurried packing, trying to
cram a little extra into overpacked bags, or taking care of
last-minute bills or chores around the house.

K2 is 8611 metres high and is situated in the Karakoram

Range in northern Pakistan. I was excited by the opportunity to climb K2 and visiting Pakistan for the first time. To make things more interesting I was to meet four new climbers in the northern city of Islamabad—the starting point for most climbing expeditions in the country.

It was an interesting group and I felt very much the outsider for the first week until I got to know everyone a little. Bill Barker was a computer programmer from England and one of the few old guard of British mountaineers still climbing. Bill had seventeen expeditions under his belt, four of them to Everest but, unfortunately, without success. Bill was always good for a story, particularly when it came to some of the stars of the mountaineering world and these stories, supposedly true, shattered some of my illusions about those heroes.

Steve Untch had trained hard for this climb and looked as if he could understudy for Stallone in *Cliffhanger*. I wondered if this was the reason he had lost his enthusiasm for organising the expedition. Steve had climbed a new route on the extremely difficult South Face of Annapurna, and lost a toe or two due to frostbite on Shishapangma's South Face. It was comforting to see someone else limping along at the end of a long day's walk like me.

Dave Bridges was more like me—small and compact and looked underweight. He had my sympathy right from the start as I knew what it was like to be the expedition leader, and while everyone else pitches in to help whenever possible, there are some things that only the person designated as the leader can do.

Wayne Thompson was a friend of Steve and Dave and

was joining us for the walk to BC; after spending a week there he would return home to California to fight house- and bushfires for a living.

Of the Americans Bruce Burns was the odd one out with his Beatles-style haircut and ability to operate at 100 kilo- metres per hour, except when sleeping. He loved his rockclimbing, particularly Big Wall climbing (multi-day, con- tinuous rockclimbing) and was a bit out of his league with K2. However, with Bruce's noticeable self-confidence, he was willing to try anything, including setting anyone up for the brunt of his practical jokes. Sometimes it was hard to tell if he was in fact joking, except that he had the habit of let- ting a wry grin slip from the side of his thin-lipped mouth.

Bruce's expertise was invaluable in breaking down the all too common barriers that exist on expeditions between the climbers and the Liaison Officer (LO). Whether climbing in Nepal, China or Pakistan, the government issues the expedition an LO, usually someone from the police force or a government department, whose role is to ensure that we climb the mountain we have permission to climb and to help with any negotiations with the locals along the way. In theory they are to help the expedition overcome any diffi- culties while travelling to and from the mountain, such as transport and porter strikes. LOs are, by reputation, noto- riously stuffy and difficult, lacking enough motivation to help themselves, let alone an expedition in trouble, even though their wages are paid by the expedition. The posi- tion of LO is considered a plum job, mainly because the wages for a six- to eight-week expedition are usually as much as they would earn in an entire year. If they sell the equipment we must supply them, it's worth twice as much as the wages. Often they sell their gear before they start the expedition and then complain they do not have enough clothing to keep them warm.

Captain Dar was our LO and quickly conformed to our expectations. He refused some of the equipment we had given him on the grounds it was inferior. He demanded that the clothing be upgraded or the expedition would not leave Islamabad. Bruce, in a long series of convincing lies, passed himself off to Captain Dar as the expedition doctor, based on one year of medical school before he dropped out in favour of rockclimbing. Captain Dar believed Bruce ran a very successful practice in the USA, specialising as a 'proctologist'. This immediately elevated Bruce to a godlike status and Dar could see his own personal benefit in being a friend of Dr Bruce, even if it might only be for future needs. In real life Bruce had difficulty applying a band-aid! The punch-line to Bruce's set-up came a few days later when Captain Dar enquired, 'And what does a proctologist specialise in, Dr Bruce?'

With a straight face Bruce replied, 'Bums.'

For a second or two the rest of us waited to see how our beloved Captain Dar would react. 'You bloody bastards! You joking on me,' he roared, slapping both hands on his knees several times. We soon joined him in a chorus of laughter and even he was laughing at himself. From then on Captain Dar lost his stuffiness and became a valuable member of our team, helping us on numerous occasions with the inherent problems of an expedition travelling through a foreign country.

Seventy of the most unruly porters I had ever encountered sat in a semi-circle around us as we tidied up the last of our porter loads. I was expecting trouble from this shifty-eyed lot, so I stepped to one side to allow those in charge to move closer to the hot spot. Captain Dar is a big man by Pakistani standards and he did not hesitate to take control. The new clothes we had bought him boosted his confidence in dealing with the men he towered over, not that he needed any more, as he was used to ordering men around in the Pakistan Army. This was obvious as he fronted the semi-circle of rabble—the noise stopped immediately. Within seconds he had the respect of every porter. He stamped his feet, raised clenched fists and preached the virtues of the Muslim religion for which he proudly acted as a self-appointed role model. He forbade indecent acts such as stealing another porter's cigarettes, hanky-panky with the local women and the consumption of alcohol. To finish his sermon he led the entire group in a Pakistani war cry that raised the dust and helped settle any aggression the porters had towards us over their wages. We were, in fact, paying them handsomely, and they wouldn't need to work much at all for the remainder of the year. A frenzy of activity started as porters scrambled to shoulder their 25-kilogram loads.

Two other expeditions gathered in the immediate area were also experiencing difficulties with their porters. Captain Dar's success had not gone unnoticed and some members from these teams asked what the secret was. We pointed to Captain Dar as seventy bare-footed men disappeared in a cloud of dust.

We followed our porters along the trail. It was a hot 42°C and clouds of bulldust billowed everywhere. Captain Dar struggled along behind us under the burden of a bulging pack. Only the expedition members knew its contents. At midday we stopped under the shade of the first tree we could find near a refuelling depot for army helicopters. Captain Dar was the last to arrive at our shady spot and, dropping his pack to the ground, he lay behind it on his stomach as if hiding from the enemy.

'Gather round, men,' he commanded to us in his best military voice.

I was comfortable where I was and was reluctant to move closer. His tone warned us that we might have done something wrong.

'Does anyone have a bottle opener?' Captain Dar enquired.

Bruce produced a pocket knife from his pack and in a flash Captain Dar produced a warm bottle of beer. Despite his warnings to the porters, hidden in his pack were three more bottles, two cartons of cigarettes and two *Playboy* magazines.

'Come a little closer,' he said as he smothered the sound of popping the beer top.

Captain Dar had no intention of offering us a drink—which I had already decided to decline if he did. He was only trying to keep out of sight of his fellow soldiers at the refuelling depot, as being caught drinking alcohol would mean a gaol sentence and losing his job. Twenty minutes and two bottles of beer later it was time to move and Captain Dar became nervous about the empty evidence.

I did not wait to see what he did with it as the heat was becoming increasingly worse.

He staggered in at the end of the day less his former dapper self, his hat tilted dangerously to one side, his sunglasses askew and his once neat handlebar moustache dishevelled.

I was taking a wash in a side stream near the camping spot of Paiju when I heard a commotion. A group of our porters was leading a cow to a spot 50 metres upstream. I felt sure the animal knew its destiny: it had a pathetic look of fear about it, but despite being pelted with rocks and having its tail twisted, it did not resist or quicken its pace. The cow's legs were pulled from beneath it by rope; once again it did not resist as eight men jumped on it, covering its entire body. The porters hollered with excitement when someone produced a knife that looked too blunt to butter bread, let alone slit an animal's throat. The cow did not die quickly, its gurgling groans carrying back to camp. I hoped it would put up a fight; perhaps gore or kick one of its tormentors, but it did not resist, it could not. Before I could gather up my belongings, the stream was running red with blood.

We took five days to reach BC at 4900 metres, beneath the South Face of K2. The day after our arrival, five Basque climbers wearily returned from the summit after making the first ascent via the South Spur. It was such an impressive route that we quickly changed our intentions from the North West Ridge to the South Spur. Although we would not benefit from any trail left by the Basques, we now knew the South Spur could be climbed.

———

Steve and I were abseiling down the ropes to BC for a rest. He was in a hurry so I let him go ahead. We had spent the night without a tent on a narrow ledge at 6400 metres and that morning we had completed a carry to the site of C2 at 7300 metres. The first stage of our climb was over and we would continue when we felt more acclimatised after our rest. I was surprised to catch Steve on the traverse but the reason for his delay became obvious—his right crampon had come off and slid down the slope. It was just within reach but not without the security of a rope. Steve thought that the stretch in our fixed rope might just get him there, and with his 90-kilogram bulk he had no trouble stretching the rope that distance. I watched the piton anchor point carefully. Will I or won't I unclip from this rope, I repeatedly asked myself. Suddenly the rock around the piton exploded before my eyes and a shower of football-sized rocks rained down on Steve. Because I was tied onto the same rope, I was pulled from my position and fell with Steve down the slope. Our only hope of survival lay with the one remaining anchor. The slack in the rope vanished in a split second, leaving us suspended from the fixed rope like a bunch of grapes, hanging from the solitary piton with an 800-metre drop below us. There followed a heart-thumping few moments as we both stared at the piton 20 metres above us and waited to see if it was going to release. We quickly took our combined weight off the rope in case it failed to hold and, trying to force some coordination into our shaky limbs, climbed clumsily up steep rock and ice to find a safe ledge for us to regain our composure.

Over dinner that night at BC, I mentioned the conversation I had had with the New Zealander, Rob Hall, that afternoon. Rob was climbing with Veikka Gustafsson from Finland as part of the German expedition. I had met both of them on Everest the year before and had spoken to them often around BC on K2. This was Rob's fourth attempt at climbing K2 and he could not believe the spell of good weather we had been having and suggested we should be making the most of it. They were both pre-acclimatised from earlier climbs and were heading for the summit in a couple of days via the Abruzzi Ridge. Bill, Bruce, Dave, Steve and I sat in our comfortable mess tent, while Captain Dar fiddled with his short-wave radio. In all of our minds K2's unpredictably fierce weather took precedence over every other aspect of this formidable mountain. We all knew that if we got one chance in the season, we could consider ourselves lucky as there were many seasons when there was no weather suitable for a summit day. Was this our first and only opportunity? Would it be better to take it, knowing we weren't fully acclimatised, and do the best we could with a slim chance of reaching the summit? If we got no more opportunities, then we could return home reasonably satisfied that we had done our best. The idea was received with enthusiasm, but there was a downside to it. Dave and I were both concerned that, as a team, we were nowhere near acclimatised for an 8600-metre peak, having been at BC for only twelve days. On the other hand, with our high-altitude experience, we were all capable and responsible enough to recognise the early warning signs of altitude sickness and descend. K2 is a mountain of storms and very few summit chances and we knew we would later regret it if we didn't make the most of every opportunity.

Morning brought a unanimous decision to at least try to see how high we could climb and we confirmed our intentions with Rob and Veikka. Although they were climbing via the Abruzzi Ridge and we were on the South Spur, the two routes converged at 7800 metres on a feature known as the Shoulder. Here it was agreed to regroup to establish our respective high camps and the next day push on to the summit. This site at the convergence of the two different climbing routes was important as we all knew that deep snow lay between the high camp and the summit, and a combined summit attempt from this point would improve everyone's chances of success. A departure day of 7 July was set. Another team also joined our combined attempt— two Poles, Voytek Kurtyka and Krzystof Wielicki, and the American Carlos Buhler who had been on the West Face. The long, hot, clear spells had played havoc with their attempt on the West Face as there were continuous rock-falls, and melting snow caused their fixed ropes to be buried deep in the ice. They too would join us on the South Spur.

In order to meet Rob and Veikka at the high camp on the Abruzzi Ridge for the summit day, we had to either cut our rest short by a day or climb from BC to C2 in one day. We chose the latter, but it was a day that would take its toll on our team. The pace was too fast for Bill and Bruce who could go no further than C1. For them the race for the summit was over. For Dave, Steve and me, our upward progress nearly came to a premature end also, for when we

arrived at C2, we found that all the food and equipment
that had been stashed there a couple of days ago had been
swept away by an avalanche. We had only enough food and
fuel to complete the climb if we didn't have anything that
night, or we could use up what we had and descend to BC
the next day. Difficult as it was to resist the temptation to
quench our thirst, we conserved what little fuel we had in
favour of continuing up the next day.

The worry of another avalanche taking us out during the
night made sleep fitful. To make things worse, the lack of
food, drink and sleep stalled our planned 5.00 a.m. departure. We dithered and delayed with sore heads and aching
limbs from the day before with little motivation left for the
coming climb. If someone had mentioned going down,
I'm sure we would have all agreed. Our late departure
meant that Carlos, Krzystof and Voytek were now ahead of
us. This was not an immediate problem; in fact it would
make our climbing easier by following their trail, but we
had a silent obligation to do our fair share of trail-breaking
at some stage. It became apparent after only a few metres,
however, that I did not have the energy or the will to cope
with the difficulties of this demanding climb. Dave and
Steve looked to be coping better than me and I resented
every step but I couldn't make myself turn around. The
golden opportunity of K2's summit lured me upwards.

Late that afternoon we were rewarded for our effort when
the climb ended suddenly and spectacularly as we crested the
Abruzzi Ridge at 7800 metres. Here we erected our tent
next to the tent of Carlos, Krzystof and Voytek. We took the
time to plot a safe route to the summit before crawling into

our tents. We could see the snow was deep without having to test it and we were glad that there were the six of us trying for the summit the next day, eight if Veikka and Rob arrived from the Abruzzi Ridge. I silently cursed Steve's decision to bring such a small mountain tent. His reasoning was that it was lightweight, but the saving of a kilogram or two meant there was not enough room for the three of us. With Dave and Steve already in the tent there was little room for me. They urged me to come in, but despite their best efforts to make room, I knew, with my knees touching my chin, that it was the doghouse for me. Squashed near the entrance of the tent I was contemplating where to dig a snow cave and how to find the energy to do it when Dave said he would sleep outside if I dug him a ledge to lie on. I would then cook dinner and prepared the drinks. I dug two ledges; the other for Rob and Veikka, who had just appeared at the top of the Abruzzi Ridge. I knew I could not impose my presence on their tent space as it was just as small as ours.

It didn't take me long in the tent with Steve to realise that Dave probably had the best spot after all. Over 180 centimetres tall and almost as wide, Steve took up most of the tent. The previous night we did not have enough to eat or drink and now we did not have enough energy to eat or drink. We made do with a cup of tea and a food bar and filled our water-bottles, hardly enough considering our deprivation. Once Rob was in his tent he called for a departure time. I suggested midnight, but this was met with weary groans from all three tents. General consensus was 1.30 a.m. The weather looked good.

In the morning I was ready first, so not wanting to stand around getting cold I started to break trail directly upwards. The snow was 30 centimetres deep and progress was monotonous and slow. For some time I thought no-one was following, but after a while head-torches appeared from the tents and started to bob and weave in my direction. I was still breaking trail by dawn, so I slowed down for someone else to take the lead. I thought Steve was going to take over but he only climbed up to tell me he was going down and so were Dave and Voytek—the cold was playing havoc with their fingers and toes.

Just below a notorious K2 landmark, the Bottleneck, I hung my head-torch from a rock, telling myself I wouldn't need it any more that day and Rob took over the lead, showing the advantage of his bottle of oxygen. He was the only one of the remaining climbers using oxygen. The Bottleneck is an airy and slippery 70-metre traverse left under a hanging glacier. In the history of K2 probably ten climbers or more have fallen to their deaths from here. At first glance it looked as if it had an unjustifiable reputation, but after a few sideways steps across I knew it could give us trouble. We managed it, but once across the traverse we became bogged down in knee-deep snow, and Rob continued the trail-breaking. With so little acclimatisation for Veikka and me the climb became slow torture and, with no motivation or energy, it was all we could do just to follow. Of the remaining climbers, Carlos and Krzystof had been on K2 for five weeks, and Rob had come straight from Everest.

At 4.20 p.m. we crested a ridge that ran off to our left.

It could have been the summit for all I knew and I glanced around each side of the ridge to see if there was a higher point. While I was distracted Veikka and Krzystof turned and started down. They muttered as they passed that it was too late in the day to continue up. Veikka showed me one gloved hand and expressed concern for his fingers. I watched with disappointment as they descended. Perhaps they were the smart ones, I thought, but I felt compelled to follow Rob as his waving hand drew me closer. As I stepped forwards, Carlos grabbed my arm—he was also concerned by the lateness of the day. The deciding factor came when Carlos mentioned that a friend of his who had climbed K2 years earlier had warned him that the summit ridge was 400 metres long. Based on our present rate of ascent at 100 metres an hour, we might reach the summit around 8.30 that night but it would leave us with little chance of coming down alive. Carlos turned his back and headed down; Rob, unaware of this information, turned his back and climbed up and I was torn between them. The fear of frostbite controls my every move in the mountains these days, so I looked towards Rob, but my mind said "Go Down".

We settled deep into the snow as Carlos and I sat for a rest before the Bottleneck traverse. I glanced over my shoulder and had to take a second look because Rob was about 100 metres above us. The summit must have been further than he thought and I congratulated myself on making the right decision to descend. As we waited for him I wondered at what height he had decided to turn around. With oxygen Rob could move quickly, so we didn't have to

wait long. Removing his mask, he hit us with the news that
we were least expecting—Carlos and I had turned around
30 vertical metres, only twenty minutes from the summit.
Carlos seemed to be a little sceptical that Rob had reached
the true summit, but I was not.

With more concern for the traverse, Rob dismissed the
temptation to prove anything to Carlos by shrugging his
shoulders and side stepping us to wait his turn on the traverse. I too dismissed the heartbreak of our near miss until
later, as Veikka and Krzystof were just starting across.
Veikka was prepared to forgo safety on this section and
opted for an unroped traverse as we had done that
morning, but I belayed Krzystof on a rope that was not
long enough to complete the traverse. Krzystof anchored
the rope at his end as best he could and was quick to follow
Veikka in the fading light. The sun was nowhere to be seen
and had probably already set behind the curve of the earth,
but because we were so high, we were still in the sun's rays,
while it was night time below. I followed Krzystof's rope,
while Carlos worried about finding better anchors for the
top end of the rope that I was on. Carlos took forever to
start moving across the traverse and a nervous voice
pleaded with me not to leave him. It was dark now and Rob
was waiting patiently just 40 metres away on safe ground.
Veikka and Krzystof were well on their way down to our
high camp. Rob broke my concentration by asking why we
were taking so long. I ignored him as I had to place my ice
axe and feet precisely, but I lost my patience waiting for
Carlos, whose nervousness annoyed me.

Finally I reached Rob who stood in a circle of light from

his own head-torch. I should be able to reach mine at the end of the Bottleneck traverse, I thought, but Rob had other ideas. To save time he wanted to bypass the next tricky section by abseiling straight down on a piece of rope he had in his pack. We knew the length of the rope, but we racked our dizzy brains for memory of the height of the cliffs we were about to abseil over. Our discussion was interrupted by a frantic call for help from Carlos hidden in the blackness of the night. With Rob's head-torch I traversed back towards Carlos. The light did not show the tremendous exposure below, but I knew it was there—one slip and I would not be coming back this way. Carlos had lost all composure when I reached him, shaking so much that he was in danger of falling. I didn't dare get close enough for him to grab me. With some light and someone to talk to he calmed down and together we inched our way back towards Rob.

Rob tied a couple of pitons to the end of the rope, to prevent us abseiling off the end, then tossed it over the edge. An unnerving rattle echoed from below as the pitons clanged against the rock. This could have meant the rope had not reached the snow slope we were anticipating it would find. Because Rob had the only head-torch he abseiled first, but as he did the unsettling rattle of metal against rock continued. The rope had not reached level ground, but a call after a long wait from the dark assured us that the last 10 metres could be down-climbed. At the bottom of the abseil I accidentally dropped my down mitt and I heard it slide over the edge below me. Now frostbite was a real danger to my right hand. While Carlos abseiled I continued down the steep slope to break a trail, having swapped my ice axe to my gloved hand and tucked my right hand inside my down suit under my armpit.

When the angle of the slope eased I sat down and waited for the others. It was twenty minutes before they appeared and I discovered the reason for their slowness. Rob had run out of oxygen and had become very weak and tired. I was able to support him with his arm around my shoulder and together we managed 20 to 30 metres before collapsing into the snow to rest. Carlos went on ahead of us searching for our tent. With the light from the head-torch fading, so came the urgency to find our tents as soon as possible. The occasional shout to Veikka and Krzystof brought no reply.

In the early hours of the morning with the likelihood of the three of us spending the night in the open my mind was full of worried calculations. What would tonight cost me? I had no more toes to sacrifice. Would it be my ears, nose or fingers this time? I expressed concern that we might have passed our high camp and that we were heading for the end of the Abruzzi Ridge. Rob and Carlos disagreed, maintaining it was only 100 metres away. As if someone had been listening to us, a tent light appeared out of the darkness 100 metres below and slightly to our right. They were right.

It was 1.45 a.m. We had been going non-stop for twenty-four hours. The extra tents at our high camp confused me and I wondered which one was mine. Four members of a Ukraine expedition, who had arrived and set up their camp the day before, were setting out for the summit. They were the ones to thank for unintentionally showing us the way home. As I broke the ice from the opening of my sleeping-bag, the Ukrainians left for the summit, but a short time later I heard one of them return. In hindsight he would be the lucky one.

Dave and Steve had descended to BC the morning before, leaving us a tent and some food but I was too tired to bother, even though a litre of water was all that I had had in the last twenty-four hours. The next thing I knew it was morning; not a pleasant one, but windy, dark and forbidding as a storm had struck and was tightening its grip on the upper slopes of K2. I could just hear Voytek in the next tent hustling his mates to get ready. They asked if I wanted to go down the South Spur with them and I hesitated, thinking of the dangerous upper slopes avalanching. Instead I favoured a descent with Rob and Veikka down the easier Abruzzi Ridge. The storm hit my tent with such force that I was pushed off balance while sitting. There was no time to pack anything except my camera—thousands of dollars' worth of gear had to be left. Only by shouting could I communicate with Rob and Veikka as we agreed to crawl from our tents at the same time. I pulled the poles from my tent to collapse it and save it from further abuse in case we couldn't find our way down and had to return. Veikka led the way. I felt uncomfortable relying on Rob's and Veikka's knowledge of the Abruzzi Ridge to get me down. I wished I had more control over the situation but blindly I followed. After a few wrong turns in the white-out conditions, Rob made the correct one and the storm gradually decreased in intensity the lower we went. At their C3 we were safe for the time being and we used this shelter to have something to eat and drink. It was also our first opportunity to communicate with BC. Veikka was too tired to continue but Rob wanted to get to the safety of C2 that afternoon. As there was a line of fixed

ropes between the two camps we were happy to leave
Veikka, but promised to wait for him at C2 the next day.

That night in my borrowed sleeping-bag I tried to hide
my envy of Rob's summit. Rob could go home satisfied
that he had climbed K2. He deserved it after four expeditions to this mountain. I could do the same, if I was prepared to accept that stopping short by twenty minutes was
good enough. Climbing all the way back up for a lousy 30
or 40 metres would be a nightmare. Now, utterly defeated
from exhaustion, I doubted my resolve to try again.

Next morning Veikka bounded down the ropes to C2,
showing little sign of a summit hangover and the three of
us continued to BC. It seemed every person from the four
or five expeditions on K2 this season was on hand to meet
us, everyone except the Ukrainians. They were still waiting
to hear from their summit team, which had not made contact since its departure for the summit the previous
morning. The German team which Rob and Veikka were
attached to put on a banquet for all who were involved in
the last summit attempt, to celebrate Rob's success. On the
advice of Krzystof, who said I had lost a lot of weight, I had
more than my share of the food and drink. Voytek was sympathetic about my failure and offered advice. 'Sometimes it
is good to fail.' But with the effect of the rum and peach
juice drinks I had little clue of the true meaning of Voytek's
words. With more rum over the next couple of hours I
slumped lower into my chair, totally forgetful of the three
Ukrainian climbers hanging on to their lives three vertical
kilometres above us.

It snowed that night and continued to do so for the next

four days and any chance of the Ukrainians coming down alive decreased with the passing of each day. Rob left for home on 15 July and I had been tempted to join him, but on 16 July the weather began to improve. On 17 July we prepared for another attempt on the summit. As I was making my way to the mess tent for some lunch a sudden movement on the South Face caught my eye—the biggest avalanche I had seen on K2 had just broken loose and was tumbling down the South Face taking most of the top part of our route with it. It was an impressive sight, showing the immense power these avalanches generate, but it also brought a rash of goose bumps at the thought we could have been in it if our timing had been wrong. As it gathered momentum it seemed likely that the shock wave would reach BC, so I rushed back to secure my tent and zipped the door shut. We did receive a shower of ice crystals but nothing like I had anticipated. However, after witnessing the avalanche I had to confess to Dave and Steve that I was no longer interested in the South Spur which I considered too risky. When I mentioned my Everest episode with the avalanche they understood my situation, but remained intent on climbing the South Spur. This problem was easily solved as Veikka was looking for a partner to climb the Abruzzi Ridge, so Veikka and I struck an arrangement with Steve and Dave to meet them at the high camp for a summit attempt together.

As I had climbed the South Spur, climbing K2 a second time via a different route was the only motivation I had to go back. At 11.30 p.m. on the night of 17 July Dave, Steve and I left our BC and picked up Veikka along the way from his camp. An hour and a half later we parted ways as Steve and Dave headed up the South Spur and Veikka and I continued around to the base of the Abruzzi Ridge. We climbed well together and made quick progress to C2. That night it snowed and the morning sky brought indecision. Should we move up or stay put? The longer we waited, the easier our decision became. Our afternoon radio call to BC revealed that Steve and Dave were stuck at C2 on the South Spur.

More bad weather arrived on 20 July and our food supply was running out. At midday it looked as if it might clear but we had to make the decision whether to climb up to C3 where there was more food and fuel and hope the weather cleared or descend to BC for more supplies and wait for the weather to settle in the comfort of BC. In the next half hour we changed our minds three times, but common sense eventually dictated we head down.

By the time we reached BC I had resigned myself completely, in motivation and energy, to the fact that I would be going home soon and I despairingly dumped my pack at the entrance of my tent. In some way it was a relief to know now that I wasn't going back up. Dave and Steve were also down and talking of going home. Our only consolation that day was that for the first time on the expedition our cook, Ali, actually cooked a meal we liked. We hadn't quite finished our dinner when Veikka and Ralf Dujmovits, the leader of the German expedition, appeared at our camp bringing with them a report that the weather was clearing for the next three days. They thought they were delivering

some good news, but it was met with frustrated abuse
because, if we were to take advantage of this predicted fine
weather, we would have to move up in the next few hours
after having just come down from C2 that afternoon. Dave
and Steve showed less than their usual enthusiasm, as did
Bill and Bruce. I wanted to agree with my American
friends, but for some strange reason I agreed to join Veikka
for one last attempt.

Sleep came easily that night, considering the physiological problems involved in getting ready for another summit
attempt so soon, but I was up at midnight to face another
day on K2. I was careful in my rustling not to wake the
others. Ralf had invited me to his camp for some breakfast
and while a meal was unappealing at this time of the night,
I ate as much as I could in the company of Veikka and Ralf,
and Micky and Axel, also from the German team. There
would be five of us moving up the Abruzzi Ridge.

Veikka and I were the first to reach C3 the following day
and we had difficulty finding Veikka's tent. I had drawn a
hasty conclusion that it had been blown away but after a
half an hour of digging we located the top of it buried
under where we were standing. It took another two hours
to completely uncover the tent, which had been buried by
an avalanche.

On 22 July the Germans erected their tent at the site of
our old high camp, while Veikka and I repaired the remains
of the tent that we had so hastily abandoned two weeks earlier. Veikka then set about melting snow for drinks and I
excavated the site of my old tent in search of my sleeping-
bag which I eventually found. I had to take great care

pulling it from the ice that glued it to the floor of the tent. This time I won with my suggestion to start for the summit at midnight and we set our alarm for 10.30 p.m. A long rest was what we needed but by the time we settled in and had something to drink it was time to start getting ready.

I felt no need to wait while the others made their final preparations so I started breaking trail. It was 12.30 a.m. After an hour or two Ralf took over until he reached the Bottleneck traverse. He belayed me across and I secured the rope at the other end for our safe return. It was a bitterly cold morning, much colder than last time, so we all headed for an island of rock where I shed my boots to rub some feeling back into my feet. We tried following the line of ascent that Veikka and I had made two weeks earlier, but steep, deep snow meant we made virtually no progress in twenty minutes. Despite the efforts of my two previous attempts, I was feeling much stronger this time, but the deep snow cast a shadow of doubt on our summit chances. The turning point in our despair came when Veikka abandoned the route we were on in favour of what we hoped was firmer snow to our right. Reaching it, however, involved a dangerous traverse across an avalanche gully. I breathed as nervously as Veikka while I watched. Each step he took put his neck further into a noose that would pull tight should the slope move from under him. I searched the slope for any cracks appearing, but prior warning in this situation would have been futile as a fall or avalanche would be fatal. Veikka's prediction of hard snow on the other side proved correct, but the rest of us were in no less danger while making the same crossing. I watched anxiously as Axel crossed last and I vowed not to return this way.

I was not fooled by the false sense of security that this perfect day on K2 presented, nor the fact that it was 9.30 a.m. with only 300 metres to the summit. I urged my friends to continue our pace which under these better snow conditions was now ten to twelve steps at a time. Although it was hard work, it was not the debilitating struggle of our first attempt or some of the other 8000-metre peaks that I have been on, and the sun warmed us to the point where it was becoming almost too hot.

I was dreaming of the summit view as it became increasingly likely that we would make it, but this feeling quickly evaporated as a short, steep ice pitch led us to the frozen bodies of the Ukrainian climbers. It was a confronting, grim sight of figures frozen in awkward angles, tangled ropes and scattered gear. It did not take much imagination to see that it was a slow death. We guessed by the intensity of the same storm that forced Veikka, Rob and me to make a hasty retreat two weeks earlier, that the Ukrainians were forced to tie themselves to the rock face to avoid being blown off the mountain. Perhaps in their keen desire for the summit, they ignored the impending storm and crossed the point of no return in the belief that the weather would improve rather than get worse. Their tomorrow never came. I felt for my pocket knife in my climbing-suit. I felt compelled to do something about their unfortunate position as being some sort of photographic display for others who might climb this way. It was hard to believe we once knew the climbers whose contorted bodies hung like the aftermath of an execution. With a single stroke of the blade against their taut ropes, I could send them on their way to the valley floor. Distressing as the fight for survival scene was, I felt only a little grief as I questioned their decision to climb on under any circumstances, while one of the original party of four had turned around from the impending danger. But then who was I to judge the correct decision as no-one will ever know the true story? I collapsed the blade of my knife, judging my action to be too callous. The Ukrainian team had a search party coming up that day, so we left their countrymen in peace.

Above and out of sight of our dreadful discovery everyone except me stopped for a rest but I was consumed by my eagerness to reach the summit. This attack of energy lasted only 100 metres and here I waited for the others to follow, drinking the last of my 2 litres of water. Ralf and Axel arrived and surveyed the slope ahead. Now at over 8500 metres there was none of that morning's energy left in any of us and Axel soon handed the lead back to Ralf, who subsequently passed it to me at the base of a steep 15-metre pyramid of snow. It was only when I reached a few metres higher that I understood his parting comment, 'You deserve to do this bit.'

For a moment I thought I had been set up to do the back breaking work until I looked down and recognised, just below us, the place where we had turned around two weeks earlier. So I was on the last twenty minutes, I thought, and smiled to myself at Ralf's gesture of encouragement. Axel sat in the snow supporting his head in his hands. He looked exhausted, and Micky and Veikka were 50 metres behind, so it was just Ralf and I on this last section. It wasn't easy. The steepness of the slope and the loose snow meant that my steps collapsed underneath me and I lost the 3 metres that I had just gained. There was no way around this last obstacle but I finally used a trick that I was shown in my mountaineering course twelve years earlier. I stepped high into the slope and, before putting my full body weight into the step, counted to ten to allow the snow to consolidate and refreeze under my boot. At this stage of the climb it took more than ten seconds for me to stop panting like a dog after just one step. For the next 12 metres this continued until my mindless trance was broken without warning after taking the next step up—I was at eye level with the chiselled edge of the summit of K2.

It was almost a rockclimbing move to leave the deep snow and step up onto the concrete-hard snow and ice of the summit. I turned to the others who were placed at various intervals in the 100 metres below me and waved my ice axe—not as a victory gesture but as encouragement that they were nearly there. Although the summit of K2 was a relatively level ridge line about 40 to 50 metres long, there was a point that was higher than the rest and, filled with happiness, I ambled casually along this airy summit.

With confidence I threw my ice axe like a dart at the highest point and sat down beside it. As on the Everest summit I knew my time here would be short, even though it was only 11.30 a.m. Ralf would be a few more minutes and the others many more, so I went across to some rocks and selected a few for my pocket and returned to the high point to greet Ralf. When I shook his hand he was in tears and repeatedly told me how important this summit was to him. He was only the second German to climb K2. I continued to take photos and curiously absorb as much of the world below as possible. Veikka was the next to arrive and we greeted each other like long-lost friends.

'This time, Mike, we have done it,' said Veikka, wrapping his ice axe hand around my shoulder. Micky and Axel were the last to arrive and Ralf reported their success via radio to their BC. Although I do not understand German, I could tell by the replies that everyone at the German BC was extremely happy for our success. I asked Ralf to pass on the news to the guys in my team. Before I knew it, three-quarters of an hour had passed and it was time to head down.

Stepping off the end of the summit ridge brought some urgency back into the descent—clouds were crossing the lower part of the mountain at great speed. We avoided Veikka's avalanche-prone traverse by taking a slightly different descent, but we could not avoid the traverse at the Bottleneck.

We were glad we had fixed a rope across this section, but the sight of a human foot protruding from the snow did little for our confidence. The macabre joke that passed along the line of climbers was that there was a spare foothold if anyone needed it. Why hadn't we noticed this foot during the morning crossing? I could only put it down to tunnel vision due to the complexity of the traverse or a slightly different path. Once across we were faced with

white-out conditions on the broad expanse of the upper
Abruzzi Ridge. Veikka was about 100 metres below us
when we lost sight of him, but he had gathered all the ski
poles that had been stashed by us at the Bottleneck traverse
and was using them as markers for us to follow. Visibility
was so low that we were grateful for his thoughtfulness. We
arrived at the high camp with enough time to descend
to C3, but my suggestion was not taken seriously and,
without resentment, I fell into the tent beside Veikka glad
that the easier option had been taken.

As I had feared, the weather worsened overnight, making
it impossible for us to move in the morning, so we packed
and waited for our moment to escape. With each opening
of the tent door more snow blew in and after a few times I
questioned whether there was more snow inside the tent
than out. Our moment for escape came around 8.00 a.m.
when we could see the first marker wand for the descent
route just 50 metres away. We didn't waste time packing
our tent as line of sight on this upper ridge was crucial for
a safe descent. We found our bearings, but within half an
hour on this course we saw that the whole slope was ready
to avalanche, and would take us over the South Face. We
were too far down to turn back, and with little to hang on
to except hope we continued. We took care to disturb the
slope as little as possible by progressing with a certain distance between each climber that allowed for as little extra
weight as possible on the over-loaded slope.

At C3 the tents were already half-buried. Veikka and Axel
wanted to stop for a rest and make a hot drink, but in the
unrelenting storm Ralf, Micky and I urged them not to

linger. I was reluctant to leave Veikka and Axel behind, so I offered to wait, but when I saw that under the conditions it was going to take forever to make their drink, I had to leave them.

Gale-force winds lashed a section known as the Black Pyramid, blowing the fixed rope in wild arcs off the ridge. To abseil I had to catch the ropes and pull them back to the ground. Here there was a narrow gully to abseil that was awkward under the best of conditions. I had lost my abseiling device and was forced to tie a special friction knot that would do the job just as well, but the locking gate on my karabiner had frozen in the open position. Despite my best effort and a close encounter with a protruding rock I could not release the lock to secure the gate. As a precaution, I attached a sling to my harness and with a spare non-locking karabiner that worked, clipped it onto the rope. Holding the gate of the frozen karabiner closed with my left hand, I began to abseil, but my pack got caught in the narrowing of the gully. I could not release my right hand from the rope to shift the pack, so I tried to use my left and, as Murphy's Law would have it, caused the rope to twist in such a fashion that it came out of the karabiner. With nothing holding me, I tumbled 5 metres, the stretch in the rope leaving me hanging over a 2500-metre drop. The only thing saving me was the precautionary sling and karabiner that had caught on a rusty piton.

The full impact of my fall was taken on my right knee and when I tried to stand up, my right leg folded under me. I knew it was not broken but it was badly injured. Ralf and Micky were well below; Veikka and Axel were yet to come, but the conditions did not favour waiting. With my lucky sling and karabiner attached to the rope I slid on my backside down the line of fixed ropes to C2. I allowed myself a short rest in the shelter of the tent Veikka had left there. Veikka was the next to come down the ropes and showed a great deal of urgency in his actions to keep moving away from the worsening storm. Veikka came across to the tent. 'You're not staying here are you, Mike? The storm is getting worse.'

'I took a bit of a tumble up higher and hurt my knee. I'm just taking the weight off it for a few minutes and then I'll follow you slowly.'

'Are you sure it's OK?'

'Yes. Go on, get the hell out of here.'

I didn't follow. As I stepped from the tent I knew I wasn't going any further that day. Veikka had just abseiled from view below C2, so I crawled back into the chaos of empty food bags, gas cylinders and cooking pots and searched in my pack for the radio which operated only occasionally because of weak batteries. I warmed the batteries inside my climbing-suit and then the radio crackled into life with Dave's voice at BC. I said I would not be down that day, perhaps tomorrow. At 5.00 p.m. Axel slid down the ropes from C3. It was too late to continue further and he had no energy to do so. Unfortunately the floor in my tent was so uneven that there was not enough room for even one person to lie down comfortably, but as the Germans had a tent already erected, it was no extra work and Axel moved into the vacant tent.

There was little to eat or drink that night, so by first light

I was eager to leave as soon as possible, despite the miserable weather. It took only 60 metres for me to realise that I would not make it to BC, but even more disheartening was the thirty minutes it took to climb back up to C2, a distance that normally took only a few minutes. When Axel decided to go down, I did not ask for assistance. Weary as he was I could not burden him with more worries and there really wasn't much he could do for me. With another day's rest I could probably get myself down the next day if I didn't go crazy from the gloomy shadows and loneliness that pervaded my snow-covered tent. Thinking of Judi and calculating the days before I would be home seemed the only bright light to look forward to. I looked at my watch frequently, longing to be anywhere but here. Only the occasional radio call to BC broke the silence.

Next morning I could tell by the brightness inside my tent that it was going to be a good day. It is amazing the change in attitude some sunshine can make and I looked forward to this day with new-found energy. The wind had dropped and there was blue sky. A test run on my knee revealed that, although still stiff and sore, I might be able to get to BC. The thought of spending another night alone at C2 was all that I needed to make me try. The perfect day on K2 enabled me to find some joy in my slow progress. Halfway between C2 and C1, having just down-climbed a difficult section, I was thinking to myself what a great day it was to be in the mountains when Steve, who was hiding around the corner, stuck his head out and gave me a loud, 'Howdy!'

I nearly jumped from my small ledge with fright but after

cursing Steve for frightening me, I managed to say I was glad to see him. This act by Steve to come and help me down was typical of him—always selfless and prepared to help others—but he could also be a strong and forceful climbing partner. We sat for a while to have a summit celebration of water and chocolate before Steve shouldered my heavy pack. I won the argument on who should go first and sent Steve on his way, while I waited for a respectful distance to appear between us so as not to annoy Steve with my body weight on the same rope that he was using.

I was distracted from the act of abseiling by the pleasure of seeing Bruce standing at C1 just 50 metres below. He had no doubt climbed up with Steve. It was a happy moment seeing my friends after two days of isolation at C2, but this feeling was suddenly shattered by a sound like a whip cracking and cloud of white dust filled the air. Steve was falling backwards through the air. At first I could not believe my eyes as he fell further onto a snowslope. Was he slipping and would the rope eventually break his fall? I watched in shock as Steve tried desperately to hang on to his life, grabbing at anything as three pairs of gloves were torn from his hands. Bruce, acting on impulse, rushed to grab Steve as he slid uncontrollably past C1 to a 1200-metre drop below. Fortunately for Bruce he never made it in time, for he too would have been knocked off balance and sent over the edge.

Barely able to control my shaking hands, I found my radio and called for anyone. I immediately received Ralf who was making his way to the base of the Abruzzi Ridge to collect stashed gear. Bill also picked up the emergency call

and I told them together that someone had just fallen from
C1. For some reason I did not confirm it was Steve.
Everyone was now rushing to the base of the Abruzzi
Ridge. At the scene of the accident I found the frayed end
of an old, bleached rope that had broken. Beside it lay a new
black-and-yellow rope that one of the Abruzzi Ridge teams
had placed this season. I wasted no time in wondering why
Steve had abseiled on the wrong rope, and by the time I
reached C1, Bruce had already descended in search of Steve.

Such was the severity of Steve's fall below C1 that my
pack had split open and its contents lay strewn down the
fall line. Although I was close enough to pick them up, I
could not have cared less about my belongings, despite
their value. Instead I put all my thoughts into the hope that
Steve might have had the same luck that I had in the
Everest avalanche. But it was not to be. I could see a half-
dozen climbers standing around a body 400 metres below
on the valley floor, and from here on my lonely descent was
filled with reminiscences of past conversations with Steve.

I was suddenly brought back from my sombre trance to
the real world with the feeling that the slope I was on was
vibrating. I turned to brace myself against the permanent
mental image, etched deeply into my brain after Everest, of
a wall of snow tumbling towards me but instead it was a
briefcase-sized rock spinning end over end down the slope
like a giant axe. Its last bounce was 30 metres above and as
if someone had control over its flight path, it curved
slightly in mid-air to line me up dead centre. I fell to the
ground, careless of my delicate stance, as the rock whistled
past my left ear. For the remainder of the descent my head

rang with the sound of that near miss.

Blood dripped from the Gore-Tex bivvy bag that contained Steve's body as we carried it across to the glacier. Bill had already found a suitable crevasse to lower Steve's body into. Despite the efforts of some, no words could be found at this moment for a eulogy on Steve's tragic death, and the rope attached to Steve's body was released.

Dave, who was Steve's closest friend, recognised that I was wearing the heavy burden of guilt for Steve's death. We both knew it was a mistake in the choice of ropes that led to the accident, but because he died while lending me a friendly hand, I will live with it for the rest of my life.

LHOTSE, 1995

chapter twelve

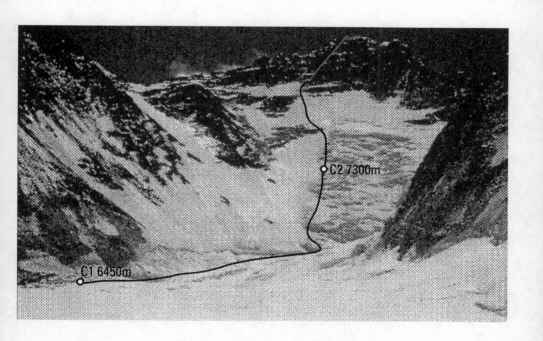

Just before Christmas 1994 I received a postcard from Veikka Gustafsson. The unexpected correspondence prompted me to suggest climbing two peaks in Nepal in the same three-month season: Lhotse at 8516 metres and Makalu at 8463 metres—the world's fourth and fifth highest mountains. They were my obvious choice to round off my ambition to climb the five highest mountains. As with Lobsang, I had developed such a good understanding with Veikka while climbing K2 that while we climbed, we actually communicated very little—we both knew what to do on the mountain and what to expect of each other. If it were not for this rapport, I would not have broken my promise to myself never again to be involved in the running of an expedition.

I faxed Veikka with the idea and received an enthusiastic response. We agreed to meet in Nepal in early April to ascend the two peaks, back to back, without Sherpas or oxygen.

It was an opportunity for Judi to be a part of the expedition and walk the eight days into Lhotse BC. Veikka's girlfriend, Elina, was also coming along. She would stay for the duration of both climbs, while Judi, due to work

commitments, could only stay a week once we reached
BC—which happened to be the same area used by the
Everest expeditions.

Because I was working as a trekking guide during March,
we arranged that Veikka and Elina would accompany the
porters carrying our supplies into BC. I would return to
Kathmandu with the trekking group and meet Judi and
the two of us would then follow the well-worn trail into
Everest/Lhotse BC, just a few days behind Veikka and Elina.

The planning for these two climbs was simple, taking just
two faxes to Veikka to work out what we needed to bring:
a tent, stove, a selection of food to last a few days and a
little climbing hardware like ice screws, pitons and a rope.
We kept it as simple as possible. There was no leader and
no pre-expedition chaos or complications—just the way I
liked it. On many expeditions the biggest and most frustrating hurdles are human-made.

I must confess to being a little nervous when I handed
over half of the expedition funds to the Nepal Ministry of
Tourism (which handles the permits for expeditions) as
Veikka had not confirmed when he and Elina were due to
arrive in Kathmandu. Was he still coming or had he
changed his mind? I paid the bulk of our expedition funds
and left to guide the trek. Veikka arrived in Kathmandu a
couple of weeks later.

––––––––––

Something made me turn around and look back along the
hill. There was a line of chortens—memorial stones—
descending in a series of steps. The chortens all looked the

same, but my eyes were drawn to one in particular. I thought of Lobsang. Fond memories of the good times we had had on Everest two years before filled my mind, marred only by the image of Lobsang's cremation just 100 metres from here. I felt very close to him.

Two days' walk up the trail we met Tashi Tenzing who was leading a trekking group of his own. He told me that he had recently spent money to build a chorten near Pangbouche for some of Lobsang's ashes and suggested the next time I went past I should visit it. I surprised him by saying I had already seen it and proceeded to describe the chorten with the necklace of prayer flags.

It was not easy for Judi to reach BC. Her first experience of altitude and a stomach bug made the going tough, but when we arrived we were given a warm reception by Veikka, Elina and our BC staff, Dil, Tshring and Ratna. All three staff had been on many expeditions and treks with me over the last half-dozen years and they prepared and cooked all our meals while we were at BC.

In the five years Judi and I had been together she had seen me disappear on many expeditions with only vague impressions of what climbing in the Himalayas was like. She had heard many tales of horror from people who had never been to the Himalayas—the armchair climbers—or wild and dangerous stories from mountaineering cowboys. This was a chance to dispel those misconceptions and to meet some of my mountaineering friends.

The week at BC passed quickly and Tshring escorted Judi to Lukla to catch a helicopter back to Kathmandu. Kissing her goodbye, I said I could be home in less than five weeks. Judi's experience told her otherwise—mountains this size often took three months to climb. But I was optimistic Veikka and I could climb Lhotse quickly. If we succeeded on our first attempt, we planned to share the 20-kilometre helicopter ride to Makalu BC with Rob Hall and Ed Viesturs, who also planned to climb Makalu. As we would already be acclimatised to 8000 metres, we could make short work of Makalu inside a week if the weather was kind to us. Home in five weeks was possible, but there were a lot of 'ifs'.

Much of the route to the West Face of Lhotse is via the route to the South Col on Everest. Veikka and I knew the first part of the climb well—the Khumbu Icefall. Above this we intended to use two camps for the climb, bypassing C1 in favour of C2 and making our second camp somewhere high up on the Lhotse Face. Everest C3 is actually on the West Face of Lhotse before the route veers left to the South Col. From here it was more or less a direct line to the Lhotse summit via a narrow couloir.

The Khumbu Icefall was less menacing this year and the route to avoid the hazards not so meandering. We did not dawdle as collapses were still occurring. Once on top of the Icefall we dug a small snow cave and buried some equipment before heading back to BC. A week later we returned, added the extra 8 kilograms to each of our already heavy packs and continued the climb up to 6450 metres, the C2 for Everest. By mid-morning the following day we were at 7300 metres on the West Face, but here our energy evaporated. Instead of climbing even higher as intended, we dug a ledge for our tent with the promise of moving higher the next day.

We planned to use Veikka's bivouac tent for our highest camp. Designed to accommodate two, it is like a coffin and under even the best conditions I find this style of tent claustrophobic. I prefer to carry the extra couple of kilograms of the roomier mountain tents for the greater comfort they afford. Luckily Veikka and I are not big in build. We wedged ourselves into the tent, then proceeded to work out where to place our boots, cameras, stoves and food in the limited space left. Being the last into the tent, I had drawn the outside edge and I quickly discovered that the ledge was too narrow, and I was more off the ledge than on. The only thing that lay between me and the 600-metre drop down the Lhotse Face was the thin fabric of the tent. I had survived a fall down this same face four years earlier and I knew I would not be so lucky a second time. The thought of bursting like a pea from a pod down the Face in my sleeping-bag helped keep me awake most of the night. The next morning the cramped conditions, terrible headaches, thirst and a sleepless night influenced our decision to abseil down, rather than move our camp another 400 to 500 metres higher. This could wait until another day and we considered the preparation for our climb now complete.

We yielded to our nervous energy and shortened the rest period we had planned at BC by a week. We knew we could climb Lhotse in a single push from BC without stopping for more than an hour's rest. At 4.00 p.m. on 2 May we left BC with 3 litres of water each and a few chocolate bars. These were the last things we felt like carrying as we had spent the entire day eating and drinking. It had been a week since we were last on the Icefall and some sizeable collapses meant disorientation and unexpected detours.

Night time one hour above the top of the Icefall brought with it strong wind gusts. Flurries of snow made seeing by head-torch difficult. It was 8.00 p.m. when I arrived at our first camp. Veikka had fallen some distance behind, unable to maintain his normal pace—a stomach upset was causing him to vomit. There was no question of continuing that night.

Veikka's sudden but short illness couldn't have happened at a better time as the weather deteriorated for the next three days, confining us to our tent. Luckily I had brought a book to read, *The Rise and Rise of Kerry Packer*, and our stash of food and fuel was adequate. The dawn of 5 May was clear and cold. We wanted to leave early, but small chores delayed our departure. Nevertheless we climbed quickly and soon made up for lost time, reaching our high camp just after 11.00 a.m. The American Everest team had a spare tent, and this would make living at our high camp more comfortable. But before erecting it, we still had plenty of time to move our camp 500 metres higher up the Face for a better chance of a shorter summit day. The thought held little appeal and we ignored the prospect of a 1200-metre marathon summit day in favour of a leisurely lunch of crispbread with ham and cheese followed by some fine Finnish chocolate.

We spent the remainder of the afternoon preparing for the summit bid, checking gear, filling water-bottles, changing head-torch batteries and films in cameras. I powdered my feet and changed to dry socks to help prevent frostbite. Boots, pee-bottle, water-bottle and sunburn cream were placed in my sleeping-bag to stop them from freezing. Noodle soup was all we felt like for dinner and we cooked this early so we could be in our sleeping-bags before the afternoon sun had left our tent.

The alarm woke us at 9.30 p.m. and I struggled to remember who had cooked dinner. Unfortunately it was Veikka, which meant I had to prepare breakfast. Veikka could normally have slept for another three-quarters of an hour, but tonight I did not allow him this pleasure and woke him to listen to the tremendous roar above us. We recognised the sound of the jet-stream winds blasting the summit of Everest at speeds in excess of 200 kilometres per hour. A summit attempt of Lhotse was out of the question.

Although it was not windy at our camp, we knew we would be blown onto our knees once we climbed from behind the shelter of the West Ridge of Everest and Nuptse. We resolved to rest for another two hours to see what our chances were. As chief billy-boiler my rest would not be so peaceful as I had to keep the stove going and scrape snow from the snow slopes outside our tent to melt for tea.

Despite the roar of the jet-stream winds and the hiss of the gas stove I easily fell asleep again. The sound of our alarm roused me. It was midnight. I sat up quickly, guilty that I had not been a more diligent watchdog over our camp. My carelessness went unnoticed by Veikka, but the silence above us did not.

As I crawled from our tent I wished we had made the effort to move it 500 metres higher. It was minus

20°C and 1200 metres to go to the summit—nearly twice the normal distance for a summit day. I was carrying 40 metres of small diameter rope, some ice screws and pitons, but for the first part of the climb we followed the ropes of the Everest expeditions, until they curved left towards the South Col. Here we climbed directly upwards in search of the steep couloir that would lead us to the summit, but we went the wrong way in the dark. The rock walls of the snow gully we were following closed in around us, leaving no place to go but down the way we had just climbed, or to follow a narrow ledge that the wash from our head-torches had picked up to our right. The ledge did widen but was not wide enough to prevent a tumble down the West Face should we trip over the many loose rocks scattered along it. This airy traverse was completed just on dawn and the extra light showed us the correct way to the couloir. A short distance above us was a brightly coloured object, possibly a body.

My feet were painfully cold and Veikka, understanding my condition, allowed me to place my socked feet onto his stomach inside his climbing-suit. Ten minutes of massaging each foot achieved little warmth but the throbbing pain was a good sign. It meant that the nerve endings were still functioning and had not yet tipped the scales towards the numbness of frostbite. Caring as Veikka was, I felt his urgency to begin climbing again, so I eased my tortured feet back into my double boots.

The object half-buried in the snow turned out to be the ruins of a former expedition's tent and I promised myself to have a closer look at it when we returned this way. The sunrise over Everest and Lhotse caught my photographer's eye as it was by far the best I had ever seen. I wanted to take a photo but it was too dangerous to stop and remove my pack.

At around the 8000-metre mark we were funnelled into the narrowing couloir. We knew from photos we had studied that this unmistakable scar on the West Face of Lhotse would lead us all the way to the summit, but we could only guess the difficulties inside it. A narrow tongue of ice barely 1 metre wide led us deep into the couloir. I took just one step onto it and instinct told me to get off. It sounded hollow and brittle, rigidly frozen across the width of the couloir. It spelled avalanche. We were forced to climb the steeper rock on the left.

As we followed the exposed rock, I tried not to knock rocks down on Veikka as my crampons scraped on the rock slabs. Eighty metres up I tentatively placed a foot back into the snow-filled couloir and, raking the surface of the hard snow with the points of my crampons, I listened for more warning signs. There were none so we moved back onto the snow of the couloir. By now all my fingers were bent stiff with cold and the stumps of my feet felt like ice blocks. I considered the cost of continuing up but reasoned that so long as they continued to hurt like hell, I would be safe from frostbite. My right thumb had gone numb so I kept wriggling it and constantly changed the grip of my ice axe from my right hand to my left to avoid absorbing too much cold from the metal, despite the handle being insulated with foam.

In one place the couloir was barely shoulder-width and

the snow base was broken regularly by short, steep sections of rock. Around each corner I searched for the sun or the summit; either would lift the spirits. Eventually I saw both 100 metres away. It was 9.30 a.m. One hour later I reached the top of the couloir that separated two almost identical twin summits. Fortunately we knew that the left summit was the higher by several metres. It took another twenty minutes to climb the last few metres of loose rubble to the small snow cone that formed the summit. It was too precarious to stand on and it was a case of sticking my chin up over it for a look at the other side. It was just a quick peek as I discovered just how finely balanced I was on the summit. I quickly climbed down to a small ledge to wait for Veikka. I was glad that he made short work of the last few metres because the unrelenting wind made waiting a misery, even though I was sitting in the sun. There was no summit handshake or time spent enjoying the view. We had to keep moving.

We could only descend so fast because some of the steeper rock sections needed slow and deliberate down-climbing. The long summit day was beginning to take its toll and we stopped regularly for rests whenever we could find a place to sit down. Veikka's rests were longer than mine and I soon found myself some distance in front. He seemed to be more tired than on K2, if that were possible, so I waited to ask if he was OK. He assured me he would manage the remainder of the descent easily and, as there wasn't much I could do to help, I continued to keep my own pace. Before I climbed under the ice cliffs sheltering our high camp, I took one last look to see how Veikka was going. He would be at least another hour and a half, so I headed for the tent to prepare tea for his arrival.

I fell asleep while boiling the billy and was woken by Veikka's arrival at 5.30 p.m., exhausted but happy. After a few hot drinks and still dressed in our down suits, we shared the only sleeping-bag we had, unzipped like a blanket, and slept soundly till the morning.

———

'It feels bloody cold this morning,' I said. Neither of us wanted to move from under the sleeping-bag, least of all get up and light the stove for our morning coffee.

'Let's wait until the sun hits the tent before we start packing,' suggested Veikka.

'So you don't want to try to reach BC today?' I asked.

Veikka thought for a few seconds. 'I think we can still reach BC before dark, even if we start late.'

'You may be able to reach BC tonight, Veikka, but my feet are trashed. I'll be lucky to get to our first camp.'

We both continued to doze until the sun's rays hit the camp and then it started to rain inside the tent as the frost lining the inside started to melt. Frozen boots are always a problem first thing in the morning, so I carefully placed both in the sun on the small ledge outside our tent. For a second or two the thought of losing one boot off the ledge amused me. We would be in serious trouble, but given it was unlikely, I returned to my packing. I finished this long before Veikka and was becoming slightly agitated by his delay. I can't say I was feeling any stronger than him, just more motivated to get off the mountain. Finally we coordinated our efforts and pulled down the tent.

It was 10.00 a.m. when we started our descent and I was tempted to drop my heavy pack down the Lhotse Face and pick up the pieces at the bottom, but the gap across the bergschrund at this point was wider than I could throw my pack. A few metres below our high camp we came across some blood stains in the ice and as we continued we saw the distance between the splashes of blood become wider. We both knew that someone from one of the three Everest expeditions had taken a tumble on the Face. It immediately brought back memories of my near-fatal fall down this same Face four years earlier and I questioned the chances of survival for this unlucky soul.

I'm not sure why, perhaps I was too tired to talk, but I tried to sneak around the outskirts of the Everest C2 without being noticed. Thinking I had succeeded, I sat down behind a block of ice but was suddenly ambushed by a couple of members from the various Everest expeditions. More followed with cups of tea and their congratulations, but I could sense an air of sadness among them. I have seen it before—a sadness etched on the faces of expedition members who have just lost a friend in the mountains. Trying hard not to spoil our accomplishment, someone quietly told me of the climbing Sherpa who had slipped and fallen to his death from their C3 the day before.

It was 9.30 that evening when we reached the bottom of the Icefall. Dil, Ratna, Tshring and Elina were there to meet us with a thermos of tea. Dil and Ratna escorted us

back to BC carrying our heavy packs. Just 30 metres from
our camp Veikka and I were distracted by the welcome we
received from Rob Hall's New Zealand team and for the
next hour we ate and drank as guests of the generous New
Zealanders. The heavy hand of guilt grabbed firmly at my
heart the moment I stepped from the New Zealand mess
tent—below me shone three lonely torch lights in an ocean
of darkness. I prayed Dil, Ratna and Tshring would forgive
me. Our success also belonged to them and they had
wanted to celebrate with us, but we had left them standing
there in the middle of the night. One of them had baked a
cake, another had run down the valley to buy some bottles
of rum and it was all laid out carefully on our dining-table.
Unfortunately the cake and rum remained as table orna-
ments until the next morning. Although dog tired from
our climb, I lay awake for many hours wondering if my
careless actions had offended my friends and affected our
friendship. Thankfully it did not.

It was a luxury to sleep in the next morning and Tshring
offered me breakfast in bed. Not wanting to encroach further on his generosity, I declined and hobbled with bruised
feet to the mess tent. Half of my right thumb had turned
black from frostbite and no amount of medication could dull
the pain. I had lost too much to frostbite already and I might
lose more. It would almost be guaranteed if I went to
Makalu. With regret I told Veikka over breakfast that I
would not be going to Makalu and we discussed his options.
It seemed likely that he could still team up with Rob and Ed.

Veikka, Rob and Ed went on to climb Makalu a little over a week later and I returned home as promised within the five weeks.

———————

As we packed up Lhotse BC on 8 May, my friend David Hume from the 1993 Everest expedition died while descending from the summit of Makalu.

10 MAY 1996

chapter thirteen

The events that transpired on Mount Everest on 10 May 1996 involved many climbers from different expeditions, in various places and times on the mountain. It's a complicated story to give a complete overview of. Therefore in writing this chapter I have chosen to record the events that involved me directly. What happened around me, what I heard and saw.

I found myself joining a commercial expedition to Mount Everest in the spring of 1996 when Rob Hall needed another guide. Guiding clients up mountains has been an occupation for the last century, most notably when Edward Whymper employed two Swiss guides to make the first ascent of the Matterhorn in 1865. Unfortunately this ascent ended when four of their party fell to their deaths. In recent times some degree of criticism has been aimed at commercial expeditions for poor service and unsafe practices, or at guides who drag inexperienced climbers willing to pay large sums of money to the summit of their whimsical dreams. The situation also raises the question: Where does a guide's responsibility for a client stop in a life-or-death situation? I gave it considerable thought as I mulled

267

over Rob's offer, but could not find a confident answer.

The days of sponsored expeditions are well and truly over and the large sums of money needed to mount an expedition to any of the world's highest mountains have to come from somewhere. Any climber with the experience and motivation to attempt Mount Everest must also have a network of like-minded climbing friends, all with disposable incomes and plenty of time, not only for the climb but for the planning stages as well. Anyone lacking any of these requirements is forced to look at other options. One is to look for a private expedition willing to sell off positions on their permit. This sometimes means a number of smaller teams operating under the one expedition permit, often with little overall planning, a mishmash of experience levels and to the detriment of such things as safety, food and equipment. Such expeditions can become a risk to other teams on the mountain, as well as to themselves. Of course, it can work well, as I have experienced, but it is far better for someone who does not have the network of resources and a high level of experience to join a professionally run (commercial) expedition.

In the world of commercial expeditions Rob Hall had an aura of respectability that was hard to match. I had become friends with him on the K2 climb and had enjoyed his generous hospitality at various base camps in the world's greater mountain ranges. Rob had shown me his clients' impressive climbing résumés, but the final incentive came when a friend of mine, John Taske, was accepted on the climb as a paying member. In fact a few of the climbers had more experience than some of the members of the noncommercial expeditions I had been on in the past. I would be the third guide along with Rob and Andy Harris, a professional guide, whom I had not met but who, by all accounts, was an excellent guide and a likeable fellow. I would need no introduction to the quality of an expedition Rob organised and, as I had witnessed on many occasions, there would be no shortage of good food, worldwide satellite phone and fax communications, and the best equipment money could buy. It would be sheer luxury compared with my previous expeditions. As a guide I would be using oxygen, a foreign experience for me, so much so that I was embarrassed to admit I could not screw a regulator onto an oxygen bottle. Rob had to show me in the privacy of our mess tent. To compare an ascent of Everest using oxygen to one without was an interesting experiment.

I had been in Nepal for most of March co-guiding a trek to a couple of smaller peaks that unfortunately became a non-event due to a heavy snowfall. I left the trek a couple of days early, in the capable hands of my co-leader Mike Wood, to be in time to meet the Everest team in Kathmandu. The bus trip back from the foothills of the Himalayas was a dusty and exhausting ride, and to test my patience further I had difficulty finding a hotel room when I arrived. Looking worn and grubby means you are a less likely victim of streetside salesmanship, so it was with considerable ease that I made my way through the backstreet alleys to the barber. My barber friend knows me well from many visits and I have always felt comfortable in his rickety chair, even though we can only exchange a few words of greeting. I had only just submitted to his razor, when John Taske bounced in to have his pre-expedition haircut. He had climbed with me a couple of times in Nepal and Tibet and had a million and one questions about the pending climb and regaled me with gossip from home. I could only afford the occasional response, as the barber did battle with my two-week growth.

On my way back from the barber I called in to Rob's hotel to announce my arrival. It was then that I met the first of our eight members, Stuart Hutchison. I took an immediate liking to the tall, handsome Canadian who was working in the USA as a cardiologist. His considerable mountaineering experience had seen him on Broad Peak, Denali, K2 and the North Face of Everest.

Food fantasies are a common torture on climbing expeditions and why climbers persist in tormenting themselves by talking about food they cannot have until they return to civilisation, I do not know. On this expedition there would be no such problems. Helen Wilton, our BC manager, took great pride in overseeing the preparation of every lavish meal and she had a shopping list of fresh vegetables, meat, bread and the occasional beer brought in on a weekly basis. As this was my first luxury expedition, I was determined to make the most of the food, but I met tough competition from Lou Kasischke, a US attorney with numerous ascents of the world's smaller but better known mountains to his credit. He liked his food as much as his climbing, as he had a big engine to run it was usually Lou who won the silent battle over the last piece of tomato or dollop of chocolate mousse.

With the spring climbing season in full swing a record number of teams had gathered at the southern side of the mountain. It represented an enormous social scene which I normally enjoy but on a much smaller scale. Catching up with old friends and making new ones is part of the social activities at BC. But with any community of between 100 to 150 people there are inflated reputations, egos, one upmanship and the inevitable false rumours. These elements I deplore in such a fine setting and purposely avoided them by keeping to myself.

BC had more home comforts than I was used to. A hot shower on call was just one of the many luxuries. It only made it difficult to leave and start up the hill. These comforts were thanks to Rob's meticulous planning and Helen, who took care of everything each time we came off the mountain. Caroline MacKenzie was our qualified doctor and at any given time of the day she could be seen treating someone, often from other teams. Her speciality, to use another doctor's expression, was coughs, colds and sore holes.

I had now been away from home for two months and I took full advantage of the phone and fax on a daily basis. This alone made being apart for so long a little more bearable. Little did we know what a key role our small phone would play towards the end of the climb.

Beck Weathers, a pathologist from Texas, and I had something in common—we liked to start the day with an early breakfast. Often it would be only Beck and I enjoying an early bite together in the BC mess tent. Without doubt Beck had the gift of the gab and my only opportunity to change the subject would come when someone else entered the mess tent. His unmistakable southern accent

could often be heard on the mountain while he climbed—
a considerable talent at altitude.

I first met Doug Hansen the year before when Veikka
and I shared the same BC area while attempting to climb
Lhotse. It was his second opportunity to attempt Everest
with Rob. He had previously reached the South Summit
but was forced to turn around due to bad weather. This
time he was determined to climb the last 80 metres.

Jon Krakauer was a journalist on assignment for an
American outdoor magazine. With considerable climbing
experience at lower altitudes, his brief was to cover the
increase in popularity of commercial expeditions to the
world's highest mountains. Jon certainly had a way with
words as his sign on our BC toilet shows. YO! Dude! If you
are not a member of The New Zealand Everest Expedition
Please don't use this toilet. We are a way serious bunch of
shitters, and will have no trouble filling this thing up
without your contribution. Thanks, The Big Cheese.

Despite popular public belief that Everest has become a
giant rubbish dump modern day climbers have taken it
upon themselves to clean up the rubbish left behind by
expeditions who believed no-one would be following in
their footsteps. Everest is cleaner now than it has been for
a long time. Every expedition is obliged to take out what it
takes onto the mountains otherwise heavy fines are enforced. In the case of our expedition we included the
removal of human waste from BC.

Rounding out our team of eight clients were Frank
Fischbeck and Yasuka Namba. Frank was a middle-aged
Hong Kong publisher who seemed to be very much at ease

with climbing Everest. He had attempted it 3 times before. I liked his reserved manner and after sharing a tent with him at C1 I discovered he was a real gentleman.

Yasuko Namba was a Japanese woman of feather weight build and gritty determination. She was the hardest to get to know. Although everyone tried to draw her into a conversation she responded with limited English. At times I felt for her, hoping she wasn't a raving extrovert bursting to have a conversation with someone.

The heavy work for our team settled on the shoulders of the strongest Sherpas around. The team of Lhakpa Chiri, Kami, Arita, Norbu, and Chuldrum were led by Ang Dorje. Over the next four weeks our group of individuals grew to become a harmonious team.

Scott Fischer's American expedition and ours had decided to team up for a combined effort in the belief that we would make a powerful force in trail-breaking to the summit. We met to finalise a date both teams could work towards for a summit attempt. As we discussed the next five or six days, it seemed increasingly likely that 10 May was the big day. As it happened, Rob and I considered the 10th to be our lucky date. Rob had summited Everest twice on that day, and I had summited a collection of the world's highest mountains on that day too.

Frank Fischbeck and I were the last to arrive at C4 late in the afternoon of 9 May, having spent most of the day climbing up from C3. It was windy on the South Col with light snow falling; this did not surprise me, nor was it cause for concern for our summit attempt beginning at 11.30 p.m. Although the day had started off under exhausting conditions weighed down with a heavy pack of personal gear plus rope and oxygen bottles, once I started to breathe bottled oxygen from midday onwards, the climb became a cruise. I experienced little of the stress I was used to when climbing without it, and I could see how climbers who become dependent on bottled oxygen can run off the rails when the supply abruptly runs out.

Arita, the designated cook at C4, shared a tent with Chuldum to prepare the basic noodle soup and cups of tea. It was far easier for them to do this and pass the mugs of hot drinks from door to door than each tent try to do their own. Ang Dorje, Lhakpa, Chiri, Kami, Norbu and Chuldum would accompany us to the summit.

The calm that I was hoping for arrived a couple of hours before our departure. Rob asked me to lead. We aimed to keep our eight climbers, three guides and five Sherpas within a distance of 100 metres from front to back. Ang Dorje, our head Sherpa, explored the climbing route ahead of us. Scott Fischer's group of a similar size would leave fifteen to twenty minutes after us. Frank had been considering an early failure for the last 24 hours but I had urged him to at least make a start for the summit in the hope that he might find some new lease of energy and motivation as I had done on previous attempts. Frank's gut feeling told him that today was not the day. He turned back early in the night, too tired to continue, but the rest plodded on in the light of a half moon and the occasional flurries of snow.

Certain landmarks prompted memories of my 1993

ascent and the debilitating cold which at the time froze any thought of reaching the summit. Now with oxygen I was comfortably warm and progress was relatively easy. At some stage, surrounded by many of the summits I had climbed, I marvelled at the luck which the 10th had brought me. On the eastern horizon was Kangchenjunga, climbed on 10 October 1987; then Everest, climbed on 10 May 1993; around the corner, Cho Oyu, climbed on 10 May 1990; and now, with the coming of dawn, 10 May 1996 was shaping up to be another great day. I quickly reprimanded myself for using luck to climb on. So brilliantly clear was the dawn that I stopped frequently to take in the view, something I was rarely able to do in 1993 when I could barely find the energy to take the next step.

This climbing was fun, and when we broke out into sunshine on the crest of the South East Ridge, I must confess feeling so confident that I put the summit 'in the bag'. We changed our oxygen cylinders and the sun was so warm I could change mine with bare hands.

Rob's arrival on the ridge meant we were together again as a team. Everyone had coped well with the pre-dawn hours, which psychologically can be the toughest, and after a long rest we set off for the steepest part of the climb to the South Summit. It was such a great day that it was almost deceitful in its promise of continuing good weather.

Summit fever. I have seen it in others on many occasions and have experienced it personally on my earlier climbs. Sometimes it can be the boost needed for that final push to the summit but often it can be a dangerous state with fatal consequences. Yasuko had told me she was well known in

Japan and hoped to emulate her country-woman, Junko Tabei, the first woman and the only Japanese woman to have climbed Mount Everest. I could see signs of summit fever in Yasuko's eyes and actions. I worried that her overwhelming desire to climb this mountain could end up killing her if she ran her race before her time. I purposely climbed in front of her to impose a more suitable pace.

The oxygen mask and goggles cover most of your face and hide your true feelings and expressions. All morning I had been bothered by bad stomach cramps. They were growing so bad, I was regularly doubled over in pain. To everyone else it would have looked like the normal resting position for high-altitude climbing, leaning heavily on your ice axe for support. It was becoming a threat to my position as a guide and my summit chances. Some members of the Fischer group, including the guide, Neal Beadleman, had passed us while we changed our oxygen cylinders. At the base of a steep rise leading directly to the South Summit we caught up to Neal who was about to fix a rope to this difficult section. I intended to help uncoil the rope for Neal and belay him but a sudden attack of stomach cramps stopped me in my tracks. Bent over in pain I seriously contemplated heading down. 'Tie this end to something solid will you,' yelled Neal as he tossed the end of the rope. It fell across my back as I was fearing losing control of my bowels. Impatient at my seemingly unhelpful attitude Ang Dorge snatched up the rope from my back and secured it to something solid. Fifteen minutes later I started up the rope that Neal had just fixed. I was feeling

Into the Icefall, September 1993, on my third attempt of Everest.

Camp 4 on the South Col of Everest, with the South Summit at 8763 metres the high point. The climbing route goes up the obvious gully before veering diagonally right to pick up the skyline ridge, which is followed to the South Summit. In recent years climbers and Sherpas have cleaned up the rubbish left behind by earlier expeditions.

Lobsang's cremation.

Sunset at Makalu Camp 1, 6000 metres, September 1993.

K2, 8611 metres, June 1994.

Dawn on 9 July 1994. Rob Hall and Veikka Gustafsson 300 metres above our High Camp on the first K2 summit attempt.

A very skinny author at K2 Base
Camp after the unsuccessful
summit attempt on 9 July 1994.

Camp 3 at 7600 metres on the
Abruzzi Ridge, K2. Broad Peak
at 8047 metres is behind.

Veikka Gustafsson and Ralf Dujmovits at 8500 metres on K2. Hanging from ropes
connected to the rocks in the background were the bodies of the three Ukrainian
climbers who died in the storm two weeks earlier.

On the summit of K2 at 11.30 a.m., 23 July 1994. Ralf Dujmovits, Veikka Gustafsson, and Micky and Axel from the German team follow. The second person down the ridge is at the approximate position where I turned back on 9 July on my first attempt.

The upper slopes of Everest as seen from the summit of Lhotse, 6 May 1995.

Veikka Gustafsson at the 1995 Lhotse Base Camp, sorting food for our climb.

Everest, 1996. Crossing the Khumbu Icefall by the usual route of ladders. I was one of three guides in this expedition.

On Everest at 8500 metres, early on 10 May 1996, using bottled oxygen for the first time. Makalu at 8481 metres stands in the background.

Jon Krakauer and Yasuko Namba on the South East Ridge of Everest after our first change of oxygen cylinders.

Andy Harris and me (left), mid-morning on 10 May, on Everest's South Summit at 8763 metres, only 85 metres to the summit.

Just 30 metres below the summit of Everest. The South Summit is visible below.

Makalu, 16 May 1999. Dave Bridges at 8400 metres with Makalu's North Summit in the background.

Me, a friend and my wife, Judi in November 1995.

Me with my son, Harry, Christmas 1997.

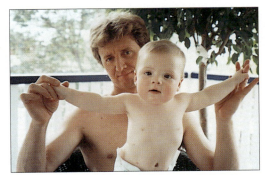

marginally better. It was 10.00 a.m. when I arrived at the South Summit. Jon was not far behind and while I waited I passed on the good news of our progress and position to Helen and Caroline who were monitoring our radio calls at BC now 3.2 kilometres below us. I remarked to Jon that we had only 85 metres to go; in fact, we could almost see the summit. I was barely able to control my temptation to push on. Rob, however, wanted us to regroup at the South Summit and assess the situation from there. Yasuko arrived next, followed by Andy, with Rob and Doug not far behind, but the steep unrelenting climb to the South Summit had taken its toll. Two hundred metres below us Stuart, John and Lou had reached their highest point at around 8600 metres before descending with one of our Sherpas. I felt sad for my friend John but he had climbed as far as he could and that is all one can hope for. I hoped he could salvage some satisfaction from this fantastic day we were experiencing. At this stage I don't remember any comment on Beck. He had, however, succumbed to problems with his sight and Rob had instructed him to stay near where we first changed our oxygen bottles until we returned. The attrition rate for both teams had been very high by the time we reached the South Summit. As the remaining members of both teams regrouped there, they became well and truly mixed together and it was difficult to tell who was who behind the oxygen mask and goggles.

The standing arrangement was that both teams of Sherpas would swap leads in fixing the sections of rope on the trickier sections. This system had not worked with Ang

Dorge doing most of the trail breaking and Neal fixing the odd piece of rope. The Sherpa from the Fischer group had not materialised so at the South Summit Ang Dorge, and rightly so, considered he had done his share and refused to do anymore. The question now seemed to be who was going to relent and do that little bit more. The sections to fix were not overly difficult with only a couple of short sections between us and the summit and I felt inclined to fix them myself, but Rob had given me instructions not to get involved. He would rather I stayed with our group. Precious minutes ticked by at the accountable rate of 2 litres of oxygen per minute. A rest of fifteen minutes was acceptable, given the time of day, but it was now starting to extend past that. I fought an internal battle, should I ignore Rob's instructions not to fix ropes and for the team to regroup at the South Summit by heading for the summit now? The wind was also playing heavily on my mind, it had increased in strength making it difficult to decide if we should go up or down. Repeated calls on the radio to Rob for help to answer my dilemma were met with silence. No doubt he was climbing in the transmission shadow cast by the South Summit. Finally the problem was solved when Neal and Anatoli, two guides from the American team, decided to fix the ropes themselves.

Another call to Rob revealed he was just below the South Summit and he said those of us waiting should go on up to the summit. I had been watching Jon who reminded me a little of myself, although I never really got to know him. For an American he was quiet, almost reserved. It seemed he preferred to listen and think about an ongoing conversation, contributing a little only if he had to. During our forced delay on the South Summit Jon and, to a lesser degree, Andy could not hide their eagerness to continue. I knew the feeling well from 1993, but this year I had none of that driving ambition. Andy, with his usual thoughtfulness for others, suggested Jon and I should go on ahead but I knew the importance of an Everest summit for Andy and told him to go instead. The two of them would make short work of the distance to the summit; besides, he had some rope which might be useful above the Hillary Step. This would leave me to discuss with Rob my concern about the rest of us continuing. Yasuko had slowed dramatically leaving me to wonder if she had the strength and speed to reach the summit before our turn around time of 1.00 p.m. Doug was certainly dragging the chain too. Rob remained out of radio contact.

The wind on the South Summit continued to increase but was certainly very mild compared to the wind on the summit ridge of Kangchenjunga. I was checking the oxygen supply in Yasuko's bottle when Rob arrived. 'Where are the others?' he asked.

Had he forgotten our chat just a few minutes earlier or had I misunderstood him? I pointed in the direction of the Hillary Step and offered no explanation for letting Andy and Jon go ahead, preferring instead to change the subject.

'What about this wind?' I asked. He considered my question carefully before he answered.

'It'll be all right, provided it doesn't get any worse. Why don't you and Yasuko go to the summit, while I wait for Doug. He's not far behind.'

The corniced and narrow ridge connecting the South Summit to the Hillary Step seemed more difficult this year than I remembered it, perhaps because there was less snow, so we took our time over this airy traverse. Every foot placement had to be spot on and backed up with our ice axes driven as deeply as possible into the hard-packed snow. Yasuko had regained her gritty determination and by the time we had overcome the final obstacle of the Step itself, Andy and Jon were returning from the summit. Meeting them on the narrows of the summit ridge created a delicate passing manoeuvre and Andy wanted to make our meeting even more memorable by greeting me with the 'high five'. He was justifiably pleased with his summit and he knew we were only minutes away from ours. His parting words were lost in the confines of his oxygen mask.

Yasuko and I went on to summit at around 2.15 p.m., just ahead of some members of the other team. The view did not compare with the morning's but it was still better than in 1993. The usual low-level cloud for this time of the day had flooded the valleys as the warm air of the plains rose to meet the cold air of the mountains. Yasuko's spirited arrival at the summit meant she had now reached the highest points on all the seven continents. I was pleased for her but personally felt little emotion. The summit had come too easily this time with the use of oxygen, and even though Everest was the highest point in the world, it felt like just another summit. I was not even interested in taking photos, but Yasuko was, so I tried to capture the moment for her: a panoramic shot of her sitting on the summit and a second filling the frame with her delighted smile.

Rob arrived on the summit as we were packing up, and he said that Doug was not too far behind. I gained some pleasure from this unrewarding achievement by shaking Rob's hand. In the short time we had known each other I had always enjoyed our partnership in the mountains and we had become good friends. I had purposely left the pleasure of speaking to Helen and Caroline for Rob as I knew that this moment was one of the highlights for Helen in her role as BC manager. No doubt they had already received a call from Andy and Jon and were waiting for the final summit tally so they could contact our family and friends. Once Rob had broadcast the good news, Yasuko and I started down as it was becoming quite crowded on the summit with five or six of the other team arriving. Rob would follow with Doug. As Rob predicted we met Doug not far below the summit just above the Hillary Step. I slapped Doug's shoulder in encouragement and said the summit was 80 metres up the gently sloping ridge. It would come into view around the next corner and from there there would be no stopping him. It has been reported that Doug didn't reach the summit until after 4.00 p.m. This meant that Rob would have waited on the summit for another one and a half hours and presumably for a lot of that time watching Doug shuffle agonisingly slowly towards the summit.

Yasuko handled the descent to the South Summit with much more ease than the ascent. I was not so lucky. Halfway down the abseil of the Hillary Step I was caught with an acute urge to have a pee. Looking down to the fly of my climbing-suit, I saw the long cord attached to the zipper was tangled in a mixture of harness straps and buckles. Bent over double I waited in vain for the urgency to pass. I would have to abseil to the bottom of the Step and untie as quickly as possible. But in my haste I lost control and a pleasantly warm flood trickled down the inside of both legs, mainly to the left boot. I realised my left foot was the warmest it had been all day. I suffered none of the embarrassment of my childhood pants-wetting days, but I did worry that any icicles dangling from the crutch of my climbing-suit might raise Yasuko's curiosity! Thanks to modern-day fabrics, nothing could be seen.

Every second step squelched to the sound of a boot full of urine; I may have found this amusing, if it were not for finding Jon slumped on the ridge beneath the Hillary Step. He was in a very distressed state, having run out of oxygen—a crippling event at such altitude, made even more critical for Jon when Andy told him there was no more. This comment by Andy signalled that he was also affected by oxygen deprivation. I unplugged my bottle and connected it to Jon's hose. The benefit was almost instantaneous and the three of us continued to join Andy on the South Summit. Here I easily located our eight bright orange cylinders that we had stashed for our return. It would have been easy for Andy, in oxygen debt and in the euphoria of a post-Everest summit, to mistake full cylinders for empty as there is little noticeable difference in weight. However, I knew that Andy was behaving irrationally and I was keen to get him back on oxygen as soon as possible. I expected the same remarkable return to normality as I had seen from Jon just a half hour earlier.

At any other place in the world these full cylinders may have been looked upon as scrap metal or useless pieces of junk, but at the second highest summit in the world, they were priceless and they represented a return ticket to the real world below. I carefully distributed the cylinders to Andy, Jon and Yasuko as if they were new-born babies. This left four full ones in the stash for Rob, Doug and two of our Sherpas, Ang Dorje and Norbu, who were now accompanying Rob. My priority for attention was for Andy, I wanted to turn Andy's flow rate up to the maximum of 4 litres a minute for five minutes so he could recover, but I was distracted by Yasuko who fumbled with her cylinder dangerously close to the edge. Her tiny hands had difficulty grasping the cylinders so I helped her change. After this I was distracted again from helping Andy by Jon who wanted me to check the flow rate on his regulator which should have been on 2 litres a minute but was on 4 litres, which explained why he had run out prematurely. By now Andy had his mask on and things seemed to be under control. I still wanted to check with him but I had now been without oxygen for some time and felt it was important for me to get back on the Os.

Many months after this climb someone asked me how I could function without bottled oxygen while everyone around me couldn't. I put this down to the fact that I had done so much climbing above 8000 metres without bottled oxygen that my system could cope better than theirs when the oxygen was gone. I also, therefore, didn't have the emotional dependency on oxygen. This was the first time I had used oxygen above 8000 metres; for the others it was their first time above 8000 metres.

With everyone appearing to be comfortable with their new bottle of oxygen I stood up to see Rob's lanky figure standing patiently at the top of the Hillary Step waiting for someone to clear the ropes. Doug was standing there too, leaning heavily on his ice axe and no doubt Ang Dorje and Norbu weren't too far away. They were in for a long wait as five or six of the Fischer group were in the process of abseiling the Hillary Step. I waved to Rob, who acknowledged with the thumbs-up signal; this visual contact between the guides was common and a short wave of the hand had meant the situation surrounding them was under control. We could have easily used our radios to do this, but we were constantly out of breath, and when we had a clear sighting of each other, a simple hand signal was all that was needed. Satisfied everything was in control, I turned to Andy and said, 'Let's get out of here. Rob and Doug are just above the Hillary Step and they are going OK.'

'Go ahead. I'll follow you in a minute,' said Andy, who seemed to be in no hurry to move. Again I should have checked on him more closely but now there seemed to be nothing outwardly unusual about his behaviour.

Yasuko and Jon followed me off the South Summit and we lost height quickly and so our line of sight to Andy, Doug and Rob. In hindsight we had just entered a more serious game of Russian Roulette. It was about to start and Everest was running the game. All the climbers still above the South Summit—Rob, Doug, Ang Dorge, Norbu and some of the Americans—were now targets. For Jon, Yasuko and myself, one wrong move, falter or a sign of weakness and the sights of the loaded gun would fix firmly onto us. Just 70 metres above the point on the South East Ridge where we had exited from the gullies that dropped to C4, the radio inside my climbing-suit came to life with Rob's voice. I let Jon and Yasuko continue while I listened intently. He wanted to know where the spare oxygen bottles had been left on the South Summit. Before I could transmit, Andy, from wherever he was at the time, replied that there were none left on the South Summit. This I knew to be incorrect as I had personally checked and stacked the remaining four full bottles in a conspicuous place on the South Summit. I replied quickly. 'Rob, listen to me. This is Michael. I have left four bottles for you at the South Summit. Do you understand?' There was no reply. Repeated transmissions failed, only Andy's and Rob's confusing conversations could be heard. On many occasions earlier in the expedition I had spent idle minutes chatting on my radio but now, when I needed it most, it failed me. I tried BC, then C2 and finally C4, but there was no response. After more calls Caroline at BC picked up my signal and said she would pass on my message on her clear line of transmission to Rob. Content that everything was under control, I caught up to Yasuko and Jon and we continued descending with one of the Americans from Fischer's team, who was trying an unorthodox passing move in an uncontrolled tumble off to our left. From where I stood he looked out of control and in no hurry to regain it, preferring instead to slide happily towards the edge and into Tibet. He stopped abruptly in an explosion of white from a thick bed of snow 30 metres below us with no sign of injury. Jon was anxious to keep moving, so I told him and Yasuko to go ahead while I helped the American. They had only just left on their way down the gullies to C4, when on my way over to the stunned American, I picked up Rob's call again for oxygen. I did not understand why there was still so much confusion. I waited with my gloved finger poised over the call button ready to steal some time in between the now desperate calls between Rob, Andy and BC. It was obvious that my radio was not working properly as conversations dropped in and out. It was not the batteries, as I had changed them the day before. Whether it was my position on the mountain or something more technical than that, I couldn't tell. After persistent tries in between their conversations I eventually got through to Rob. I once again repeated the position of the oxygen bottles. I reassured him they were there. He seemed, however, quite convinced they weren't. He begged for help and I replied that I was on my way back up. It would take hours to get to him. I yelled to the American that the trail he needed to be on was over near me and then started to climb. It was 4.30 p.m.

I had climbed 100 metres. There was a light wind and snow fell softly settling on my shoulders. Above me I saw two people descending fast and for a few minutes I felt relieved as I believed them to be Rob and Doug—they must have found the oxygen and everything was okay. It wasn't. Our Sherpas, Ang Dorje and Norbu, materialised out of the falling snow. I asked if they had seen Rob, Doug or Andy, but they hadn't seen them since the South Summit.

'What about the oxygen? Is it still on the South Summit?'

Ang Dorje replied. 'Yes. Two cylinders are still there. We have two full ones with us.' His response only confirmed what I already knew and I wished it could be as simple as that for Rob. I had left four bottles up there. Ang Dorje and Norbu now had two of those four. Rob and Doug only needed the remaining two. I couldn't understand why they had not found them. I asked Ang Dorje where he had collected their two bottles.

'Same place as this morning,' he replied.

I grabbed my radio. Thankfully it worked and I told Rob exactly where the bottles were. This time Rob did not seem so stressed and his immediate problem seemed to be solved. He only had to traverse 30 or 40 metres to the stash of oxygen on the South Summit, whereas I would need to climb up 200 metres to get the cylinders. If Rob now knew where the cylinders were, I saw no sense in continuing up, so I followed Ang Dorje and Norbu in their hasty descent. The fact that they had been with Rob and had come down indicated that things weren't as desperate as I thought they might have been. On reflection, I believe my call to Rob came at a moment when things were coming slightly back under control for him. There was a calmness in his voice and perhaps Andy, who was closer to Rob than me, had returned to the South Summit to help. He was certainly more lucid. However, it was never going to be quite that simple. Rob and Doug had been without oxygen for far too long and the three of them were still extremely high at a depressingly late hour of the day.

It continued to snow. Lower down the ridge the American who had passed us with such haste was amazingly only just getting to his feet after all this time and moving again, veering dangerously close to the wrong side of the mountain in a series of drunken flops into the snow, one of which could end up over the edge into Tibet. I detoured off my path to get close enough to speak with him. I could see that his oxygen mask had slipped off beneath his chin and clumps of ice hung from his eyebrows and chin. Lying half-buried in the snow, he was giggling—a result of oxygen debt to the brain. I told him to pull his oxygen mask over his mouth. In a fatherly sort of manner I then coaxed him closer and closer to the ridge crest, and as I did so I was interrupted by calls from BC. Every attempt to respond failed and from then on I heard no further talk on the air waves.

With the American now following me closely, we continued down the ridge a little way until we reached the exit point into the gullies that led down to C4. 'Now, see those two climbers down there in red? Just follow them,' I said pointing to Jon and Yasuko still visible in the gully below. He stepped off the ridge in such a haphazard manner, I wondered whether he cared if he lived or died. Concerned about his judgement, I decided to stick with him. All this time Beck Weathers had gone unnoticed standing beside me.

'Is that you, Mike?' The Texan accent startled me. Beck was camouflaged perfectly in a light sprinkling of fresh snow. He must have been standing still for some time, judging by the amount of snow that had settled on him. He looked like a tatty scarecrow, his bulky down suit pushing his arms awkwardly out to the sides.

'What are you doing here, Beck? I thought you would have been well and truly back at C4 by now.'

'I can't see, Mike. I have been waiting for you to come down.' He didn't have to say any more. I knew we were in trouble when I looked into his blank and unfocused eyes.

'How bad is it, Beck? Can you see anything at all?'

'Everything is a blur. I can't seem to focus,' said Beck in a remarkably calm voice, considering our position.

'Okay, Beck. We'll see how you go on this first bit, which is fairly easy. I have a rope if you can't manage. Follow me if you can.'

A year or so earlier Beck had had radial keratotomy to improve his failing vision. The sudden drop in barometric pressure, however, severely impaired his now delicate eyes.

Within the first few metres I knew I had a difficult task on my hands to get us both down alive as Beck fell over twice on easy ground. I pulled a rope from my pack and hastily tied it to Beck's harness because from here on the gully became much steeper and more difficult to negotiate. Just 2 metres of tight rope separated us, and just one wrong move separated us from certain death. I directed our progress from behind, 'Left! Right! Stop!' were the only words I used for the next couple of hours as Beck often balanced dangerously close to walking over the edge with many a step into thin air. I tried to predict his falls by bracing myself and driving my axe deep into the snow. This worked well, considering my disadvantage in weight—64 kilograms to Beck's 80 plus. On several occasions, however, caught on bare rock slabs, I was pulled forwards, my crampons scraping across the rock, and only just managed to stop Beck from toppling over the edge. There was no doubt that I was more nervous than Beck, for he could not see the exposure below us. I knew if there was any lapse in my concentration, Beck would pull us both over the edge. For one instant I thought of my friend, Lobsang, who had fallen from around here in 1993. I quickly put it out of my mind.

For hours I shouted my instructions to Beck as we weaved our way down through the endless rock and ice gullies. It was just on dark when we stumbled thankfully onto the easy snow slopes that led to C4, but they were still steep enough for Beck to sit and slide while I lowered him. I stopped for a few seconds to get a bearing on C4; we now looked across to it rather than down on top of it. Under normal conditions it would have taken half an hour, but for us it would be at least an hour. Here a few members of the Fischer group caught up with us, the only one that I knew being Neal Beidleman.

By now Beck was exhausted. It was still snowing and in the last few minutes of light I got my visual direction on C4. If we kept our bearing, we would walk straight into it, but the distractions were many as I shouldered a good deal of Beck's weight to try to make any sort of progress. The falling snow now had a sting to it brought about by a steadily increasing wind, and with Beck's regular requests for a rest I soon lost any sense of C4's position.

A few metres further on we came across Yasuko sitting in the snow. Neal had found her first and was removing her oxygen mask as her supply, like ours, had run out. No amount of persuasion could convince her that she had run out as she persisted in putting her mask back on, which only suffocated her more. Finally we ripped the straps from her mask and shoved it into her pack. Thankfully Neal and his group were able to descend with her, while I continued very slowly with Beck. Visibility was now down to a few metres as high winds lashed the upper slopes of Everest and with it came the energy-sapping cold. I was afraid we would lose sight of the others.

'Come on, Beck. We have to keep up with the others,' I yelled.

'Mike, I need to rest. Just a short rest,' he begged.

I relented, silently cursing with every second that passed. Beck was going nowhere without a rest. Meanwhile the others were moving further away from us.

Quickly the situation became critical: we lost sight of Neal's group and any shouting to contact them was carried off by the wind. Beck and I were alone. I had done everything I could to keep up with the others, but our pace was far too slow. I sat Beck down as the 70 to 80-kilometre-per-hour winds threatened to blow us off our feet and snow stung my eyes, temporarily blinding me. Thoughts of what to do shrieked through my mind at a million miles an hour. At best I could see 3 or 4 metres. I used my radio to call C4 but there was no reply on my useless piece of junk; nevertheless I continued my transmission in the hope that they could hear me. Even if they did respond it would have been difficult to hear them above the roar of the wind. We wanted a direction, a light, a voice, a familiar sound, anything to help guide us in.

It's not in my nature to beg, but that night I begged Beck to keep moving—every minute we delayed for a rest put another nail in our coffins. The wind was increasing rapidly and the temperature was dropping to an unbearable level. I supported Beck's weight for as long as I could, now ignoring his requests to stop in our relentless pursuit for shelter. Again I tried calling C4 on my radio; still there was no reply. A beam of light flashed in front of us; for a moment I thought it was help from C4, but as we came closer we found Neal and Yasuko who were as confused as we were. Neal was trying to regroup his team who had scattered in all directions. You didn't have to go far in these conditions to be totally lost. Slowly they regrouped and I allowed Beck to sit. I did not get involved in the yelling match about where C4 was—I was just as confused as the rest of them. My only contribution was a request that we all stay together and there was a unanimous agreement. Finally a direction was agreed upon and Neal led off hopefully; it was as good a direction as any. Beck leaned heavily on my shoulder—he could lean as much as he liked, so long as I could keep us both moving.

When I tripped over two old oxygen bottles, my spirits soared; we were obviously close to C4 and I told Beck this. Only a couple of head-torches were working now, and their criss-crossing beams often silhouetted the distressing sight of clumsy figures struggling to stay upright. I tried not to think that Beck and I would have looked equally pitiful.

Neal stopped to allow us to catch up, all the time encouraging his team-mates to stay together and to keep moving. He asked if I had any idea of the direction of C4, but I confessed that I didn't as the constant attention to Beck and the white-out conditions had distracted any sense of it. Others also voiced their opinion, but they often conflicted. Today, looking back, I realise we had staggered depressingly close to C4 before veering away in the opposite direction.

I struggled with Beck but the dread of losing the others was enough incentive to keep moving. I was tempted to try my radio again but the fact that it had been malfunctioning made me think it was a waste of time. We continued to chase the others in their search. Up front the two leaders had come to an edge, their head-torches shining into a black void. Between us and them lay four or five exhausted climbers, some were kneeling, some had collapsed and were lying motionless in the snow. The edge marked the most significant landmark we had found in the last couple of hours, but was it the edge leading into Nepal or was it the edge dropping into Tibet? No-one knew, although there were some wild guesses. The situation was seriously grim now. Beck had lost one of his gloves, leaving a bare hand exposed to the elements; I searched in the snow and rocks in the immediate area, but no doubt the wind had carried it off, so I gave him mine and then checked on Yasuko. She was still standing, still keen to push on, but she was incoherent, unable to tell left from right. Now I had a chance to use my radio. It worked! Stuart answered my call from C4. I asked him which direction the wind was blowing from at C4, as it might help me get some idea of where we were on the South Col. If I had been warm and rested with a sea level supply of oxygen, I would have easily made use of the small amount of information he was able to give me, but tonight it made little sense at all. Once Stuart had picked up my call, he wasted no time in coming out to look for us, banging metal and shining his head-torch in wild arcs into the night sky to give us the best chance of seeing him. But he could only travel a short distance from camp for fear of becoming hopelessly disoriented too. Stuart tried desperately to find us before having to return to his tent to recover from the cold. He came back out time and time again, but all to no avail.

I moved closer to the edge to look for any clues. There was nothing but a black hole where only the wind dared to go. It could easily have been the edge of the earth. I stepped back quickly; it was no place to stand braced against the gale. For a moment I paused, confused. I had to try to think of a new plan of action but that action was more or less decided for us, because lying on the rocks at our feet were the pitiful figures of three or four climbers who had been pushed beyond their limit with the torments of the cold and exhaustion. We desperately needed to find C4, but we were going nowhere, we had nowhere to go. Neal yelled to a couple of his team-mates who were still standing to lie low to try to shelter from the bitterly cold wind that was showing us no mercy. He asked if I agreed with his decision to shelter as best we could and I nodded my agreement. There were maybe twelve of us altogether and Yasuko lay down among the other climbers on the rock and ice, tucking her hands in between her legs and pulling her knees up to her stomach. My fingers had long since stopped performing any delicate tasks and had become useless attachments. I grabbed a handful of Beck's clothing and pulled him to the ground beside me, unapologetic for the way I was handling him. I didn't want to lose sight of him now, as I doubted I had the energy to repeat any unnecessary action. Up until now the uncertainty of whether or not I'd find C4 had remained a finely balanced question but now the broad expanse of the South Col as jet stream winds blasted across it bringing crippling temperatures well below –40°C. Any sense of control over the elements was lost to me. I was trapped in a giant wind tunnel, that was equal to the most desolate place in the world.

I lay on my side in a small depression and pulled Beck in behind me to protect him from the wind. From this position he was able to put his frozen hands inside the chest pockets of my climbing-suit where I tried to rub some warmth into them. Although I had run out of oxygen some time before, I kept the mask on to protect my face from the cold. This prevented me from speaking clearly to anyone, but the wind made sure of that regardless. The wind was now unrelenting in its bid to drive the cold deeper into our bodies and for hours we shivered uncontrollably. I felt totally alone and, even though I had no intention of dying, my thoughts did turn negative from time to time. It did not bother me to think about it for I have had plenty of practice over the years. Unfortunately freezing to death doesn't happen quickly; it torments your mind and body with a slow and painful suffering for hours before finally

showing some mercy in allowing you to go to sleep, never
to wake again. For long and wandering periods I thought of
Judi, and of our hot and humid holiday in Fiji just a few
months earlier, when a sudden and uncontrollable shiver
made me lurch from my rocky resting place. With this
sudden movement came a terrible stinging pain to my right
ear. I had been using my pack as a pillow and my ear had
become glued to it with ice. I rubbed the palm of my gloved
hand up and down the length of my pack to feel if the top
part of my ear was stuck to the pack, but I came to the
drowsy conclusion that I couldn't care less; it would be just
another body part lost to frostbite. Now that I was sitting
up, I had a look around, it looked like doomsday, everyone
seemed dead until I heard some moaning coming from the
motionless bodies scattered around me. Someone was
crying, someone else was begging not to be left to die like
this. I saw Yasuko shaking from the cold but otherwise lying
silently behind one of the Americans. It was a hopeless situation and I lay back down, the pain from my ear being just
another discomfort in the whole miserable affair. I tried to
pretend it was only a nightmare, that it would all go away.

I tried my radio again, first to C4, then to BC, but no-
one responded. I turned my attention to Beck.

'Beck, how are you going?'

'I'm very cold but I'm OK,' said Beck. His distinctive
Texan accent was slurred and only just recognisable above
the roar of the wind. For me it was a small but comforting
thought to know he was still alive because I did not know
how much longer I could last protecting Beck from the full
force of the gale. I could only hope that Yasuko was equally

protected in her hollow. It was a long night and I was starting to surrender to the temptation of eternal sleep.

Throughout the night the roar of the wind brought numerous false alarms when we thought someone had found us, which sent our small group into an excitable frenzy only to be miserably disappointed. It was after midnight when the alarm was raised again. I think it was Neal who saw it first and I rose, fully expecting to be disappointed again. A gap had appeared in the cloud that was whipping across the Col and left a short but adequate sighting onto the south-east slopes of Everest. To get a better view I had to break away the ice that hung from my eyebrows and around the rim of my hood. From this unmistakable landmark we were able to gain some idea of where we were in relation to C4. We were too far east— closer to Tibet than Nepal.

Neal gathered those in his team that could still walk and headed off in the direction he thought C4 should be in.

I pulled Beck to his feet. Yasuko had managed to get to her feet with the other climbers. Beck had lost his glove again and as my head-torch had expired because of the cold, I had to search the ground with my hands. Luckily I found it stuck to Beck's cramponed boots, otherwise it would have surely blown away with the wind. Beck suggested that if he had his head-torch on, the beam might give him some direction to focus on. I shoved my frozen hands into his pack in search of it, but it was a fruitless effort as my hands had no feeling.

All this had consumed precious minutes and by the time we were ready to move, the others were out of sight. Yasuko had tried to go with them but had collapsed not far in front of us. She stood up again, swaying precariously on her feet as if she had been hit with a knockout punch. Staring stubbornly into the teeth of the storm brought no answers for her. There were three more bodies in our vicinity sitting in the snow. At first I thought they were dead, but one of them started crying. It was a female voice and again I heard the plea. 'Don't leave me. I don't want to die here,' she begged.

I ignored the pleas for help as I fought against the wind to gather in Yasuko before she wandered off into the night.

By this time Yasuko had collapsed again, so I pulled her back onto her feet and removed the rim of ice around her hood so she could see. By now the three Americans had moved off and disappeared. I stretched Beck's left arm around my shoulder and supported his weight as best I could, but I had become so incredibly weak in the last few hours that we swayed like two old drunks. Yasuko fell yet again. Leaving Beck to stand unsupported like a statue, I picked up Yasuko; this time as I stood her up, her arms moved in a swimming fashion, so I pulled them down to her side and held them there, yelling at her to follow Beck and me. 'Camp Four is not far away,' I said for encouragement, but I doubt she understood me. I still had no idea where C4 was.

The three of us began to move, leaning heavily into the full force of the gale. After a few metres Beck needed to rest. This time I was thankful as he was becoming far too heavy for me to support any longer. Yasuko stumbled and fell face down. I didn't dare let go of Beck as I knew I would not have the strength to lift him to his feet again.

'Come on, Yasuko. Keep moving. Follow me,' I yelled,

but I expected little response from her. None of us was able to walk a straight line as we teetered on the edge of total exhaustion. Only the recent sighting of the upper slopes of Everest gave me some motivation to keep trying. Step by step we moved on if ever so slowly.

We had been out in the elements for twenty-six hours and I doubted we could last much longer. If the wind increased its intensity, it would bring the wind chill factor down to an unbearable level and this would finish us off quickly. Beck, Yasuko and I had stumbled just 15 metres when we encountered the three Americans again, two of them had fallen to the ground and the other was pleading with them to keep moving. Here Yasuko stumbled and fell. The American male and I both knew that we were not going to make it under these dreadful conditions and he asked if I could go and find C4 and bring back help. I hesitated, pretending for a second or two that I hadn't heard his request, but it seemed like our only chance for survival.

Yasuko was now lying motionless behind us; Beck stood, barely, and my fellow path-finder had his two companions lying semi-conscious in the rock and snow. I only agreed to go on the condition that all of them stayed put and did not separate. The American agreed and I slapped Beck hard across his shoulder to make sure I had his attention before I explained my request.

'Stay here with Yasuko. Don't let these people out of your sight.' I immediately felt stupid, as I had forgotten Beck could not see.

'OK,' mumbled Beck. I repeated my request to the more able-bodied American. It was even more important that he understood my instructions concerning Beck's and Yasuko's condition.

My frozen hands made it extremely difficult untying the rope that bound me to Beck. I was very reluctant to leave Beck and Yasuko behind while I went in search of help. The short piece of rope had forced Beck and me to work as a unit and now I felt I was giving up on him. On the other hand it was our only choice, if anyone was to survive. I propped Yasuko up against a rock. Of all of us she was probably the closest to death. I yelled my instructions to stay with Beck and the others directly into her face. She nodded agreement but she didn't stop nodding as I walked away—I doubted she had understood any of it.

I drew on the limits of my reserves to make some headway into the wind. I leaned heavily into the gale and protected my eyes from the high-velocity ice particles that had the sting of a thousand needles. It dawned on me that the people I had just left could well be the lucky ones. Perhaps the others who had left us about twenty minutes earlier had already found C4 and were sending back help; perhaps I would be the one who remained lost and alone; perhaps in the near-zero visibility I would walk over the edge, never to be seen again. I had no idea where I was going and every second rock looked like the outline of a tent.

My crampons skidded uncontrollably across the rocky terrain of the South Col; each stumble only confused my sense of direction even more. At some stage I stopped and stared at two head-torch lights bobbing and weaving high up on Everest, somewhere in the vicinity of the gullies that led down to C4. My immediate thought was that it was

Rob and Doug making their way down, but on reflection I know it wasn't; I suspect I was longing for the lights to belong to them and therefore imagined it. In my lonely search I stopped to rest, believing I had been , wandering for hours and that soon it would be morning. I even considered stopping altogether because I couldn't remember what I was searching for. By now I had lost all sense of urgency. I had forgotten about Beck, Yasuko and the others, the wind no longer bothered me and, worst of all, I felt comfortably warm. As far as my body temperature was concerned, I could not have been more seriously cold.

I wanted a nice place to sit and wait for morning. This special place couldn't be just anywhere; it had to be big enough for two of us. I sensed his powerful presence: Lobsang was with me now and we had a lot to talk about since we said goodbye on the summit ridge of Everest in 1993. As we looked for a place that would give us the best view of the sunrise, a sudden clearing in the turbulence of the wind-driven snow and ice extended my visibility to 40 or 50 metres.

'There it is!' I said to Lobsang. 'Over there!' I had just spotted the unmistakable outline of our wind-crushed tents at C4, and I suddenly remembered the reason I was here alone.

I don't know why but I went past the first tent, preferring instead to go to one in the middle of the huddle. There was a long moment of disbelief on both sides as I crouched outside the door belonging to Stuart and Jon. Did they know who the ice-encrusted apparition was? Or was I the one that was dreaming? I am not sure if I spilled out the speech that I had so carefully rehearsed in my mind during those crazy

hours of wandering around on the Col. If I did say something, it probably sounded like a drunken slur. Whatever I
said, I hoped I gave some accurate directions and instructions to help find Beck, Yasuko and the others.

I was convinced that as a result of whatever conversation
took place between us, rescuers would be rounded up to
help me get Beck and Yasuko back into camp. Somehow I
was confronted with another closed tent door. Had Stuart
closed the door on me to prevent the tent being filled with
snow? Or had I just imagined my conversation? Or was
this a different tent? If anything was clear to me at this
moment, it was that I didn't have a clue where I was. I only
remember kneeling outside the tent trying to unzip the
door that I had thought was open. Stuart may have even
directed me to my tent. It was a frustrating exercise in
coordination, a skill I no longer had. If Stuart was playing
a joke, it was a bad one. I yelled for help and Frank
responded from inside the tent. I was trying to remember
where the full oxygen bottles were to take back for
Beck and Yasuko, but Frank operated with the efficiency
of a battlefield medic and pulled me inside the tent. It
was then I gave up trying. Frank swore at me and I thought
he was abusing me for being late. Before I knew it I
was being wrapped and buried in a sea of down sleeping-
bags. The questions continued while he broke away the
ice from around my face. If I answered them, I answered
very few.

Everything seemed to be happening in slow motion,
most likely because the cold had drained every ounce of
energy. Speaking was difficult and confusing. I tried to sit

up to answer a voice that I thought came from outside the tent—it was probably Stuart wanting to confirm directions for Beck and Yasuko—but I couldn't even find the strength to sit up. At some stage Frank went outside, leaving me in the hands of John, an anaesthetist by profession. I was not an easy patient for him that morning as I shook uncontrollably while he tried to keep an oxygen mask on my face. I settled down slowly, and in the belief that a search party had gone for the others.

The next thing I remember it was early morning on 11 May and high winds continued to batter our tent. I immediately looked for Yasuko, hoping to see her dark eyes peeping out from the bulk of her over-filled sleeping-bag, but there was nothing except a shambles of ice-encrusted gear littering our tent. John told me that Frank had gone to keep Lou company, as his tent-mates Beck, Doug, Andy and Rob were still missing. I asked what had happened to Beck and Yasuko—they should have been here by now—but John had no answer.

In the meantime I continued to drift in and out of reality, with one dreamlike conversation after another. The few real events I remember were John's persistent efforts to supply me with more and more drinks—a difficult task of coordination and strength. However, in the back of my mind I was still aware of those unaccounted for. I tried to gather my wits and strength to get up to at least look for Beck and Yasuko but John, who could judge my condition better than me, said there was nothing I could do. I suspect he knew everything that could be done in these dreadful conditions was being attempted.

It is my understanding that after alerting Stuart he set out alone to find Beck and Yasuko but once again, like so many times before, he found himself in danger of becoming hopelessly lost in the blizzard conditions. The guide Anatoli, who was Neal's counterpart in the Fischer group and who had returned to C4 from the summit by late afternoon, was alerted by Neal's desperate arrival at C4 with a few surviving members of his team. In a long and sweeping search of the South Col Anatoli found no-one and returned to the tent. Undaunted by his fruitless search he set out again. This time he found the three Americans, and Beck and Yasuko who lay motionless he presumed they were dead.

At dawn Stuart and Lhakpa Chhiri went out in search of Beck and Yasuko. Later Lhakpa Chhiri and Ang Dorje made a determined but hopeless attempt to reach Rob, who was still trapped up at the South Summit. Too weak to move, Rob was known to be still alive due to his intermittent radio calls that had been picked up by BC and Jon and Stuart who had our spare radio.

Throughout the expedition I had felt uncomfortable about using the Sherpas to do the back-breaking work; their tireless efforts and cheerful attitude made me feel lazy and guilty. Without them our expedition would not have existed and they were as much a part of our team as anyone else. I found out that these rescue attempts were being made when I regained some degree of consciousness, and I was crushed by a heavy weight of guilt as I lay incapacitated in my tent. No amount of persuasion or money had made Stuart, Ang Dorje or Lhakpa Chhiri do what they were doing; it was their nature to do so.

I learnt later that the Fischer group had left C4 that morning in an effort to get to safer ground. How they made progress under those conditions, I do not know. Stuart and Jon had our only working radio in their tent and they kept Helen and Caroline at BC informed of our situation and of the high winds that continued at C4.

Jon thought he had last seen Andy Harris only a stone's throw from C4 just before 5.30 p.m. of 10 May, when Andy made a sudden turn to the right towards the Lhotse Face saying, as he disappeared, 'I'm going straight to BC.' Jon, however, has since changed his mind and thinks that, in the confusion of the moment, he saw someone else. An expedition that summited much later in May found Andy's ice axe at the South Summit. It is widely accepted that Andy was behaving abnormally from hypoxia and could easily have left the South Summit without his axe just as he believed there was no oxygen on the South Summit. However, I believe he returned to the South Summit to help Rob. This explains why Rob sounded in control of the situation when I made that final call to him from below the South Summit: Andy had returned to help. Sadly, we will never really know.

———

The struggle of someone wrestling his way into the tent woke me from my hazy existence. It was around mid-morning, 11 May. I was alarmed at the sight of Stuart, exhausted and wind blown. Above the roar of the wind that continued to hammer our tents he yelled out that he had found Beck and Yasuko. He said that in the time it took for

him to return to the tent, Yasuko would most likely be
dead but Beck might yet be alive. To make things worse, he
said they were close to an edge, perhaps the Kangshung
Face—not where I remembered leaving them. It was a risky
proposition for anyone to venture out to get Beck. Stuart
asked me what I wanted to do.

I was coherent enough to understand what was going on
and the implications of Stuart's question. Without doubt it
was the most difficult question I have ever been asked.
Lhakpa Chhiri and Ang Dorje had been beaten back by
violent winds higher up; Stuart had done everything he
could for Beck. Who among us had the strength to go out
again and operate a rescue? Was it worth risking other lives
to rescue someone who would most likely be dead when
found or would die soon after? I couldn't ask another to go
if I couldn't go myself. This was the ruthless way I had to
look at it. My priorities had to shift to the surviving members of our team. It was crucial for me to regain some control of the situation and get our team out of C4 and
descending as soon as possible, otherwise more would die.
John's antidotal comment about decisions being made in
the Vietnam war to save the lives of surviving soldiers by
abandoning their less fortunate and critically injured team-
mates was only mildly comforting.

Around early afternoon there was a lull in the gale, which
allowed a rescue party to reach C4: Pete Athans and Todd
Burleson were members of an independent expedition.
Their mission was two-fold, to lend assistance to us and to
try and rescue Rob. They tried to coax me into getting the
rest of my team down to a lower camp, preferably to C2 as

soon as possible. It was the correct decision but it was not possible—I was barely able to sit up in my sleeping-bag or think clearly, let alone descend to C2; also Lou was snow-blind. I nearly suggested that Pete and Todd take the remaining members down while I stayed, but Lou would most likely have to remain too and I did not know if I would improve enough by the morning to get myself moving and to help a blind person down. Both of us would need assistance, and we needed more time to recover to be able to help ourselves down. Time at this altitude, however, was also a killer. I asked Stuart to count the remaining full oxygen bottles. There were enough for the six remaining team members and our four Sherpas to survive one more night and descend the next day.

I explained our situation to Todd and Pete; considering the late hour of the day, I felt we would be moving too slowly with our disabilities to reach the safety of a lower camp before nightfall. I believed it was better for us get an early start the next morning. There was a risk, however, that the jet-stream winds might intensify and pin us down even longer at C4. I made the assumption that Lou and I would have recovered enough to be able to descend the next day without assistance and if the winds did increase, it would be up to the individual disabled climber to struggle down into the shelter of the Western Cwm without hindering the others. Pete and Todd reluctantly agreed to let us stay one more night and they set up a tent next to ours.

Around mid-afternoon Jon and Stuart brought the radio into my tent. They had been maintaining contact with Helen and Caroline at BC, who were relaying the information, most of it not good, to Madeleine, Rob's personal assistant at the office of his guiding company in New Zealand. It was not a clean and simple connection of two phones—all the guides had two-way radios which allowed us to speak to each other and to BC. At BC the incoming phone calls could be patched to the incoming two-way radio calls via the satellite phone. Madeleine then had the unenviable task of giving news of our individual team members to their families. I was warned by Jon that an earlier conversation with Rob, who was still trapped on the South Summit, had revealed that Doug had gone. No explanation was given, none was asked for; we all knew what it meant. When Rob came on line, all the radios between BC and C4 tuned into his channel. I managed to get through to him only once before I was cut off by another caller, and in a hopeless effort of persuasion to get him moving in our direction, I told him we were all waiting for him at C4 to come down. It was the last time I spoke to him and no amount of encouragement by anyone else could make Rob move. The radio conversation gave little hint of the real misery he was suffering. Why hadn't he made an effort to continue? Perhaps the answer lay in my own condition—exposure to the cold had sapped all my energy and the motivation to move. I thought of the time a couple of years earlier when Rob, Veikka and I had to fight our way down from the high camp on K2 in conditions similar to these. I was trying to think of what to say next when the radio crackled into life with the sound of Rob's wife, Jan, speaking via telephone from New Zealand. We listened for only a few seconds before turning off our radio. It was the last time I heard Rob's voice. Outside the deafening roar of the wind continued to trash our tents; inside a sad silence formed an uncomfortable barrier between us all. Rob was dying.

Murphy's Law prevailed. That night the terrible wind picked up in strength and it became the toughest night yet at C4. I placed my pack to the windward side of the tent and pushed hard with my feet to prevent the tent collapsing in on top of John and me. Much-needed sleep and rest were impossible under such conditions. Unlike earlier in the day I was now conscious and fully aware of our situation. My thoughts tended to wander between those who were missing or dead and our immediate danger. I already had all my gloves on to keep my frostbitten hands warm and had tucked my boots into my sleeping-bag in case the weather turned into a full-on storm and the tent ripped open or was ripped from its tie-down points and blown away with us in it. Whose tent would we go to, if ours exploded like a balloon? What would we do if all the tents ripped open? Fortunately though, I had experienced far more serious storms than this, and I knew what to expect. I guessed the temperature to be minus 30°C and the winds to be blowing at 70 to 80 kilometres per hour. They had the potential to return to their normal velocity of over 200 kilometres per hour at any moment. A shrapnel cloud of ice and rock could shred the tents in minutes. If this happened, it would be no good praying. The emergency actions for our team's survival filled my mind until the cold, grey hours of dawn and the eventual subsidence of the life-threatening gale to nothing more than a nuisance.

It was 6.00 a.m. on 12 May. The wind had punished us severely for daring to stay another night at C4. Our once-cosy tent was a shambles of displaced food, drinks and frozen pee-bottles. John lay shaking in his ice-coated sleeping-bag. I assumed he was cold from the amount of ice on his bag, so offered him my down vest. I assured him we would be on the move to safer ground in less than an hour and to start packing.

'Bring only the essentials. Abandon everything else and leave room in your pack for a full bottle of oxygen,' I said.

Before I put on my boots, I checked my feet for frostbite. I could see the tell-tale signs appearing on both feet, and the left was far worse because it had been swimming in my urine that had since frozen. Thumbs and fingers on both hands had more advanced frostbite, with the tips of some turning a dark blue-purplish colour.

I dressed and ventured out to the other tents to pass on the same message. My instructions were simple: be ready by 7.00 a.m. with a full bottle of oxygen. In passing from tent to tent, I saw that the night had been tough on the others as well by their bewildered faces: the last forty-eight hours had not been a bad nightmare but reality. I took in the devastation of our hostile environment—torn and twisted tents were everywhere and for a few moments I couldn't help but think of the others who were still unaccounted for, and I knew there would be casualties from other teams as well. For the moment, though, I had to deal with the more immediate problems. I only looked towards the summit of Everest once that day; it was still lashed by jet-stream winds. Somewhere between the summit and me

were Doug, Andy, Rob, Beck and Yasuko—all dead. I
didn't look that way again.

It took some time to speak to everyone as each tent had
some little problem to sort out. Our team of Sherpas had
been a strong and tireless bunch and had worked unselfishly
to get us in a position to try for the summit, but now they
showed signs of exhaustion and were understandably sad-
dened by our losses. I was not used to having Sherpas on the
mountain with me and because of this I knew just how
much they had done for us. Now my only request was that
they get down the mountain as far and as quickly as possible. Casting back the door of one tent I came face to face
with Arita, bug-eyed with fear and alone with the disorder
of his tent. His look of absolute terror scared me, causing
me to deliver my instructions quickly, none of which he
could understand. I called over Lhakpa Chhiri to help pacify
Arita and explain the reason for my urgency. He soon
resolved the misunderstanding I had caused. Lhakpa Chhiri,
who is always good-spirited, rallied his team-mates into
packing their belongings. It was a difficult and tricky path
back to my tent: a tangled web of tent guy ropes formed a
high-altitude obstacle course and it required considerable
effort and coordination not to trip up. I was in mid-stride
when something urged me to look in a particular tent.

There was no obvious reason to go to the tent as it
belonged to the Fischer group, but I went anyway. It
showed signs of having been left in a hurry as the doors at
both ends of the tent flapped wildly, allowing the wind to
tunnel through. Kneeling down to look inside I was confronted by a pair of climbing boots. At first I was startled

by the sight of a body dressed in a red and black climbing-suit lying on its back, with a sleeping-bag covering the face and upper body. It was impossible to tell who it was by the clothing as every second climber was dressed in one of these particular climbing-suits. Besides I had no desire to know the true identity of this casualty of misadventure in the mountains—I had seen many like it over the years. Because the body was in the American team's tent, I believed that it belonged to one of the Fischer group. I called by Todd and Pete's tent to let them know that we would be heading down soon. Pete smiled, perhaps with a sigh of relief. It was a smile that I remember well as no-one had smiled in a long time and it helped relieve some of the pressure I was under. However, I startled Pete with the news of the dead climber I had just found. With no reply from him I returned to my tent to finish packing.

Everyone was ready: Lou, Frank, Jon, Stuart and John were crouched outside their tents making last-minute adjustments to buckles and straps, while Ang Dorje, Norbu, Lhakpa Chhirri, Arita, Chuldum and Kami finished the last of their packing. I had insisted that we abandon everything except our sleeping-bags. The clouds had cleared, leaving a bright but windy day. I guessed from previous experience on the South Col that we would be out of the worst of the wind by the time we dropped off the end of the Geneva Spur down to C3. Everyone was moving slowly from exhaustion so I had plenty of time to pull out the fixed rope that lay buried under the snow drifts. From our vantage point at 1.5 kilometres above the Western Cwm I could see the entire length of the Cwm and I noticed some movement down near C2—small black dots moving up towards C3. At about this same time our Sherpa team overtook us and continued down to C3 and later to C2, all in amazingly good spirits now that we were heading down.

The Yellow Band is the last obstacle before reaching C3 and it involved a number of short abseils to reach the bottom. Here I let the others pass so I could wait for Frank, who was the last in our line. Stuart and I shared a small rocky ledge, both of us clipped in to the same anchor, waiting for the rope to clear below us before Stuart began his abseil. Here he told me the incredible news. Beck was alive at C4! I learnt that the partially covered body I had found in the tent was Beck. Pete and Todd were bringing him down. Stuart abseiled away from me shortly after this, leaving me deeply upset and shaken. I was standing in roughly the same place where I had been cleaned up by the avalanche in 1991; even when you are used to it, it is still a dizzying fall from all that way to the valley floor. Luck had been with me then as it had been with me during the last two terrible days, but now as the missing pieces gradually fell in place, I was regretting surviving at all. Stuart's reaction was one of relief and happiness that Beck had miraculously survived; I was grateful too, but I also felt a deep sense of failure: I had helped Beck all that way down the mountain but in the ensuing complications had failed to bring him home. In the isolation of my airy ledge, I hoped for another avalanche to sweep me away.

My initial reaction was to show that I truly cared by waiting for Beck and helping him down, but below me, strung out on the fixed rope, were the remaining members of our team, all treading a fine line between safety and carelessness due to exhaustion. As the only surviving guide, my responsibility remained with them as I knew Beck was in the excellent hands of Todd and Pete.

I found out later that Beck had stumbled into C4 around 5.00 p.m. on 11 May. He recounted later that he had woken from some sort of reptilian sleep, decided he was not going to die and started to crawl into the wind, the only way he could keep a sense of direction. When alerted to Beck's arrival Todd and Pete attended to his immediate needs. I was not told of Beck's miraculous appearance and I can only assume that it was because of my condition at the time and they did not want to burden me with the added responsibility. On reflection I believe they had my best interests in mind.

———————

If there were ever such a thing as a ghost town in the mountains, our C3 was it. I sat between the two tents that once accommodated Rob and Doug in one and Andy, Yasuko and myself in the other, and felt desolate. The others had continued down to C2. As I rummaged through the personal belongings in our tent, I was overwhelmed by the haunting memories of the once friendly chatter that filled the air between the tents that sat so precariously on this narrow ledge. Andy, Yasuko and I had shared this tent on more than one occasion. Andy and I had even planned our next climbing trip from this very tent, and I got to see the funny side of Yasuko as we tried to trick her with English jokes, only to find out that she understood everything we said. I prised my personal belongings from the pool of ice that had formed in the floor of our once happy home. I freed Andy's jacket from the ice and absent-mindedly turned to pass it out the door to him before I remembered. This had become our normal packing procedure—someone inside passing various belongings through the door to the other to be packed into a different rucksack. By the time I was finished I had respectfully folded two neat piles of gear: one for Yasuko and one for Andy; these would be collected later.

We may have arrived at BC in April as a dozen different teams and a multitude of nationalities, but on 12 May there were no such barriers to keep us apart as everyone who could came up from C2 to help us down. From within a group of Sherpas and climbers who had climbed up the base of the Lhotse Face came a voice. 'Hello, Michael *Dai*. Let me take your pack.' It was Nima, a cook boy whom I had employed ten years before but who had now risen to the rank of a climbing Sherpa. I remembered how terribly sick he was then with altitude sickness. I had fetched a cup of tea for him from our kitchen tent and, with two or three Aspros, managed to offer some relief for his throbbing headache. It was the least I could do. For the remainder of the expedition he was extremely grateful. Back then he used to call me 'Michael *Sahib*'; now 'Michael *Dai*', which means 'Brother Michael'—a little less formal but equally respectful.

Nima eased my heavy pack from my shoulders and sat me down. Lou and Jon were there too, but the others had continued down to C2. We sipped tea silently, while the reception party rearranged our packs to carry down to C2.

'More tea, *Dai*?' asked Nima, who was offering me more than my fair share. Too exhausted to talk, I declined with an open palm.

By now it was a perfect day at 6500 metres on Everest. It was warm enough to strip down to our thin first layer. Only the jet-stream winds, 2 kilometres above us and still thundering across the summit, gave any hint of the harshness of our environment. Nima told me to take it slowly; he would look after everything now, even though he was employed by another expedition. I had no choice but to walk slowly as my feet were driving me crazy with the pain of frostbite and the usual bruising from over-activity. All I had to do was follow the relatively easy terrain down to C2.

Our large mess tent at C2 had now turned into a MASH unit to deal with the injured climbers who had come down from C4. I had not seen most of the climbers who maintained this service on the mountain before this day. I was attended to immediately and the news was not good. I was close to tears when one of the doctors told me I could lose more of my feet. Another 10 millimetres off each foot and it would be impossible to walk again. Although the true extent of my frostbite injuries was not yet known, the doctor was preparing me for the worst. He gently cleaned my feet and wrapped them in bandages, and I was then carried to my tent where I started on a course of circulation-improving drugs and an injection of pain relief that made me so drowsy I slept for the remainder of the day. This was exactly what the doctors wanted: to keep me off my feet for as long as possible to prevent further damage. The climbers who came to our aid took care of everything, including caring for the needs of the remaining members of our team. Their labour was tireless and sympathetic.

It was just on nightfall when I was woken by a ruckus in our mess tent next door. Beck had arrived and room was being made for him among the other injured climbers and medical supplies. I leaned on one elbow and listened through the walls of the tent; I would have disregarded the doctor's orders to stay off my feet to go and see him if I hadn't been tied to a drip and felt too dizzy to stand. John, who was sharing a tent with me, went over immediately to see if he could lend a hand. He returned later to say that Beck looked terrible but was in remarkably good spirits, considering his injuries that consisted of serious frostbite to his face, hands and feet. Occasionally I could hear his cheery Southern accent and, like me, he would have been in some sort of morphine haze.

My conscious state passed quickly to the morning of 13 May. I tried to remain patient as it took considerable time and energy to squeeze my painfully swollen feet into my boots using aching frostbitten fingers. More than any-thing I wanted to see Beck; John had warned me he didn't look good but I wanted to confirm for myself that the cheery spirit I had heard last night was really Beck. I was not to be disappointed. Although at first it was hard to recognise him, as his face was swollen and black from frostbite, I hoped a lot of it was superficial. There was nothing superficial about his hands; they were in a shocking state. Privately I gave little hope for his fingers. I felt awkward and compelled to offer some explanation for what had happened but a brief and interrupted chat was all we could manage as people pushed past in a rush to get him and an equally seriously frostbitten Taiwanese climber ready to move further down the mountain. We were all heading down to BC that day and various more able climbers from other expeditions were joining in to help get Beck and the Taiwanese climber down to the top of the Icefall, where they hoped to rendezvous with what would be the world's highest helicopter rescue.

I said goodbye to Beck. It was simple but heartfelt with none of the usual intoxicated BC or Kathmandu parties to soften the sadness of our disbandment as a team. I particularly thanked all the climbers who had lent a hand to Beck, my team-mates and me. I was given another injection for pain; it was just enough to take the edge off it and still leave some feeling in my feet. Too much and I would be away with the fairies while going through the Icefall and that was an area where I wanted to be as alert as possible. Despite the easy passage through the Icefall this season, it was still not the place to take any chances and therefore I was prepared to tolerate a lot of discomfort.

In a little over an hour since leaving Beck I stood among the towering pillars of ice in the upper reaches of the Icefall to watch Beck's helicopter labour under the heavy influence of the altitude. It reminded me of one exhausted climber going to the rescue of another. It also reminded me of John Coulton's and my experience waiting for a helicopter near Kangchenjunga and I knew how Beck would be feeling right now—anxious, exhausted and useless and maybe even regretting ever wanting to climb Everest. He would be fed up with everything and all his hopes would be focusing on the helicopter making the pick-up and getting him home. Pain, if it existed at this early stage, would be under control by his medical aids. Lots more memories came flooding back, none more memorable than my father's remark when he found out I was returning to Kangchenjunga for the second time. It was like daring 'to pull the tiger's tail twice. You're bound to get caught one day.' This time the tiger had bitten back hard and I would be scarred forever. How many more times would I gamble my life? I came to the conclusion that the key to this game of high-altitude climbing is to quit while you are in front and to resist the temptation to go back for just one more climb, but I know that will not be possible.

On 14 May 1996 I sat on a large rock about fifteen minutes walk below BC. A large dose of morphine had helped to get me here and now I stared dumbly in a narcotic daze at the large area of flat rocks that I had so meticulously levelled four weeks earlier so a helicopter could pick up one of the Sherpas who was seriously injured when he fell into a crevasse. Now it was my turn to be air-lifted out as the doctors had warned me that to walk on my re-frostbitten feet could do irreparable damage. With the exception of my fingers, no visible signs of frostbite had appeared and I could not understand the tremendous amount of pain in my feet. Although it was only a short time since they were frozen, they looked OK from the outside, but it can take a little while for the true extent of the injury to show. I was not

going to take any chances. Beck had been flown out the
day before; today there would be two landings by the same
helicopter as it shuttled people down to a more suitable
collection point in the valley before taking us all together
back to Kathmandu. I would be on the second flight out.
Although Beck's rescue the day before had been 600
metres higher it had never been attempted before and it
will always remain something out of the ordinary. Base
Camp is at the maximum level of altitude for a helicopter
landing and there are only a couple of hours during each
morning at BC when the cold air is dense enough to support an incoming helicopter. Any later than 10.00 or 11.00
a.m. and the air would be too warm and therefore not
dense enough to support a landing helicopter at this critical
altitude. Because of this tight limit in flying time the first
flight also collected the body of a Taiwanese climber who
had fallen from C3. The accompanying climbers had to
scramble in over the top of the tarpaulined body and I was
thankful to be on the second lift. It took twenty minutes
for the helicopter to return for me and I took shelter
behind the large rock I had been sitting on. This time the
helicopter flew in large decreasing circles around BC. I was
puzzled by this expensive waste of time. When it circled
closer I looked up, anxiously wanting it to land, only to
look straight into the barrel of a TV camera. As the helicopter flew back down the valley it did not dawn on me
what had happened, but Helen, who had accompanied me
to the helipad, was more attuned to the situation: news
crews were trying to get into BC to do interviews. There
was a standing arrangement among the various expeditions

at BC that a 'No comment' response was to be given to any news crews silly enough to fly straight up to 5300 metres without acclimatisation. We guessed a TV cameraman, on a mission to get footage for his network, probably offered more money to the pilot than my US$2500 ticket out of BC, showing no regard for the sick and injured climbers desperate for urgent medical help. Fortunately morphine has a remarkably calming effect and I trudged wearily back up to BC with a furious Helen.

Another helicopter was ordered for the next morning and this time John was going to come with me in case I needed further assistance to get home. In the meantime, Caroline had found a suitable alternative to the mind-numbing morphine, so that I could be more aware of what was going on around me. I was also deeply embarrassed by the trouble which Helen and Caroline were taking to get me home, but I knew that if I lost as little as 10 millimetres more off each foot, I would never be able to return to the mountains again. Overwhelmed by depression I hid in my tent.

———————

Like the morning before, it was another early start. I had little confidence that I would be out of BC that day as I limped down to the helipad. Helen and Guy Cotter helped carry our gear. Guy and his team-mates Dave Hiddleston and Chris Jillet, in a selfless act, had given up their Pumori expedition to come up to our BC to help deal with the drama that was unfolding on 10 May. They were now doing the job that I was meant to do, packing up BC and returning with the members to Kathmandu. For half an

hour I strained to hear the chatter of an incoming helicopter—it was depressingly silent and the helicopter was
late, but once it came there was no time for prolonged
goodbyes to all those that had helped. They deserved more
consideration on my part but before I knew it John and I
were in the helicopter and off to Kathmandu.

A little over an hour later we had landed in Kathmandu
and under the umbrella of the spinning rotor blades milled
a pack of hungry journalists. I could see there was no escape
and I prepared myself to face international interrogation.
When the door slid open I couldn't believe my eyes: there
was Nima, my erstwhile friend who has been my agent in
Nepal for the last ten years. He guarded the opening with
outstretched arms before jumping up to greet me. His hug
was short, his actions urgent. 'Follow me, Michael. Do not
stop to talk to these people.' I could see no escape for us as
John followed. I was pushed and poked from all directions
and surrounded by the usual media weaponry of micro-
phones, lights and cameras. I was bombarded with questions and the most vexing was, 'Do you have any photos of
the dead? I will give you a good price.' Nima pulled harder
than the rest and dragged me towards an approaching
minibus. In the crowd of thirty or forty journalists I had
noticed a dark-haired woman, who looked comparatively
unthreatening but my manners had long disappeared in
response to the aggressive crowd. As she homed in on me,
hustling to get beside me, I lined her up for a hard elbow in
the ribs—the fate of some equally aggressive journalists a
second or two before. But before I could swing into action,
Nima had hauled me into the bus. The woman doggedly

jumped in beside me. Pushed beyond the limits of my patience, I turned to serve her the full strength of my anger, but found myself defending the windows from journalists outside. John had only one foot in the bus, when Nima turned to the driver and shouted, 'Go!'

'Hello, Michael. My name is Claire. I'm assistant to the Australian Ambassador here in Kathmandu. I'm here to help you get out of the country without too much trouble from the media. Unless, of course you want to speak to the media!' It was good to hear an Australian voice and I suddenly felt I was almost home.

———

Twenty-four hours after leaving BC I really was home, still wearing the same stinking clothes from BC. This rapid return to the real world made it feel like the past few days on Everest had been nothing more than a surreal nightmare. I allowed myself to get sucked into this pretend world for a little longer, knowing full well that I would have to deal with reality sooner or later. The next day I was off to the doctor for an injection of morphine. Some worrying patches of black had started to grow in size on the ends of my feet and fingers, but thankfully time would eventually heal all the new frostbite injuries.

———

Not a day has gone by since when I haven't stopped to think about the events and the friends who died. When I returned home I was convinced that everything humanly possible was done to save the lives of our friends and

team-mates. But with the passing of time memories of the
appalling conditions we endured fade: the incredible cold
that caused crippling exhaustion, the sting of that relentless
wind, and zero visibility. As these images grow dimmer
with time, I have started to ask myself the question, 'Could
I have done more to save lives?', 'What if I had done this
or that?', 'What if …?' I have experienced the same and
worse conditions on other climbs, but never with such
tragic results. When I first arrived at BC in April 1996 our
team was one of a dozen teams attempting Everest from
the Nepal side of the mountain. A record number of permits had been issued by the Ministry of Tourism in
Kathmandu that season and I said to John as we surveyed
the construction of a small tent city from our higher vantage point at BC, 'With this number of climbers on the hill
this season, there is bound to be at least half a dozen who
won't be going home.' Perhaps it was a premonition of
events to come, but I think not. I am sure John assumed I
was referring to the members of the other teams, making
the classic assumption that it always happens to someone
else. I know I was.

In Everest's long history, 10 May 1996 will go down as
a disastrous day. So much for our lucky date of the 10th.

Six months later it was an eerie feeling returning to
Kathmandu and Nepal. I led my trekking group quickly
past the restaurants, not daring to look in the window at
those familiar tables and chairs where our Everest team had
previously enjoyed a cheerful meal before heading into

Everest. Around each corner I half-expected to see Rob walking my way with hands tucked into the pockets of his jeans, or Doug and Andy doing their last-minute shopping. I phoned home a lot during those three weeks in Nepal as Judi was pregnant with our first child—due on 10 May.

THE MISSING LINK: MAKALU 1999

chapter 14

Note: Dotted line indicates that our route was actually in the valley on the other side of the ridge.

The thought of climbing Makalu, the last of the Big Five, was always on my mind since failing to do so in 1993 and 1995. In 1995 I didn't even get to set foot on the mountain. Veikka Gustafsson and I had just climbed Lhotse, the fourth highest, and were due to fly by helicopter to Makalu BC with Rob Hall and Ed Viesturs, but half my right thumb was black from frostbite—a legacy of our Lhotse ascent. I pulled out of the Makalu climb because I didn't want to risk losing my right thumb, and the other three went on to climb Makalu on 17 May 1995. Sadly, Lhotse was the last climb Veikka and I did as partners—not because of any ill feeling, but Veikka wanted to climb all fourteen 8000-metre peaks, a quest that I had no interest in. I think it is reasonable for me to say that having climbed the four highest and the sixth highest without oxygen, I could, granted the time, money and good weather, go on to climb the remainder. Climbing the top five, which stand head and shoulders above the rest, was a worthwhile mountaineering challenge without getting bogged down in the enormous resources needed to climb all the 8000-metre peaks—a process that had become all too familiar. I preferred to try something that would continue to challenge my climbing skills. Because of my feet, I had stayed away from the small technical peaks and Big Wall climbing where you really do have to use your feet, but with the help of some special boots, this type of climbing was now looking possible.

Every time I fly into Kathmandu, the spectacular view from the windows on the right-hand side of the plane, reminds me that I have a missing link in my mountaineering career. Lined up in a neat and impressive row from east to west are Kangchenjunga then Makalu, Lhotse, Everest and Cho Oyu. All of them are shimmering giants atop the blue-purple haze of the Teria, the lowlands of Nepal, barely 70 metres above sea level. If I were going to climb Makalu then I wanted to do it in the year that I turned 40—1999 was that year.

It was 10 May and my dark coloured tent at BC absorbed the midday heat more than most tents. It was not a depressing heat but one that slowly sent me into a deep cozy sleep. Before falling asleep I had been unable to satisfy my hunger and was snacking continuously on whatever I could find—a symptom of being up on the hill for the last few days. That must have triggered the dream I was having about the lack of food on the Annapurna II climb, reliving the mental torture of being continuously hungry. On that climb, gluggy stodge had been the normal fare when we had any. I had learnt it was no use dreaming or talking about more desirable food or about the first meal that I would order when returning to civilisation. I learnt to be satisfied with whatever food we had. A full tummy is a contented tummy.

'Hey Mike, lunch is ready,' a voice said.

My dream shifted to Maila, our cook for Annapurna II, cooking up a storm of rice and lentils in the kitchen tent. Onchu, the expedition clown, was helping out by adding a few rodent droppings as extra condiments to a plate of tomato sauce, salt and pepper.

'Mike, lunch is ready.'

I woke up, and there at the entrance to my tent was Lincoln Hall. He politely apologised for waking me but the food was ready. The coat that I had used as a pillow was stuck to my right cheek and I quickly snatched it away. My mind raced. Seeing Lincoln after dreaming about Annapurna II had me momentarily concerned that I really was back on that mountain in 1983, then I realised it was just a dream.

Lincoln waited while I put on my boots. He asked about the clothing I had planned to wear between CI and C2, what personal equipment I would be taking, and would I climb from BC to C1 or BC to C2 in the same day? Sixteen years ago on Annapurna II, it had been me who had asked these questions. Sixteen years ago I had been the cub of the wolf pack. As we ambled over to the mess tent, it dawned on me that my climbing career had just turned full circle. Over two decades ago I had stood in awe of Lincoln and his climbing achievements. After my father's advice to learn from the best mountaineers that I had access to, my initial contact with Lincoln and Tim Macartney-Snape had been somewhat hesitant, believing they were beyond approach. I had been pleasantly surprised. Now in 1999 on Makalu we were climbing as friends and equals.

There were only four of us left at BC by early May. There had originally been eight climbers plus two American film crew and one Australian cameraman, but all of them had left because of other commitments or ill health. The four who remained were Lincoln Hall, Dave Bridges, Bob Sloezen and me. Dave and I were the founding members of the expedition, with Dave putting together the American contingent and a great deal of the climbing equipment and food, while I organised the Aussie climbers. Dave and I had built up a great friendship while climbing on K2 in 1994, and it was our personal ambition to climb Makalu that had started this expedition eighteen months earlier.

Both Lincoln and Bob were last-minute additions to the team. A chance meeting with Lincoln the previous August had planted the Makalu seed in his brain, but it wasn't until the end of January 1999 that he could finally commit to coming. For me it was one of the highlights to be climbing with Lincoln again after all these years. Bob, on the other hand was a regular climbing partner of Dave's in Aspen, Colorado. He was to have been on another expedition to search for George Mallory's body on the North Ridge of Everest but due to circumstances way beyond his control he suddenly found himself without an expedition. Dave did not have to do much talking to get Bob to join our team in the last couple of weeks before our departure.

Lunch that day was excellent by high-altitude standards. Rhatna, who has been with me on every trek and expedition to Nepal for the last eight years, had prepared an excellent meal—lots of potato chips with fried rice and fried tinned meat. We did our best to hide the taste of the meat with copious amounts of mustard and tomato sauce. This was followed by Rhatna's specialty—a freshly baked cake.

We all agreed that despite a number of the team leaving a couple of days earlier, we were delighted that it was now just the four of us. We had not been comfortable with the original size of the team, but it had been necessary because the cost of climbing in Nepal has skyrocketed over the years. To climb a mountain the size of Makalu there needed to be a team of eight to ten climbers to help absorb the tremendous cost. As it would turn out, the reduction of the team would work in our favour, bringing the four of us closer together.

This was my third expedition with Lincoln, but it had been sixteen years since the last. During these long years he had been drawn to the Buddhist religion. My first impression of Lincoln had been of someone with a very caring sense for others and an easy-going manner. Following the beliefs of Buddhism had only enhanced these qualities. He had also become a successful writer, and his quick wit and use of words made his sense of humor and 'pardon the pun' expressions a welcome part of everyday life on an expedition.

But Lincoln's laid-back affair with life could also get him into a little trouble, particularly with respect to time. We had called a meeting at BC to discuss our climbing plans. Lincoln was already late as he casually strolled over to the 'Throne Room', our spacious pit toilet which was covered by a small tent. He had been in there for some time when someone, becoming impatient, picked up a rock and threw it at the toilet tent. It was meant to be a gentle reminder that we were waiting, but it was thrown with such unintentional force that if it hit the tent it would surely hurt Lincoln, maybe even knock him out and he would fall into the pit. Fortunately the rock ricocheted harmlessly past the entrance of the tent. I expected Lincoln to not take this incident lightly and waited nervously for an angry response. A few silent seconds passed, then Lincoln, still squatting, poked his head from the tent and said, 'Hey, fellows, I could be here some time. Why don't you bring your chairs up here and we can have the meeting here.' We all fell about laughing—so much so that some of us needed to join him.

Compared with Lincoln and Bob at forty-two and forty-six and me at almost forty, Dave, at twenty-eight, was the baby of our team and had the energy to go with it. His inner stength had improved dramatically in the four years since K2 and his enthusiasm to climb Makalu was infectious. Some of it rubbed off on me, which was just as well because my motivation had waned considerably in the past couple of years.

Bob warned me when I first met him in Kathmandu that he was not called 'The Slow Man' for nothing. The nickname was hardly appropriate because, as a professional mountain guide for eighteen years, he had learned that by setting a slow pace, he was able to keep on going and rarely stopped for a rest. With so many years of climbing and guiding, he had his fair share of horror stories to tell. Like his climbing, he was slow to start but once he got going, he never stopped. For most people, they were riveting stories but on more than one occasion I had to politely excuse myself from the mess tent when some of them became all too familiar. I could get altitude sickness or frostbite just listening to his experiences. At first Bob thought he had offended me, until I explained that through the telling of his epics, I relived some of my own. Some of my epics I would rather forget. Nevertheless we already had a great mutual respect for each other's climbing ability as between us we had five ascents of Everest and nine of the other 8000-metre peaks. Between the four of us we had a collection of something like forty to fifty expeditions. But there was something that separated Dave and Bob from Lincoln and me—we both had wives and children. Dave seemed to be in a steady relationship, but Bob was considered a reasonable bivouac by many ladies. For Lincoln and me, the increased responsibility of having families meant we would accept a much lower level of risk than in the days we shared on Annapurna II. Despite this difference we made a strong and happy team.

On the mountain, the four of us had taken a physical and psychological beating at the hands of Makalu's sledge-hammer winds and bad weather. For Dave and me, the hammering had been twice as severe. On 2 May, Dave and I were in a position to make an early summit attempt and establish the way for the rest of our team. This was before the sudden departure of half our team and the film crew. We set up our high camp at 7600 metres, leaving an 800-metre ascent to the summit. By 9.30 p.m. we had given up hope of the summit, as jet-stream winds had returned, transforming our haven into an icy hell. Throughout the night, tent poles quivered and buckled at abnormal angles, tent fabric stretched as tight as a drum skin on one side, while on the other it flapped like a flag.

Next morning, we fought intense cold and jet-stream winds to dismantle our pathetically small tent. Dave hovered over the hole I was digging in the snow, ready to throw the rolled up tent in, but I was going to be some time; I was going to bury this miserable excuse for a tent and the memories that went with it as deeply as possible.

'I won't be coming back here,' I said as I threw the last rock onto the cairn that marked our tent and the memorial to our first summit attempt. I just wanted to get out of there and down to the warmth and comfort of BC. The cold had seeped deep into my bones, and this terrible wind was tugging annoyingly at every inch of my clothing.

But we were back on the mountain a few days later, after we had said goodbye to those who had chosen to leave. Bob, Lincoln, Dave and I had sheepishly returned to the mountain, not yet trusting the Makalu weather. We did not get very far. During 7 and 8 May, heavy snowfall and high winds prevented us from climbing above C2. Again the long hours of inactivity while lying in a small tent for two stormy days nearly drove me crazy. Fortunately, there were some funny stories to be told, and the moments of happiness shared in difficult situations were priceless. However, there is only so much two people can talk about in the confines of a storm-lashed mountain tent before it becomes boring. Silent conversations in your head can become self-defeating—places you would rather be and food you would rather eat are definitely taboo subjects. On the morning of 9 May, I had to do something, go up or go down. There was a clear blue sky but the remnants of the previous day's storm lay in the valleys below Makalu like a thick prickly carpet. Dave and I were at last outside our tent, dressed in our down suits ready to head up, with Lincoln and Bob following and carrying a light load of food and fuel to our high camp for their summit attempt which was to follow ours. Returning to C2 after the day's carry was their preferred option as they felt the need for further acclimatisation time before spending a night at C3. But there was a sudden movement of air around the mountain, clouds were starting to rise, the weather was changing again. Dave and I looked at each other for an answer. Bob and Lincoln returned to their tent to shelter from the wind. I raked the snow with the points of my crampons, but the answer was not there, it was 1.4 kilometres above our heads. The flags of jet-stream cloud had been hoisted high on Makalu's summit. 'Don't even bother climbing higher,' it said.

We dithered with indecision for a few more minutes but it soon began to snow. We all descended, weary and despondent at having failed again.

'Could I come back up here again?' I asked myself. My aching feet said no.

'This is not the time or the place to make an important decision like that,' I thought, silently berating myself for such a hasty decision. 'Wait until you've had a few days rest at BC.'

If it wasn't for our 400 metres of fixed rope hanging immediately beneath C2, we would have been forced to stay at C2. Every step that I took down the ropes, I pushed a small powder avalanche ahead of me. Loose snow from the storm lay on a foundation of polished blue ice and, worst of all, a large catchment area lay above us. We wasted no time getting back to BC, concentrating solely on speed and changing our abseil device at the anchor points.

'When Lincoln and I go back up, we're going to C1 instead of all the way to C2 in a single day. It's too long a day and I personally don't have the motivation or the energy to continue upwards the next day,' said Bob in a manner that indicated no amount of persuasion could change his mind. The mess tent was silent for a few seconds. I chased some chips around my plate with my fork, contemplating Bob's decision. I wanted to agree. My feet were telling me too—they could not take another marathon effort by climbing to C2 in a single day—but my mountaineering mind said it was still the best option to capitalise on the short spells of good weather that had been occurring.

'So, Mike, how do you feel about going back up in a day or two?' asked Dave.

'We've only just come down and you're already talking of going back up. I'll need a few days just for my feet to recover and, secondly, we're not getting the breaks in weather. We need to see some real sign the weather is settling, otherwise we'll just be bashing our heads against a brick wall.' Everyone nodded in agreement.

Dave was keen, too keen. I knew that it was going to take

a great deal more patience than strength to climb Makalu while the weather still seemed to be all over the place.

'Mike, I know you are used to getting up these mountains by 10 May. Now that we've passed that date, you're probably feeling a little lost and don't know what to do,' said Dave with a cheeky grin. Dave was partly right, I was used to going home at around this time in May and that's what I desperately wanted to do. For years people have asked where I got the motivation to reach such lofty heights. I thought it was a natural urge to achieve worthwhile goals. But now I had been finding it hard—hard on my feet and hard to keep coming up with the same drive needed to get up and down these big mountains safely. I missed Judi and Harry.

That afternoon I fell into a bout of depression and hid in my tent. I was on the verge of packing when I was saved by a phone call from Judi. I have had only one other like it and that was on K2 after what was my second failed summit attempt. Demoralised and exhausted then, I used Rob Hall's satellite phone to call Judi and tell her I was on my way home.

'So you should have a long rest and try again in a few days,' she said. These were not the words of sympathy that I had been looking for.

'You've done so much to get to K2 it would be a pity not to give it your best shot and in years to come regret not doing so.' She knew that I had it in me to keep trying K2 until the season and the weather changed. I just needed to be reminded.

Judi said the same sorts of things to me about this climb.

She added that everything was fine at home, Harry was well and growing fast. Wilbur, the Corgi, had taken up his usual position as the man and guardian around the house while I was away. In other words everything was in its normal expedition mode, nothing had changed, there was no need to hurry home. 'I know how much you want to climb Makalu. You're on the verge of achieving your mountaineering ambition. Don't throw it all away by coming home too early,' were her final words. As has often been the case, an outside influence had inspired me to continue. And so 10 May 1999 had become another memorable anniversary and a turning point in this expedition. I had been trying hard all day to think only of the positive things that had happened on this day in 1990, 1993 and 1996. The phone call with Judi had kick-started my motivation to climb Makalu and put a bounce back into my step. There is no doubt in my mind that every step I take on every mountain Judi climbs with me, if only in spirit. She can sense my highs and lows, the effects of bad weather, and of frustration, exhaustion and aching feet. She knows when I have had enough and when it's time to come home. She knows me better than I know myself sometimes.

For the next couple of days, jet-stream winds blew across the upper part of the mountain with relentless monotony. On the morning of 13 May it was calm. How long it would stay like this we hadn't a clue. We had experienced a couple of calm days early in the month but they did not run consecutively, nor did the window of opportunity last much longer than twelve hours. We had an early breakfast and discussed the possibility of another summit attempt and wondered if the weather would hold for a three or four day spell.

'This yo-yoing up and down the mountain, trying to catch the weather, is getting to me, but I would feel better if we were doing something. We can either sit here and wait for a more settled spell or we can chance it that today is the start of something good and it will continue for a few more days,' said Dave. Although Bob, Lincoln and I could have used another rest day, and we felt like waiting for a more positive sign of good weather, we all knew from our experience of the last few weeks that a prolonged period of calm weather was unlikely. Our best chance of success would be to sit and wait at C2 for one of the summit days to appear and try and make the most of this opportunity. It was a unanimous decision that another summit attempt would start today although we had serious doubts about the weather holding for the duration. But at least we were doing something.

There was one problem, Dave and I were going to separate from Bob and Lincoln. We were going to climb to C2 in one day while the others had a more leisurely day planned to C1. My feet and body preferred the C1 option as it was less tiring, and I enjoyed the company of everyone and could draw on their motivation in time of need. However, I felt the best chance of success was to climb straight to C2 and be in position to continue should the weather hold, or more likely, be forced to wait for a brief calm and make a dash to the summit. I had to follow my gut feeling. Dave and I packed quickly for the long climb to C2 while Bob and Lincoln could afford to leave for C1 after an early lunch. As Bob and Lincoln wished us the very best of luck, I was aware that, despite separating, we could end up on the same timetable thanks the unpredictability of the jet-stream winds.

It was a rare perfect day high on Makalu as Dave and I climbed towards C2. The calm above brought a newfound inspiration, an air of excitement that made me dizzy. 'Maybe we'll get up this thing,' I thought. We could not help but be happy and confident. There was no other place we would rather have been. Dave arrived at C2 at 3.30 p.m. When I arrived fifteen minutes later he was no longer happy, and he soon showed me why. A small opening in the tent door had let in a large amount of storm-driven snow. This had melted, forming a pool of water in the floor of our tent in which various items of down clothing and sleeping bags were now soaking. With every cup full of water Dave ladled from our tent poured a torrent of swearing. We cleaned up the mess as best we could and started our dinner. Above 7000 metres Dave and I knew we would not eat very much, and in preparation for this we had brought chapattis and boiled potatoes, precooked by Rhatana at BC, to mix in with our freeze-dried food for one last meal before going high.

Looking west from the door of our tent I could see Everest and Lhotse about 20 kilometres away, sitting peaceful and calm in a pink and purple glow of the late evening sun. It was not the best view of these great mountains, but even a rear-end view could not hide their immense height and a lifetime worth of memories. The prevailing winds brought voices from the past—the laughter of our BC parties, summit celebrations, or sharing a humorous situation high on the mountain. In clear view were mountaineering landmarks, the precarious summit of Lhotse that Veikka and I were not game to stand on, the South Col, the South Summit, the Hillary Step, and I could see myself taking those final steps onto the summit of Everest six years ago. As I closed the door, all thoughts of the past faded away immediately and I was struck by more pressing thoughts: what would tomorrow bring?

At 9.30 p.m. the tent started to rattle with the arrival of the wind. For most of the night it was just an irritating noise that kept us awake as the tent wrestled with the wind, but by morning it was Dave and I who were doing the wrestling as we struggled to keep our tent in one piece. By mid-morning the wind had eased, with the occasional rogue gust surprising us. Cloud rose from the valley below and it started to snow. Radio contact with Lincoln and Bob at C1 revealed that conditions were equally grim there. We resolved to sit it out for the day in our respective camps, but by late afternoon conditions had deteriorated and we suffered one of our worst nights on the mountain.

It was daylight at 4.30 on the morning of 15 May after our second night without sleep, and our mood matched the ugliness of the weather.

'What do you want to do, Mike? Stay here another night or head down?' asked Dave.

'I don't know but if we do go down I won't be coming back up,' I said.

'Yes you will, I know you better than that,' was Dave's reply.

We flipped back and forth for the next hour, trying to make a decision. Lincoln and Bob had made theirs, they were heading down. At 9 a.m. Dave had to answer a call of nature and confronted the chaos outside. Before he had re-entered the tent he called to me with a hint of excitement in his voice. 'It's clearing, Mike. The cloud is lifting with patches of blue sky everywhere and the horizon is clear too. Have a look and see what you think.'

I knelt at the door and peered around the corner. 'We can't go up in this wind' I protested.

'And we can't go down if the weather is clearing. Look how much it's cleared in the last hour,' said Dave firmly.

The reality of what Dave had just said echoed in my head. He crawled back into the tent a real sight, with iced hair and clothing after his short ordeal with his daily oblu-tions. His eyes asked the question, 'So what do you want to do?' He let me dither in indecison and battle with my personal conflict. I had had enough of Makalu, and the last two days pinned down at C2 was the nail in the coffin. I was going home. We were only halfway to the summit, so we had a long and more difficult way to go. I could go home now reasonably happy after this third failed attempt, knowing I had given it a good try. But Dave's words were haunting me, 'We can't go down if the weather is clearing.' No truer words were said on the entire expedition.

'OK, Dave, let's go.'

'Where are we going, Mike ?'

'Up.'

The higher we climbed, the better the weather looked. Scrambling up the orange-brown granite rib below the

Makalu La took the points off my newly sharpened crampons, but I gained some satisfaction in dealing with this
section with considerably more ease than on our first foray.
Once we reached the Makalu La at 7400 metres we were
officially in Tibet for the last 1000 metres to the summit.
We rested for a few minutes, piecing together the jigsaw
puzzle of steep polished ice, the occasional patch of powder
snow and spurs of more orange granite. The blue ice was a
concern; the long and exposed slopes would be difficult to
climb and dangerous to descend. I normally look for solid
ground to climb, to conserve energy, but now I started to
piece together the patches of snow that would offer better
grip.

As I climbed one of these unavoidable ice slopes, I was
concentrating hard on my immediate footsteps, when I was
suddenly shocked back into the broader picture of where I
was. There at eye level, in a band of rocks just off to my left,
were the skeletal remains of a fellow climber. For a second
or two I was mesmerised by the stare of the hollow eyes
and the half-content, half-grimacing smile. The upper body
had been stripped bare of its clothing, exposing ribs and
vertebrae and showing the real velocity of the winds that
plagued this area. A number of possible names raced
through my head but the faded and torn clothing gave no
clues to the identity. Sitting semi-composed in the rocks,
the remains reminded me just how easy it is to be careless
with your life above 8000 metres. To sit down and never
get up.

At 4.30 p.m. we reached our final camp perched beneath
a sérac at 7800 metres. For a while I felt utterly defeated. I

blamed it on the need for sleep, which I longed for, as we faced our third sleepless night. Dave started the gas stove immediately. It would take at least a couple of hours of melting snow to fill water bottles and make cups of tea. I deliberated about tomorrow and fiddled with gear, stripping my pack of any unneccesary items. The weather had remained calm and cloudless all day and now, just on sunset, the horizon was perfectly clear and the tent gave only the occasional limp flutter. On any other occasion, with weather as good as this and with only 600 metres to reach the summit, I would have been extremely confident, but my feet had really taken a beating and with the lack of sleep I questioned whether I had the motivation and the energy to get out of my sleeping-bag at 2 a.m. Despite my uncertainty about tomorrow I snuggled in with a cup of tea and a muesli bar, completely comfortable with the thought of maybe having to return without reaching the summit. Perhaps I felt this way because I was already extremely content with my climbing career. On the other hand, I sensed Dave was battling with the nervous apprehension that I normally experienced on the eve of a summit attempt. He was certainly the most motivated of all of us to climb Makalu, his first 8000-metre peak. To help calm his anxiety, I tried to be as positive as I could about tomorrow without building up any false hope that we had it in the bag.

We should have slept soundly but high-altitude insomnia set in again. Between sunset and midnight I would have slept no more than forty-five minutes. Dave fared much the same. It took the usual two hours to make a cup of tea, put on boots and harnesses, and check that we had everything we needed for the day. Dave packed 30 metres of rope in case we needed it for the final summit pyramid which we had heard was difficult and dangerous. Above our camp we chose a steep diagonal traverse to the left up a hanging glacier and we followed a sloping ramp that had collected a reasonably stable bed of snow. Despite sometimes being knee-deep, it at least allowed safe upward progress compared with scratching around on steep blue ice in the dark. The moon offered no assistance and we relied totally on the circular beam of light cast by our headlamps. For the first hour-and-a-half we made good progress and I was able to maintain body heat. Even my feet were warm thanks to Dave giving me a pair of battery-heated foot pads. But how quickly things change—the batteries to my heat pads died and my feet turned to stone within minutes. The ramp that I had been following stopped abruptly at a wall of blue ice and we were faced with descending to find a way around this barrier. Dave, who was 30 metres below me, could see an opportunity off to the right, but from where I stood I did not share his optimism. Dave followed his lead until he disappeared from my view, and I waited to see if he would find a way up. Then I heard him double-shuffling his crampons for a more secure stance on hard ice. Repeated blows from his ice axe told me he was on difficult terrain. Dave returned.

'Blue ice everywhere over there. Do you think it will go over to the left?' asked Dave.

'Wait here while I have a look,' I replied. It was now 4.30 a.m. and the first hint of sunrise was appearing on the horizon. In this minimal light I followed a narrow band of snow barely half a metre wide, and thankfully darkness still hid the tremendous exposure below me. Seventy metres on I found a cleft in the ice wall and called back to Dave that this way would work. While Dave caught up, I poked around with my ice axe at the entrance, as I suspected crevasses in the area. With no evidence, I started up the line of weakness only to fall straight into a crevasse. Thankfully it was not deep, and my face, flushed with self-conscious-ness at my stupidity, poked above the hole. I complicated my awkward extraction by stubbornly refusing Dave's ice axe to pull on. I slumped on the surface desperately panting for breath, then I started to shiver; ice water was running down my arms and legs from the melting snow that had entered my climbing suit.

We were in the sun by 5.30 a.m. and for the next two hours we enjoyed its warmth. For a while the route was straightforward, a 45-degree snow slope leading to the base of a gully at 8100 metres that in turn lead to the rocky French Rib we would follow to the summit ridge. At this rate we would reach the summit around 10 a.m. I was hes-itant to enter this gully as it looked cold and gloomy due to the shadow cast by the French Rib. We intended to climb it quickly but discovered it was full of deep crusty snow. We longingly ploughed a trench towards the sun on the Rib, only to have our progress slowed even further by loose powder plastered on the rock and hiding all foot- and hand-holds. Had it been bare rock we would have made good progress, but time was flying by. At 10 a.m. the Summit Ridge was hidden behind an endless staircase of orange-red granite. Dave climbed with a tireless energy and motivation. I followed blindly.

Eleven o'clock passed with no sight of the Summit Ridge. Fifteen minutes later it appeared, as the angle of the French Rib tapered off to a gentle slope. At 8400 metres our climb turned to an amble along the Summit Ridge to the North Summit which we had to climb to reach the Main Summit. I glanced over the other side of the ridge and instantly recognised the valley we had walked up six weeks earlier. Until now we had enjoyed an uninterrupted view, but suddenly clouds were boiling up from both sides of the mountain and hiding the tremendous exposure. I baulked at the difficulty of climbing the North Summit until my practised eye could work out a safe route, but before I could do so, Dave started up. There was no talk of getting out the rope and I followed with complete confidence that Dave would not lead us into a blind corner. In places where the east side of the mountain met the west, a true razor's edge was formed, barely a couple of centimetres wide. I climbed this section with the ridgetop at eye level, so I could easily hang my heavily gloved left hand over the other side of the mountain. Luckily the ridgetop was ice, as solid as concrete, and I was able to hang most of my body weight off it to improve the grip of my feet which had been scratching for a better hold. Hand over hand, I shuffled up the ridge and over the North Summit to easier ground.

It was noon. Dave sat four or five metres above me. His grin told me where he was sitting. I could not let my thoughts wander as I encountered the same difficulties of the North Summit on the Main Summit. Suddenly Dave had a video camera pointing at me.

'You've made it, Mike.' I think he wanted to record a profound response but all I could do was slump down beside him. The real summit, the size of a small seat, lay between us and was too precarious to stand on. In fact, the summit was on top of a razor-sharp ice fluting where the four main ridges of Makalu meet in a single point. We could not move around to take better photos; instead, I drove my axe deep into ice and put my hand through the sling in case I slipped. I felt a warm and relaxed sense of satisfaction after all the weeks of frustration. We did not shake hands. That would wait until we had really made it, back at BC where the elation of our success would slowly start to sink in.

We sat in another world. By now a blanket of thick cloud covered everything below us. Only the last 100 metres of Makalu and an equal proportion of Everest, 20 kilometres to the west, rose above the cloud. Via radio, Dave relayed our success to Lincoln and Bob who had just arrived at C2. Lincoln asked to speak to me, but I was so absorbed with having finally made it, I found it difficult to think of something to say.

I suddenly remembered that I had a hitchhiker with me. In my pack was Harry's toy elephant, affectionately known as Eric the Elephant. Harry had been helping me pack for the expedition although it was more like unpacking. Every time I placed an item of gear into one of my kit bags Harry would take it out. I became very confused with what I was taking and what I was leaving behind. Some where along the line Harry, after chewing poor Eric's trunk off, had slipped him into my kit bag. It was not until I was unpacking at BC that I discovered Eric hiding in my kit bag, it was then that I decided he would remain with me for the rest of the climb. Eric made a brief appearance on the summit of Makalu.

After videoing and photographing each other, our concern for the difficulty of the descent forced us to start down after just a fifteen to twenty minute visit to the summit.

We arrived back at our high camp at 3 p.m after a twelve-and-half-hour day. During our pre-summit conversations, I had stressed the importance of continuing the descent as far as possible if time allowed. The desire to stop and rest is an overwhelming urge to fight, but I had been caught too many times at high camps by the sudden return of the jet-stream winds. That quandary caused a delay of thirty minutes as we sat in the snow outside our tent, staring in the direction we wanted to go but unable to do anything about it. During our descent from the summit we had only been able to cover 40 to 50 metres before falling into the snow for a long rest. We now had a difficult route to descend to reach C2, the last section involving some abseiling. In our current state of exhaustion, chances were high that we would not reach C2 until late that night. The weather looked stable, the clouds non-threatening, so we decided to stay where we were.

The next day, 17 May 1999, I started packing before the sun's rays had reached the tent, as we wanted to reach BC that day. I had enjoyed the rest and had even had a couple of hours of sleep. After just one cup of tea we broke camp and started down at 6.30 a.m. We had relayed our movements and intentions via radio to Lincoln and Bob at C2.

They were hoping to follow our trail to the summit. At 7.30 a.m. Dave and I stood at the top of a steep gully that dropped straight down to C1. We were intending to abseil this gully, although in doing so we would bypass Lincoln and Bob ascending from C2. By the time we reached C1 at 10 a.m. it was snowing and the upper part of the mountain had disappeared in cloud. We could hear the wind and thanked our lucky stars that we weren't still up there. The sudden and unpredictable change in the weather stopped Bob and Lincoln from leaving C2 but they were going to wait to see what tomorrow would bring. They deserved to reach the summit as much as we did and I wished for some luck to come their way.

I wanted to be at BC as soon as possible but my feet would not move any faster than a slow shuffle. With each step I felt as if I was standing on a bed of nails. 'You've overdone it this time, Groomy. You'll be lucky if you can walk back to Kathmandu.' Dave could not hear my self-talk but could sense it, and ordered me to hand over some of the weight I was carrying. Although my mental distress eased when we arrived at BC to the warm welcome of our BC staff, the pain continued. I found some relief in an injection of morphine and after a long lunch of chips and pizza I dozed in my tent, basking in a sense of inner peace, and experiencing the usual morphine itch.

The post-summit satisfaction continued into the next morning. It is not a fleeting sensation. In the past I have been on a high for six to twelve months after a great climb. It is one of the many reasons I continue to climb. Dave and I lounged in the warmth of our mess tent, the air thick with the smell of freshly brewed coffee. Rhatna served us a three-course breakfast including a reheated version of our Summit Cake which David and I had failed to finish the night before.

Our 8 a.m. radio call to Bob and Lincoln at C2 revealed they were not enjoying equal comforts. The winds had returned and the cloud level was already low on the mountain. So was their motivation, and it came as no surprise when Bob said they were coming down. After seven weeks on the mountain it was time to go home. Bob said they would be at BC by early afternoon and they would be bringing as much gear down as they could carry. Tshring and Rhatna had come to listen to the radio call, although I suspect Rhatna really came for the coffee. He loved the smell of brewed coffee, and the taste even more. He poured himself a cup and sat quietly in the corner listening to our radio calls.

Tshring said it would take four days to send one of kitchen boys down to round up the twenty-five porters he anticipated we would need to clear BC.

'Will this be enough time for you to pack, Dai?' Tshring asked. Packing meant going back up the hill to bring down all the gear, tents and ropes between BC and C2 as well as the accumulated mess of BC. Dave and I calculated that between the four of us climbers and Tshring and Bishnu, another of our very capable staff, we could clear the mountain in a single day. 'Don't worry, Mike, you won't have to come with us,' said Dave. He knew how much my feet were hurting and was offering me a reprieve from the arduous task of clearing the mountain. I thanked him for the offer.

Bob and Lincoln arrived at BC with heavy packs early in

the afternoon. Outwardly they seemed unaffected by their misfortune, but Bob was fighting an internal battle, coming down hard on himself for making decisions that, in hindsight, put them on a dead-end path to the summit. I felt powerless to console him. Fortunately, Bob's good humour returned quickly and we all sat drinking tea and laughing at some of the stupid and amusing events of the last seven weeks. Dave and I were careful not to gloat about our success. The remnants of our Summit Cake appeared on the table for the third time.

At 6.30 in the morning of 22 May it was cold. It had been our normal practice to rise when the sun hit BC but today we were leaving and there was much to do. Our porters had arrived the previous afternoon and our gear, including rubbish, was organised into 25 to 30 kilogram loads.

I had been speaking to Judi every three or four days via the satellite phone. She was delighted at our success and, more importantly, that we were all safe and coming home soon. At the beginning of the expedition Judi had taken an important booking for me to speak at a conference on 1 June. She had purposely avoided telling me until after the summit to give me an open-ended timetable. I could have easily cancelled the booking but to do so would have been harmful to my reputation as a reliable speaker, particularly this close to the date. Now, with a six-day walk to Tummingtar, another day to catch a flight to Kathmandu and two days to fly home, I would have to move quickly.

For the first three days I stayed with the main group on the walk out. The first day I was in misery, rock-hopping down the Barun Glacier. As I jumped from rock to rock, each step felt like a four-inch nail was piercing the ball of my foot. With no morphine left, I longed for a helicopter to take me out of my misery, but I knew what an anti-climax that would be, and I did not want to end this great climb that way. Some of the sting was taken out of the trek by the wonderful feeling of coming back down to earth. The air was so thick that it alone was enough to make you float along on a high. Yaks and goats grazed side by side in alpine fields and rhododendron forests were still in full bloom of yellow and red after a long spring. I had taken all of this for granted during the walk in, but now it was something special. The scenery changed around each corner as we continued our meteoric descent from BC at 5700 metres to Tummingtar at 450 metres, dropping nearly a vertical kilometre each day.

On the second day it started to rain. By the third it was torrential and there was no doubt in anyone's mind that the monsoon had started. Once thirsty cracks in the ground now oozed with water and the trail in places turned to bog. Our porters struggled with the increasing weight of their soaked loads and clothing; our kitchen staff laboured in the most appalling conditions to feed us. For almost twenty years I have admired the unshakeable cheerfulness of the local people and we could not help but become infected by their attitude. Even today, after so many journeys to other parts of the world, I still find Nepal offers the friendliest people as well as the most spectacular scenery.

The rain eased long enough on the third day for us to cross over the Shipton Pass at 4200 metres and drop down

to the village of Tashigoan and the beginning of rural Nepal.
Those who had straggled at the beginning of the day were
punished for the last two hours of the descent by the onset
of a torrential downpour. Even with the best rain gear, my
underclothes were soaked. At Tashigoan we did not even
contemplate putting up our tents, instead we moved into a
spacious lodge. Rhatna was on the prowl early and managed
to buy four chickens, and that night we sat down to fried
chicken, assorted roast vegetables and a cold beer. Despite
the rain, it was warm and for the first time in months we
were able to wear T-shirts and shorts. At times the rain was
so heavy on the iron roof it was difficult to make conversation. Tashigoan was still 2000 metres above the Teria and
the monsoon was in full force with lightning and thunder
every minute. The lightning came in handy for negotiating
a path past our sleeping staff, in various stages of contortion
on the verandah, for the inevitable midnight pee.

I left Tashigoan and the rest of the group at 6.30 a.m.
Tshring had selected three of the strongest porters to carry
my personal equipment and follow me in my quest to reach
Tummingtar for the flight to Kathmandu. We would have
to do four days of walking in two. The first few hours were
hot and humid, a sure sign that things were only going to
get wetter before day's end. I set my own pace that put me
well in front of my porters who stopped regularly for rests.
I was glad to be alone and I was comfortable with the
thought that I would meet them again at a pre-arranged
destination. With an abundance of red blood cells still in
my system, a farmland hill offers little challenge and I
walked with great ease past a gaggle of pale-faced trekkers

wheezing their way upwards. As I did so, I attracted the question 'Where have you come from?'

'Makalu Base Camp,' I replied.

'What were you doing there?' asked the English voice.

'Climbing Makalu,' I said.

'What were you doing a stupid bloody thing like that for,' asked the trekker. I had expected a more understanding response from my fellow trekkers and my only reply was 'See ya'.

By 1 p.m. I still had five hours of walking to go. I hadn't seen my porters all day. When it started to rain I didn't bother wearing my rain gear as it was still saturated from the day before. At first it had a cooling effect and washed away some of the grime from the last seven weeks, but when the trail crested a ridge, a chilling wind made me shiver. For hours I sloshed along the trail that had become a gutter for the water. As night came, I started to look for shelter under a tree or rock, but nothing looked promising. Thankfully I came to a couple of houses, but could find no-one. At the last house before the trail entered the forest, a little old lady stood at her window and beckoned me over. She asked me if I needed shelter and, with a great deal of effort, she climbed a rickety old ladder to show me the attic where there was a bed and a blanket. Ten minutes later there was a shout from downstairs, and a bowl of noodle soup and a cup of tea was waiting for me on the table. I could not have been happier. The downpour continued throughout the night.

At 5 the next morning I could just see enough to gather my meagre belongings. I paid the lady for letting me stay in her house and stepped out onto the trail. It was still raining. There was just enough light to narrowly avoid walking straight into someone on the trail. I came face to face with one of my three porters. They had had a terrible time the day before and had found shelter in a house about one hour further up the trail. They greeted me cheerfully and again their happy disposition rubbed off on me. We continued down the trail, completely oblivious of our miserable conditions. My agent in Kathmandu, Nima, had booked me on a flight out of Tummingtar that day but I had to be there by early afternoon to catch it. By 10 a.m. I could see the airstrip at Tummingtar down through a break in the clouds. The weather was showing signs of clearing but it would only be for a few hours, as heat and humidity were building again. At 1 p.m. I was there. The first three flights to Kathmandu that day had been cancelled due to the monsoon. There was now only one possibility and Nima had me booked on this flight. It arrived at 2.30 p.m. but my porters had not. As the loading of the plant began, in an attempt at a quick turn around before the clouds enveloped the runway, my three porters, carrying 30 kilograms each, appeared running along the trail. They looked absolutely shattered but relieved they had made it time. I've never gone in for the American custom of tipping, given that we were paying our porters more than they could earn doing some other job, but it seems to have become more widely expected in Nepal. I don't normally tip, but this time sincere thanks didn't seem to be enough for their hard work and loyalty, so I gave them enough money on the pretence that it was not a tip but so they could eat, drink and be merry for the next couple of days.

In the foyer of a Kathmandu hotel I was interviewed by Reuters correspondent, Elizabeth Hawley. I had met her many times before. Since 1960, Miss Hawley has inter-viewed members of nearly every expedition that has entered Nepal and you could safely bet money on a phone call from her within two hours of your arrival. Not only is she one of the most knowledgeable people on climbing in Nepal, but she is also an excellent judge of character. If she senses a big ego or that the fertilizer is being spread a bit thick, she can be very dismissive. Towards the end of the half-hour inter-view she asked, 'So did you get to the real summit?'

For a second or two I thought it was a stupid question to ask, but decided to respond politely.

'Yes we did, although we couldn't stand on it as the summit was only this big,' I said, measuring the size of a small seat with my hands. She seemed satisfied with my description and added, 'Not everyone climbs to the real summit of Makalu'.

Two days later I arrived home. Harry had grown from a baby to a little boy in just two months, it seemed. I was worried that he would not remember me, as two months in his life would feel like two years, but Judi said that was never a problem. For the entire thirty-minute drive from the airport to home he did not take his eyes off me. As Judi and I sat on the back verandah of our house drinking tea, I asked, 'So what has happened while I have been away?'

'Nothing has changed while you've been gone,' she sighed with some relief. 'I'm just happy to have you home after all this time.'

POSTSCRIPT

Dave and I shared a tent for the walk out from Makalu BC. One afternoon, having made camp for the evening, we were confined to our tents as the monsoon started its afternoon session. We spoke about future climbs together but we spoke more about the last few weeks on Makalu. Dave said it meant a lot to him to climb Makalu—so much, in fact, that he said 'If I do nothing else for the rest of my life, or should I die tomorrow, I will have lived a very happy and rewarding life'.

Dave and I always shared a lot in common but his words that afternoon reflected just how I was feeling. Having just climbed Makalu and completed my mountaineering ambition of climbing the five highest mountains, I felt extremely content with my life. For Dave, his high-altitude climbing career was just beginning.

Sadly Dave was killed a few months later in an avalanche on Shishapangma, a mountain in Tibet.

After I recovered from the shock and sadness of the news I remembered a saying: One crowded hour of glorious life is worth an age without a name. At the age of 29 David Bridges had lived one crowed hour of glorious life.

May 2000

AFTERWORD

Harry Donn Groom was born on 5 May 1997. He was five days early. Judi and I thought he was wonderful, as most parents do. For the first six months I hardly knew he existed, as he seemed to eat then go back to sleep until he was hungry again. I enjoyed being a dad. I enjoyed the bathing and feeding times, and even changing the dirty nappies. When he was old enough I would take him for walks in a special backpack. I soon learnt I had to take some care and couldn't just fling a six-month-old baby onto my back as I had done so many times with my 20 kilogram climbing packs.

Of course many people expect Harry to follow in his father's footsteps. Judi and I hope that he doesn't. He has certainly started on his way to becoming a mountaineer. Occasionally he asks to leave the comfort of his cot to sleep in his play tent. It's only now that I start to understand the worry Mum, Dad and Judi must endure while I'm away climbing, and I thank them for their tolerance. If Harry wants to climb then I will certainly teach him, but no doubt there will come a time, as came for my father and me, where I won't be able to teach him any more. It will then be up to him to go out and learn from the best climbers around and do the long apprenticeship so that when it counts he will be able to make the right decisions at the right time. Judi and I don't mind what he does so long as he is living a rewarding and fulfilling life. I know that bringing Harry up in this world will be the most frustrating and difficult adventure of all. It will also be the most rewarding.

When I was home I helped Judi as much as possible, but 1997 was a big year as I was travelling around Australia speaking at conferences. Fortunately no-one asked me to speak about the Everest disaster of 1996. I had a lot of equipment to handle and set up for each show. Graham Howlett, an expert in projectors and sound systems, travelled with me. We had finished a presentation at the Cairns Casino, and with time to kill before flying back to Brisbane, we went for a walk round town. We came to an indoor rock-climbing gym and Graham was so intrigued by this artificial climbing that we had to go inside. We went straight to the practice wall where I proceeded to show Graham the various shapes of the plastic holds. A young female instructor came bouncing over. 'Would you like to have a go at climbing or abseiling?' she asked. Graham took a step to one side to see how I was going to handle this one.

'We are just having a look,' I said, not wanting the conversation to go too much further.

'It's a great workout for the upper body,' she said suggestively glancing at my timid stature. 'It's the latest craze, everyone is into this these days,' she added.

'Oh really?' I replied. Silently I thought, 'I was doing this before you were born'. By now Graham was wetting himself and trying not to laugh by shuffling nervously on the spot.

'Who knows where this could lead. Today Cairns, tomorrow the summit of Everest,' she said with a polite giggle.

That was it, I had to leave. 'No thanks, I'm really scared of heights,' and with that I headed for the door with Graham laughing all the way behind me.

'But it's really safe,' just squeezed through the door as I closed it.

To make matters worse I had to do an interview with the local paper that afternoon. Graham couldn't help but mention the episode to the journalist who was going to headline it in the next day's local paper. I never did see the paper.

Another interesting situation happened during question-time after one of my presentations, and, sadly, it shows the real lack of knowledge about mountaineering and adventure. I was asked in all seriousness, 'Is there a restaurant at the top of Everest to have lunch when you get there?' Another was 'Which state [of Australia] is Mount Everest in?' On a more serious note I have been asked about the powerful presence of another person when, in fact, I was alone. I have never had hallucinations of ghost-like figures. The presence is more like the powerful sense we all have when we feel someone is staring at us.

Since the first edition of this book was released two years ago, many people have written to me or passed on their comments. Some people jokingly say that 'Sheer Luck' would be a more appropriate title. Others don't understand that luck had little to do with it. In some instances it did, but for the greater part I created my own luck. For twenty expeditions over the last seventeen years I have toiled over months of training for each climb. This was nothing com-pared with the climb itself, where I tested my physical and mental skills close to the limit, each time finding new boundaries. All the time I was developing a mountaineering instinct that has allowed me to make the right decisions in life-threatening situations. However, I am not immune from overstepping the mark—fortunately I have been able to recognise it before I have done so. Those people in life who do not take risks will never understand the spirit of adventure. They will always see the great adventures of others as careless risk taking and the Houdini-like escapes as nothing more than sheer luck. People who do understand the spirit of human endeavour will know that, when faced with a difficult or life-threatening situation, the human spirit relies on a great untapped reserve of sheer will to overcome all obstacles. We all have it; it's human nature. It's how you use it that counts.

Today my plumbing tools lie virtually untouched, their use limited to the occasional tap repair. One day I will give them the good oiling they deserve, as this trade long subsidised my climbing aspirations. Except to like-minded people, I feel uncomfortable trying to explain why I climb. I doubt there will ever be a satisfying answer for the non-climber and 'Because it's there' is only the frustrated response to a difficult question.

My losses from mountaineering cannot be hidden from this book but the gains are too numerous to mention, from the countless magical moments to an extraordinary sense of achievement. The teamwork and mateship shared while climbing under such extreme hardships is unparalleled in any other sport. I have made many great, life-long climbing friends.

Some people ask whether I am affected by the death of climbing friends. I am, but for seventeen years Himalayan climbing has been my life. Every climber learns at the start that it's a dangerous game, but we have a choice: either climb, understanding the risks, or don't play the game. My Himalayan years have been by far the most difficult but also the most rewarding of my life, and I have learnt that few rewards are worth having without overcoming difficulties to achieve them. I would not have swapped this time for all the tea in China.

With success comes recognition and I enjoy receiving it. Countless awards are given out each year in recognition of sporting achievement and since childhood I have had many sporting heroes and always hoped to become one. When I was in hospital recovering from my climbing injuries, however, I discovered another playing field of heroes who do not choose their opponents, and who receive little public admiration and no awards. My respect is boundless for those who suffer physical or mental handicaps with little hope of improvement, and who have their own Everest to climb just getting through each day.

Sponsorships and speaking engagements around Australia pay the bills these days and a lot of people ask me how have I been so lucky to have done so many things in such a short period. My reply is generally that luck has had little to do with climbing the world's highest mountains, but opportunities presented themselves and I had to put in the hard preparation and persistence to make them work. I *have* been lucky though. After losing my toes and being faced with life in a wheelchair or on a walking frame I was given a second chance to lead an active and rewarding life. It made me aware that I have been guilty of taking some things for granted, none more so than the value of time. No better words can sum this up than these from Phillip Adams:

When people say to me: 'How come you do so many things?', I often answer them, without meaning to be cruel: 'How do you do so little?' It seems to me that people have vast potential. Most people can do extraordinary things if they have the confidence or take the risks. Yet most people don't. They sit in front of the telly and treat life as if it goes on forever.

Michael Groom, Brisbane

GLOSSARY

Abseil A method of descending a rope using a special device to act as a friction brake.

Acclimatisation The time needed for the human body to adjust to the lack of air pressure at high altitudes.

Anchor A point to which a rope is fixed, e.g. a piton, ice screw or snowstake.

Belay To make a safe stance in an exposed position with anchor points. 'Belaying' means the feeding out of rope by the second climber to the lead climber.

Bergschrund The crevasse formed when a snowfield or glacier pulls away from the steeper face or buttress of the mountain.

Bivouac A night spent out in the open without a tent.

Bridging Method of climbing using the back and shoulder to push against one wall and the feet and hands against the opposite wall.

Buttress A pillar of rock protruding or extending beyond the normal line of the cliff face.

Chimney A wide, vertical crack.

Climbing permit Pakistan, Nepal, China and Tibet require expeditions to buy a permit from either the

Ministry of Tourism or the Mountaineering Association.

Col   A dip or low point in a ridge.

Cornice   An overhanging section of snow from the top of the ridge, formed by prevailing winds.

Couloir   A gully with a base of snow or ice.

Crampons   Usually twelve or more metal spikes strapped to the bottom of the boot for grip on snow or ice.

Crevasse   A crack in the snow formed by movement, often very deep and sometimes hidden by a covering of snow.

Cwm   A high mountain valley.

Fixed rope   A rope that remains fixed on various parts of the mountain for the duration of the climb. It is held in place by ice screws, pitons, etc.

Frostbite   The freezing of cells, usually in the body's extremities, at extremely low temperatures.

Glacier   A river of ice.

Harness   An arrangement of straps around the waist and legs while climbing, used to connect the climber to the rope and absorb the shock of a fall.

Hypoxia   Inadequate oxygen reaching the tissues.

Ice axe   Usually around 60–70 centimetres long, it has a pick for gripping the ice and snow and an adze for chopping steps. It is also used as an anchor and for belaying.

Ice screw   A threaded screw with an attachment on the end for a karabiner. Comes in varying lengths and penetrates the ice when turned by hand.

Jumar   A mechanical device that when attached to a rope will slide up but not down. It is attached to the climber's harness via a sling.

Karabiner   An alloy, chain-type link with a spring-loaded gate which can be pushed open to allow the rope to pass through.

La   The Nepalese word for a low point in a ridge that is sometimes used as a pass.

Moraine   A steep wall or ridge of rock and earth pushed ahead or to the side of an advancing glacier.

Piton   A sturdy blade of metal hammered into a crack in the rock to secure rope.

Sérac   A tower or wall of ice.

Summit pyramid   The final slopes to the summit. Some mountains have a final pyramid-shaped slope leading to the summit. Can vary in distance from 100 metres to 1000 metres.

Snowstake   An angled piece of alloy between 50 centimetres and 1 metre long. When hammered vertically into the snow, it can be used as an anchor.

White-out   When visibility disappears due to dense cloud and/or falling snow.

THANKS TO MY SPONSORS

As I have already mentioned in this book, I had to lead a frugal existence in the early days of my climbing career so I could afford to pay for the next expedition. A high percentage of my yearly income was invested into these expeditions and as the size of the mountain increased so did the financial burden. There came a time when I could no longer afford to fund these expeditions from my own earnings and therefore, it appeared the world's highest mountains were beyond my reach.

Fortunately, I received support and encouragement from organisations who not only believed in my ambition but shared my vision to reach the top by taking well calculated risks. Without that support, most of the chapters in this book would have remained just another dream. I would like to thank those organisations listed below.